Homophobia: An Overview

The *Research on Homosexuality* series:

Series Editor: John P. De Cecco, PhD, Director, Center for Research and Education in Sexuality, San Francisco State University, and Editor, *Journal of Homosexuality.*

Number 1

Homosexuality and the Law, edited by Donald C. Knutson, JD

Number 2

Historical Perspectives on Homosexuality, edited by Sal Licata, PhD, and Robert P. Petersen, PhD candidate.

Number 3

Nature and Causes of Homosexuality: A Philosophic and Scientific Inquiry, edited by Noretta Koertge, PhD

Number 4

Homosexuality & Psychotherapy: A Practitioner's Handbook of Affirmative Models, edited by John C. Gonsiorek, PhD

Number 5

Alcoholism & Homosexuality, edited by Thomas O. Ziebold, PhD, and John Mongeon

Number 6

Literary Visions of Homosexuality, edited by Stuart Kellogg

Number 7

Homosexuality and Social Sex Roles, edited by Michael W. Ross, PhD

Number 8

Bisexual and Homosexual Identities: Critical Theoretical Issues, edited by John P. De Cecco, PhD, and Michael G. Shively, MA

Number 9

Bisexual and Homosexual Identities: Critical Clinical Issues, edited by John P. De Cecco, PhD

Number 10

Homophobia: An Overview, edited by John P. De Cecco, PhD

This series is published by The Haworth Press, Inc., under the editorial auspices of the Center for Research and Education in Sexuality, San Francisco State University, and the *Journal of Homosexuality.*

Homophobia: An Overview

John P. De Cecco, PhD
Editor

The Haworth Press
New York

Homophobia: An Overview has also been published as *Journal of Homosexuality,* Volume 10, Numbers 1/2, Fall 1984.

The Haworth Press, Inc., 28 East 22 Street, New York, NY 10010

Library of Congress Cataloging in Publication Data
Main entry under title:

Homophobia: an overview.

    Published also as v. 10, no. 1/2 of the Journal of homosexuality.
    Includes bibliographies and index.
    1. Homosexuality—United States—Public opinion. 2. Public opinion—United States.
3. Homosexuality—Law and legislation—United States—Bibliography. I. De Cecco, John P.
HQ76.3.U5H64   1984   306.7'66   84-8959
ISBN 0-86656-356-3

Homophobia: An Overview

Journal of Homosexuality
Volume 10, Numbers 1/2

CONTENTS

The *Journal of Homosexuality* is devoted to theoretical, empirical, and historical research on homosexuality, heterosexuality, sexual identity, social sex roles, and the sexual relationships of both men and women. It was created to serve the allied disciplinary and professional groups represented by psychology, sociology, history, anthropology, biology, medicine, the humanities, and law. Its purposes are:

a) to bring together, within one contemporary scholarly journal, theoretical empirical, and historical research on human sexuality, particularly sexual identity;

b) to serve as a forum for scholarly research of heuristic value for the understanding of human sexuality, based not only in the more traditional social or biological sciences, but also in literature, history and philosophy;

c) to explore the political, social, and moral implications of research on human sexuality for professionals, clinicians, social scientists, and scholars in a wide variety of disciplines and settings.

EDITOR

JOHN P. DE CECCO, PhD, *Professor of Psychology and Human Sexuality and Director, Center for Research and Education in Sexuality (CERES), San Francisco State University*

MANUSCRIPT EDITOR

NORMAN C. HOPPER, *Center for Research and Education in Sexuality, San Francisco State University*

ADMINISTRATIVE ASSISTANT

TONY DONATONI, *Center for Research and Education in Sexuality, San Francisco State University*

ABSTRACTS AND BOOK REVIEW EDITOR

RICHARD BEATTY, *Center for Research and Education in Sexuality, San Francisco State University*

FOUNDING EDITOR

CHARLES C. SILVERSTEIN, PhD, *New York City*

EDITORIAL BOARD

EVELYN BLACKWOOD, MA, *Anthropology, CERES, San Francisco State University*
PHILIP W. BLUMSTEIN, PhD, *Associate Professor of Sociology, University of Washington, Seattle*
EDWARD BRONGERSMA, JD, *Founder, Dr. Edward Brongersma Foundation, The Netherlands; Former Senator, Dutch National Parliament*
ROGER BROWN, PhD, *John Lindsley Professor of Psychology, Harvard University*
VERN L. BULLOUGH, RN, PhD, *Dean, Faculty of Natural and Social Sciences, State University College at Buffalo*
ELI COLEMAN, PhD, *Assistant Professor and Coordinator of Education and Training, Program in Human Sexuality, University of Minnesota*
LOUIS CROMPTON, PhD, *Professor of English, University of Nebraska at Lincoln*
MARTIN DANNECKER, PhD, *Klinikum der Johann Wolfgang Goethe-Universitat, Abteilung für Sexualwissenschaft, Frankfurt am Main, West Germany*

Foreword

This monograph represents the largest collection of articles on homophobia to be published to date. It includes theoretical analyses of the concept of homophobia, critiques and innovations pertaining to its assessment, and its relationship to the biological sex of respondents, their self-perceived sex-roles, and their etiological theories of homosexuality. At the level of applied research, one article describes an attempt to rid university students of homophobia. Two articles deal with the organizational aspects of homophobia, one with the military and the other with perhaps the first political stirrings of organized homosexuality in the United States. Finally, it includes a comprehensive, annotated bibliography of publications of the United States Federal Government pertaining to homosexuality, covering a period of over sixty years.

Speculation and research on homophobia as a clinical, social, and psychological phenomenon are approximately 15 years old. The two theoretical articles in this collection survey that work in an effort to supply it conceptual and methodological clarity and direction. The empirical studies, for the most part, expand our knowledge of how homophobia is related to particular characteristics or beliefs of individuals and to organizational policies and attitudes.

I wish to thank the several authors for their contributions and their generosity in responding to our proposed revisions and to the manuscript editor's telephone entreaties for information. A special note of appreciation is owed to Gregory Herek, Wayne Plasek, and Janicemarie Allard for their extensive theoretical examinations of homophobia. The referees of the manuscripts were very helpful in providing advice to the contributors and the editor. They included Alan Bell, Stanley Harris, Gregory Herek, Walter Hudson, Mary Laner, A. P. MacDonald, William Owen, and Richard Smith. Finally, I wish to express my gratitude to the new manuscript editor of the *Journal*, Norman Hopper, for his bravery and skill in assisting me in the management of these voluminous materials.

With the first issues of the *Journal's* tenth volume we are inaugurating an abstracts section devoted to articles and books that have recently appeared. It is our hope that readers conducting research of their own or who merely wish to remain *au courant* will find the abstracts useful. I thank Phillip Hecht for his assistance and inventiveness in launching this section of the *Journal*.

John P. De Cecco, PhD
Editor

Beyond "Homophobia":
A Social Psychological Perspective
on Attitudes Toward Lesbians and Gay Men

Gregory M. Herek, PhD
Yale University

ABSTRACT. *Homophobia,* a term often used to describe hostile reactions to lesbians and gay men, implies a unidimensional construct of attitudes as expressions of irrational fears. This paper argues that a more complex view is needed of the psychology of positive and negative attitudes toward homosexual persons. Based upon a review of previous empirical research, a model is proposed that distinguishes three types of attitudes according to the social psychological function they serve: (1) *experiential,* categorizing social reality by one's past interactions with homosexual persons; (2) *defensive,* coping with one's inner conflicts or anxieties by projecting them onto homosexual persons; and (3) *symbolic,* expressing abstract ideological concepts that are closely linked to one's notion of self and to one's social network and reference groups. Strategies are proposed for changing attitudes serving each of the functions. The importance of distinguishing attitudes toward lesbians from those focused on gay men is also discussed.

Until fairly recently, the basis for heterosexuals' hostility toward lesbians and gay men was not studied by social scientists. Homosexuality was assumed to be a form of psychopathology and researchers generally aimed to discover its "cause" or "cure" while taking for granted its negative evaluation by society. During the 1960s, however, the nascent North American gay movement matured and took a militant turn (Marotta, 1981). When lesbians and gay men began to protest their low status, a natural focus for their efforts was the psychiatric-psychological establishment, which had popularized and maintained the notion that homosexuals are sick.

Through intensive lobbying and political activism, bolstered by the growing body of scientific literature challenging the psychopathological

Dr. Herek is a postdoctoral research fellow in social psychology at Yale University. Requests for reprints should be sent to the author, Department of Psychology, Yale University, Box 11A Yale Station, New Haven, CT 06520.

1

view of the homosexual orientation (e.g., Freedman, 1971; Hart et al., 1978; Hooker, 1957), lesbians, gay men, and their supporters eventually pressured the American Psychiatric Association to remove homosexuality from its Diagnostic and Statistical Manual as a form of mental illness (see Bayer, 1981). That decision, along with supportive resolutions from the American Psychological Association, the American Anthropological Association, the American Sociological Association, and others, helped to promote new directions in research on lesbian and gay issues by social and behavioral scientists. Unlike previous research, which was dominated by a sickness model (Morin, 1977), the new body of empirical and theoretical inquiry addresses problems faced by individuals as a consequence of their homosexual orientation.

A particularly important focus for this new research is the topic of prejudice against lesbians and gay men, which has been categorized under various names: *homophobia* (Smith, 1971; Weinberg, 1972), *homoerotophobia* (Churchill, 1968), *homosexphobia* (Levitt & Klassen, 1974), *homosexism* (Lehne, 1976), *heterosexism* (Morin & Garfinkle, 1978), and *homonegativism* (Hudson & Ricketts, 1980). These different terms reflect the multiple theoretical assumptions and political orientations intertwined in this research. Characterizing hostility toward homosexual persons in terms of a phobia implies that those attitudes are based upon an irrational fear, similar to the fear some people experience when confronted with snakes, spiders, or open spaces. Alternatively, tying negative attitudes to sexism, racism, and other forms of prejudice highlights the social context in which the attitudes develop and are maintained. The use of *homonegativism* by Hudson and Ricketts (1980) as an umbrella term includes both the phobic and sexist aspects of prejudice and leaves room for other facets as well. I agree with their view that there are many factors underlying these attitudes (not to be confused with the single statistical factor that describes the relationship among attitude items; see Herek, this issue). But even *homonegativism* seems to me too restrictive a term because, like the others, it limits our focus to negative attitudes.

This emphasis on prejudice rather than tolerance is understandable. Since homosexual persons in our society historically have been viewed as sick, immoral, antisocial, or otherwise bad, asking instead what is wrong with people who persecute them represents a political stance. But given the prevailing norms in the United States and many other countries today, it is not surprising that the person-on-the-street usually expresses unfavorable opinions about homosexuality. Recent polls indicate that only one-third of the adults in the United States feel that homosexuality is an acceptable alternative lifestyle (Newsweek Poll, 1983) and more than one-half would exclude homosexual persons from particular occupations (Gallup, 1982). It is necessary, of course, to ask why these views are widespread and why some persons hold attitudes that are even more negative than average. Why, for example, do some individuals physically brutalize gay men or lesbians, or join political campaigns that seek to deprive them of equal opportunity for employment, housing, and services? But an equally important question is how, despite overwhelming social pressures to the contrary, some heterosexual people manage to develop positive and accepting attitudes. If social scientists are to conduct research relevant to changing public opinion, we must be guided by theory sufficiently broad to explain the psychology of both positive and negative attitudes.

In this article, I shall organize recent empirical research on the psychology of individuals' attitudes toward lesbians and gay men in order to lay the foundation for a theoretical perspective. My goal is to integrate disparate empirical findings to provide testable hypotheses for future research. I will also discuss strategies for attitude-change studies and the need for distinguishing attitudes toward lesbians from those directed at gay men. As a first step, I shall locate my discussion within its cultural-historical context.

THE CULTURAL CONTEXT OF ATTITUDES

Social groups create social categories which define subgroupings of people. These categories (e.g., class, caste, race, gender) can be so deeply ingrained in individuals' understandings of the world that they appear to be "natural" rather than the products of social interaction. "Sexual orientation" is one such category. In the United States today, we categorize people as primarily heterosexual or homosexual, with some allowances for bisexual and asexual individuals. We often impute our categorization to other cultures and historical periods as well. It is necessary, however, to distinguish specific sexual behaviors from the social roles and psychological identities attributed to them (see Foucault, 1976/1978; McIntosh, 1968; Goode, 1981a, 1981b; Omark, 1981).

In cultures where sexuality is situationally organized, it makes little sense to impose labels such as gay, straight, or bisexual. For example, in several New Guinea tribes, adolescent boys engage exclusively in homosexual behavior for years as part of their initiation rites until eventually they marry as adults and engage in heterosexual intercourse (Herdt, 1981). In some groups the men revert to homosexual behavior when a new group of boys is to be initiated (Williams, 1936). A historical examination of North American and Western European societies further illustrates the specificity and recent origins of our present notion of sexual orientation (see Weeks, 1977).

I do not suggest that people have homosexual or heterosexual behavioral preferences only in societies where sexual orientation has been culturally defined (on this point, see Dannecker, 1978/1981; Whitam, 1977, 1981, 1983), but I think it is necessary to understand sexuality within the terms defining it in a particular culture. As primates, human beings are capable of great plasticity in sexual behavior (Herek, in press), but the roles, identities, and attitudes surrounding sexuality (what we usually call sexual orientation) should be understood as culturally constructed rather than innate or fixed by nature.

Thus attitudes toward lesbians and gay men must be understood with reference to our own culture's institutions and the psychological issues related to them. In attacking this problem, at least three levels of analysis are relevant. First, using historical and anthropological perspectives, we must ask how the heterosexual-homosexual dichotomy developed in Europe and North America, why homosexuality has come to be defined primarily in negative terms, and what circumstances might bring about a change in this evaluation (see Boswell, 1980; Davies, 1982; Greenberg & Bystryn, 1982; Weeks, 1977). Second, treating our own contemporary society as the unit of analysis, we must ask how the negative evaluation of homosexual persons is perpetuated through specific components of the social structure, such as cinema (Russo, 1981), theater (Carlsen, 1981), and textbooks (MacDonald, 1981; Newton, 1979). Finally, at the social psychological level, we must ask what individual and situational factors permit some persons to oppose the societal ideology by maintaining tolerant or even favorable attitudes toward lesbians and gay men, while others keep exceptionally hostile attitudes. This last question provides the focus for the present paper.

PREVIOUS EXPLANATIONS OF REACTIONS TO LESBIANS AND GAY MEN

Theoretical Accounts

Social scientists attempting to explain why so many people hold negative feelings toward homosexual persons have tended to offer either theoretical speculations or empirical data, with little synthesis of the two. The theoretical accounts often have revealed more about the writer's personal prejudices toward homosexuality than society's reaction to it. For example, William James (1890) assumed that being repulsed by the idea of intimate contact with a member of the same sex is instinctive, and exists more strongly in men than in women. Interestingly, in cultures where such forms of "unnatural vice" as homosexuality are found, James supposed that the instinctual aversion had been overcome by habit. In other words, he assumed that tolerance is learned and revulsion is inborn, rather than vice-versa. This is particularly surprising in view of his hypothesis that a "germinal possibility" for same-sex attraction exists in "most men" (pp. 437–439).

There are similarities between the thinking of James and Edward Westermarck (1908), but the latter went beyond instinct-based explanations in his cross-cultural study of morality. He was willing to assert that societal censure of homosexual practices is due to "the feeling of aversion or disgust which the idea of homosexual intercourse tends to call forth in normally constituted adult individuals whose sexual instincts have developed under normal conditions" (p. 483). But he thought this explanation was inadequate in accounting for the particularly violent reaction against homosexuality displayed by the Jewish, Christian, and Zoroastrian religions. Their strong hostility exists, he said, because homosexual practices were associated historically with idolatry and heresy, and so were condemned by way of laws and customs.

Psychoanalysts offered a more social-psychological view. Sigmund Freud (1905/1961) asserted that an exclusive heterosexual orientation does not only result from biological causes, but also is influenced by societal prohibitions on homoerotism and by early experiences with parents. He assumed that all men and women had strong attractions to their same-sex parent but these feelings were usually repressed in dissolving the complete oedipus complex. In many cases, however, the repression is incomplete. Thus, Sandor Ferenczi (1914/1956) suggested that heterosexual men's feelings of aversion, hostility, and disgust toward male homosexuality really are reaction-formations and symptomatic of defense against affection for the same sex (see also Dannecker, 1978/1981). Ferenczi did not extend his analysis to women's attitudes or to attitudes toward lesbians, but similar processes might be inferred.

Empirical Studies

In the last two decades, there has been a dramatic increase in empirical research on attitudes toward lesbians and gay men, but most of it lacks a theoretical framework. Studies have documented the attitudes of particular occupational groups, such as physicians and mental health professionals (Davison & Wilson, 1973; Fort, Steiner, & Conrad, 1971; Garfinkle & Morin, 1978; Gartrell, Kraemer, & Brodie, 1974; Lief, 1977; Masters & Johnson, 1979; Morris, 1973; Pauly & Goldstein, 1970; Thompson & Fishburn, 1977; White, 1979), law students (Dressler, 1979), and police officers (Fretz, 1975; Niederhoffer, 1969). Other writers have detailed institutionalized reactions to homosexual persons in settings such as the military (Williams & Weinberg, 1971), academia (Crew, 1978), and the news media (Nelson, 1981; Pierson, 1982).

The bulk of studies have sought to uncover the correlates of negative attitudes. Some findings are contradictory, such as the relationship between sex-role conformity (i.e., masculinity, femininity, androgyny) and attitudes (see Black & Stevenson, this issue; Hansen, 1982b; Millham & Weinberger, 1977; Minnigerode, 1976; Siegel, 1981; Weinberger &

Millham, 1979). In general, however, some consistent patterns have been observed across different samples. When compared to those with more favorable attitudes toward lesbians and gay men, these studies have found that persons with negative attitudes:

1. are less likely to have had personal contact with lesbians or gay men (Bowman, 1979; Glassner & Owen, 1976; Hansen, 1982a; Millham, San Miguel, & Kellogg, 1976; Weis & Dane, 1979);
2. are less likely to report having engaged in homosexual behaviors, or to identify themselves as lesbian or gay (Kinsey, Pomeroy, Martin, & Gebhard, 1953; Mosher & O'Grady, 1979; Weis & Dain, 1979);
3. are more likely to perceive their peers as manifesting negative attitudes, especially if the respondents are males (Herek, 1984b; Larsen, Reed, & Hoffman, 1980);
4. are more likely to have resided in areas where negative attitudes are the norm (e.g., the midwestern and southern United States, the Canadian prairies, and in rural areas or small towns), especially during adolescence (Hansen, 1982a; Irwin & Thompson, 1977; Levitt & Klassen, 1974; Nyberg & Alston, 1976; Stephan & McMullin, 1982; Turnbull & Brown, 1977; Whitehead & Metzger, 1981);
5. are likely to be older and less well-educated (Bowman, 1979; Glenn & Weaver, 1979; Irwin & Thompson, 1977; Nyberg & Alston, 1976; Snyder & Spreitzer, 1976; White, 1979);
6. are more likely to be religious, to attend church frequently, and to subscribe to a conservative religious ideology (Alston, 1974; Bowman, 1979; Cameron & Ross, 1981; Glassner & Owen, 1976; Hansen, 1982b; Henley & Pincus, 1978; Herek, 1984b; Irwin & Thompson, 1977; Larsen et al., 1980; Larsen, Cate, & Reed, 1983; Nyberg & Alston, 1976; Weis & Dane, 1979; White, 1979);
7. are more likely to express traditional, restrictive attitudes about sex roles (Brown & Amoroso, 1975; Dunbar, Brown, & Amoroso, 1973; Dunbar, Brown, & Vuorinen, 1973; Krulewitz & Nash, 1980; Laner & Laner, 1979, 1980; MacDonald & Games, 1974; MacDonald, Huggins, Young, & Swanson, 1973; Millham & Weinberger, 1977; Weinberger & Millham, 1979);
8. are less permissive sexually or manifest more guilt or negativity about sexuality (Brown & Amoroso, 1977; Dunbar, Brown, & Amoroso, 1973; Dunbar, Brown, & Vuorinen, 1973; Levitt & Klassen, 1974; MacDonald & Games, 1974; Mosher & O'Grady, 1979; Minnigerode, 1976; Nyberg & Alston, 1976; Sorenson, 1973; Weis & Dain, 1979; Young & Whertvine, 1982), although some researchers have not observed this pattern (Larsen et al., 1983) and others have reported a substantially reduced correlation

with the effects of sex-role attitudes partialled out (MacDonald et al., 1973; Minnigerode, 1976);
9. are more likely to manifest high levels of authoritarianism and related personality characteristics (Hood, 1973; Karr, 1978; Larsen et al., 1980; MacDonald & Games, 1974; Smith, 1971; Sobel, 1976).

Sex differences in the direction and intensity of attitudes have been observed fairly consistently. It appears that heterosexuals tend to have more negative attitudes toward homosexuals of their own sex than of the opposite sex (Burd, 1983; Cuenot & Fugita, 1982; Herek, 1984b; Millham et al., 1976; Steffensmeier & Steffensmeier, 1974; Weinberger & Millham, 1979), with more negative attitudes manifested by males than by females (Brown & Amoroso, 1975; Conley & O'Rourke, 1973; Dressler, 1979; Gurwitz & Marcus, 1978; Hansen, 1982a; Herek, 1984b; Kite, this issue; Larsen et al., 1980; Millham & Weinberger, 1979; Nyberg & Alston, 1977; Price, 1982; Turnbull & Brown, 1977; Weis & Dain, 1979; Young & Whertvine, 1982). Some researchers have not found a sex difference (e.g., Bowman, 1979; Glenn & Weaver, 1979; Irwin & Thompson, 1977; Levitt & Klassen, 1974; Nyberg & Alston, 1976), usually in national opinion polls, which may not be comparable to more psychologically oriented studies.

These empirical findings have yet to be integrated in a coherent theoretical perspective. Although several writers have sought to account for hostility toward homosexual persons (e.g., Ehrlich, 1981; Lehne, 1976; Morin & Garfinkle, 1978; MacDonald, 1976; Plummer, 1975; Rich, 1980; Weinberg, 1972), they have not sufficiently combined social psychological theory with empirical data to explain how individuals form, maintain, and change their attitudes. A synthesis of data and theory is needed, however, in order to move beyond simple correlational studies and to generate testable hypotheses concerning the reasons why people express favorable or hostile attitudes. In the next section, I shall propose such a synthesis.

ATTITUDES TOWARD LESBIANS AND GAY MEN: A FUNCTIONAL APPROACH

The social psychological perspective proposed in this paper is based on the premise that different people can express similar attitudes for entirely different reasons and that one person's attitudes toward different social objects may each serve different functions. Within this functional approach attitudes are understood as strategies for meeting psychological needs (Katz, 1960; Smith, 1973; Smith, Bruner, & White, 1956). Any one person's attitudes toward lesbians and gay men can serve more than one function, and the functions described here are not necessarily exhaustive. They provide a parsimonious framework, however, for integrating extant empirical research.

While different theorists have postulated varying numbers of functions most often served by attitudes (Elms, 1976), three major needs appear likely to be met by individuals' attitudes toward lesbians and gay men. First, such attitudes may be *experiential,* categorizing social reality primarily on the basis of one's past interactions with homosexual persons. Second, attitudes may be mainly *defensive,* helping a person to cope with some inner conflict or anxiety by projecting it onto gay men and lesbians. Finally, attitudes may be *symbolic,* expressing abstract ideological concepts that are closely linked to one's own notion of self and to one's social networks and reference groups.

Experiential Attitudes

Experiential attitudes develop when affects and cognitions associated with specific interpersonal interactions are generalized to all lesbians and gay men. A person with positive experiences, therefore, expresses generally favorable attitudes and a person with negative experiences reports unfavorable attitudes because of the experiences. Note that experiential attitudes do not inevitably follow interactions. It is necessary also that those interactions themselves (rather than, for example, ideological considerations) provide the primary basis for the attitude.

Interactions have consequences for both beliefs and affects associated with lesbians and gay men. Because they provide information, face-to-face interactions tend to refute stereotypes and reduce ignorance, which Marmor (1980) identified as the most important sources of hostility toward homosexual persons. At the same time, interpersonal encounters have an emotional impact that individuals can generalize to all lesbians and gay men. Thus, heterosexuals who know lesbians and gay men are better able than others to recognize stereotypes as inaccurate (Simms, 1981), and are more likely to express tolerant attitudes as well (Glassner & Owen, 1976; Hansen, 1982a; Herek, 1984b; Weis & Dain, 1979). Since only about one-fourth of the adults in the United States report that they have homosexual friends or acquaintances (Newsweek Poll, 1983), it can be hypothesized that attitudes will become more favorable overall as more lesbians and gay men disclose their sexual orientation to friends or family. For the present, however, we must assume that only a minority of people in the United States have attitudes based on experience. The remainder have formed their opinions and beliefs without the benefit of personal contact. Consequently, stereotypical beliefs about gay men and lesbians are prevalent, and it is appropriate here to discuss their forms and effects.

Most common stereotypes are related to cross-sex characteristics (Taylor, 1983). Additionally, significant numbers of individuals characterize male homosexuals as mentally ill, promiscuous, lonely, insecure, and likely to be child molesters, while lesbians have been described as aggressive and hostile toward men (see Casas, Brady, & Ponterotto, 1983; Gurwitz & Marcus, 1978; Heinemann, Pellander, Vogelbusch, & Wojtek, 1981; Karr, 1978; Rooney & Gibbons, 1966; Simmons, 1965; Weissbach & Zagon, 1975). Positive characteristics are also part of the homosexual stereotype, including such traits as sensitivity, intelligence, honesty, imagination, and neatness (Staats, 1978).

Recent research in social cognition has revealed the importance of stereotypes as cognitive categories for imposing order and predictability on the world (e.g., Hamilton, 1981). Some people feel the need for categorization so strongly that they increase their liking for a person simply because she or he labels another as homosexual (Karr, 1978). Homosexual persons who violate stereotypical expectations (e.g, masculine gay men and feminine lesbians) may actually be disliked (Laner & Laner, 1979, 1980; Storms 1978). Such nonconformity may not be noticed, however, since labeling itself can lead people to perceive stereotypical behaviors, whether or not they occur (Gross, Green, Storck, & Vanyur, 1980).

Distortion may be manifested in memory as well. Snyder and Uranowitz (1978) found that when respondents read the case history of a woman named "Betty K." and were later told that she was a lesbian, they recalled information from the case study consistent with the stereotype of lesbians. Other students who thought that Betty was a heterosexual remembered information consistent with that label. This sort of retrospective restructuring of information about homosexuals also was noted by Kitsuse (1962) in his interviews with respondents who had interacted with lesbians and gay men. But Casas, Brady, and Ponterotto (1983) found that accurate recall of characteristics that had been associated with lesbians and gay men was not affected by the extent to which those characteristics were congruent with popular stereotypes.

In contrast to studies of cognitive errors due to stereotyping, Langer and Imber (1980) argue that perceptions of minority individuals as different may be due to highly accurate rather than distorted perceptions. They suggest that people usually perceive their environment in a "mindless" or passive fashion and ignore most details of behavior. But when they become "mindful" of another (actively scrutinizing the other's characteristics and behavior), they pay more attention, they perceive common gestures and traits as atypical, and they perceive the person as somehow unusual. This was demonstrated by Langer and Imber (1980) in a study where respondents were asked to view a videotape of a man. When the man initially was labeled as a homosexual (or a millionaire, cancer victim, or other sort of unusual person), respondents recalled more information about him than when he lacked a label. Further, they rated the correctly recalled characteristics as more atypical.

Defensive Attitudes

The essential function of defensive attitudes is implicit in the widely held belief that heterosexual men and women who are genuinely secure about their own gender identity and sexual orientation feel less threatened by homosexuality than do those who are insecure (Marmor, 1980, p. 19). It frequently is assumed that feelings of personal threat result in strong negative attitudes toward homosexuality, whereas lack of threat leads to neutral or positive attitudes. This perspective often is associated with the term *homophobia,* and it derives from a psychodynamic view that prejudiced attitudes serve to reduce tension aroused by unconscious conflicts (Adorno, Frenkel-Brunswik, Levinson, & Sanford, 1950; Katz, 1960; Sarnoff, 1960; for a liberationist interpretation of this perspective, see Altman, 1971; Hocquenghem, 1972/1978; Mieli, 1977/1980).

Attitudes are likely to serve a defensive function when an individual perceives some analogy between homosexual persons and her or his own unconscious conflicts. Subsequently, that person responds to gay men and lesbians as a way of externalizing inner conflicts and thereby reducing the anxiety associated with them. The conflicts specific to antihomosexual prejudice presumably involve a person's gender identity, sexual object choice, or both (e.g., Hoffman, 1968, pp. 183–184). For example, unconscious conflicts about one's own sexuality or gender identity might be attributed to lesbians and gay men through a process of projection. Such a strategy permits people to externalize the conflicts and to reject their own unacceptable urges by rejecting lesbians and gay men (who symbolize those urges) without consciously recognizing the urges as their own. Since contact with homosexual persons threatens to make conscious those thoughts that have been repressed, it inevitably arouses anxiety in defensive individuals. Consequently, defensive attitudes are likely to be negative.

Several psychodynamic explanations offered for attitudes toward lesbians and gay men fit with the defensive function. Heterosexual men may envy gay men because the latter are not constrained by the masculine ideal (Weinberg, 1972). Heterosexuals may also envy the sexual freedom presumably enjoyed by lesbians and gay men (Cory, 1951). In either case, the envy is presumably translated unconsciously into hostility. In a similar vein, Cory (1951) also proposed that negative feelings toward opposite-sex homosexuals result from heterosexuals' feelings of rejection as potential sexual partners. Weinberg (1972) hypothesized that since many people strive for vicarious immortality by having children, and since lesbians and gay men are perceived (incorrectly) as having rejected this means for eluding the finality of death, the latter evoke an unconscious fear of death.

Many particular empirical findings I have mentioned make sense if we assume that negative attitudes often are based in part on a defensive function: the finding that people are more negative toward homosexuals of their own sex than toward those of the opposite sex (since same-sex homosexuals presumably are more threatening); the positive correlations between hostile attitudes toward homosexuality and variables such as authoritarianism, cognitive rigidity, intolerance of ambiguity, and dogmatism (all of these personality traits presumably indicate higher levels of defensiveness); and the positive correlations between hostility and sex-guilt, sexual conservatism, and nonpermissiveness (all of which might indicate conflicts about sexuality).

Other studies shed additional light on the defensive function. Weis and Dain (1979) found a positive correlation between ego-development and tolerance for homosexual persons. San Miguel and Millham (1976) found that antigay males were more punitive toward a man labeled as a homosexual if that man had also been identified as highly similar to the subject than when he was identified as dissimilar. This pattern can be explained psychodynamically. An insecure heterosexual male would experience increased threat because similarity would imply that he may resemble the homosexual man in sexual orientation.

Defensive attitudes should produce anxiety in individuals interacting with homosexual persons. In line with this hypothesis, Heinemann et al. (1981) noted physiological arousal (measured by skin-resistance) and reduced eye-contact when male subjects thought they were talking to a gay man. Cuenot and Fugita (1982) found that subjects talked faster when they perceived the interviewer to be homosexual than when he or she was presumed to be heterosexual. This increased arousal in the presence of homosexual persons might indicate anxiety resulting from unconscious conflicts. Alternatively, it may simply be due to the novel social situation created by the experiment.

One study that contradicts the psychodynamic view was conducted by Breger and Liverant (1961). In a perceptual defense experiment, they found no relationship between males' reaction times to homosexual words and their attitudes toward homosexuality. No attempt to replicate the study has been reported, however.

Symbolic Attitudes

McConahay and Hough (1976) defined symbolic racism as "the expression [by whites], in terms of abstract ideological symbols and symbolic behaviors, [of] the feeling that blacks are violating cherished values and making illegitimate demands for changes in the racial status quo'' (p. 38). This definition can be used to delineate the third functional category of attitudes toward lesbians and gay men. As with symbolic racism, symbolic sexual attitudes express the feeling that cherished values are being violated and that illegitimate demands are being made for changes in the status quo. I will expand the definition, however, to include favorable attitudes that are based upon the belief that discrimination and prejudice themselves violate the values of freedom and equality.

Whether favorable or unfavorable, symbolic attitudes derive from socialization experiences, past and present (McConahy & Hough, 1976). They express values important to one's concept of self, thereby helping individuals to establish their identity and affirm their notion of the sort of person they perceive themselves to be, while simultaneously mediating their relation to other important individuals and reference groups. This is part of an ongoing social dialectic through which one's sense of self develops while it also defines interpersonal relationships (Mead, 1934). Plummer (1975, chap. 8) has described in detail the relevance of this perspective to understanding reactions to lesbians and gay men.

Symbolic sexual attitudes tend to be consistent with a larger ideology supported by important reference groups. For example, a woman who conceives of herself as a liberal committed to individual rights and social justice is likely to express favorable attitudes toward homosexuals as part of this self-image. Negative attitudes might be expressed by a man who thinks of himself primarily as a devout fundamentalist Christian. For both individuals, expressing their attitudes reinforces their self-conceptions, publicly identifies them with important reference groups, and probably elicits acceptance or avoids rejections from significant others.

The symbolic pattern is apparent in the empirical data already summarized. Heterosexuals who express hostile attitudes toward homosexual persons also tend to endorse traditional ideologies of family, sexuality, and sex roles, and often are prejudiced against other minorities as well. That some of these same findings also apply to the defensive function underscores the complex, overdetermined nature of attitudes toward homosexual persons. Attitudes serving different functions can be correlated with identical behaviors.

For persons with symbolic attitudes, certain reference groups appear to be particularly influential. As already mentioned, people who are involved in church groups (as indicated by frequent attendance at church services) reflect the historical religious bias against lesbians and gay men, and this is especially so for Christians. People who grew up in areas where higher tolerance exists for diversity also hold more positive attitudes toward lesbians and gay men; these include city-dwellers and people from the northeastern and Pacific coastal regions of the United States. The same studies report that more tolerant attitudes are held by younger persons (whose cohorts' values reflect the liberalism of the 1960s and 1970s) and by persons with more education (who presumably have been exposed to liberal values on a college campus). Finally, people are more tolerant of lesbians and gay men if their parents also displayed tolerance (Glassner & Owen, 1976).

Because the studies cited here did not differentiate respondents according to the functions served by their attitudes, they provide only indirect support for the functional support. Future research should treat attitude function as an intervening variable (my own preliminary work suggests the utility of this approach; see Herek, 1983). For now, the functional perspective is a useful heuristic for understanding the psychological processes underlying both positive and negative reactions to lesbians and gay men. The goal, however, should not be simply to understand these attitudes. Additionally, research should be action-oriented, directed toward influencing opinions in a positive direction. Some observations relevant to this point are presented in the next section.

ATTITUDE FUNCTIONS AND ATTITUDE CHANGE

The few studies that have examined the efficacy of various attitude-change strategies have found more positive attitudes toward gay men and lesbians after the rather simple intervention of a course of study on homosexuality or general human sexuality (Larsen et al., 1983; Morin, 1974; Serdahely & Ziemba, this issue). Although sex-education courses often ignore homosexuality or treat it in negative terms (Levitt & Klassen, 1974; Newton, 1982), favorable discussion can provide information about lesbians and gay men that undermines negative stereotypes and establishes norms of tolerance and positive attitudes (see Chng, 1980; Greenberg, 1975; Price, 1982). Research is needed, however, to develop additional strategies that will be effective in changing attitudes, especially on a large scale outside the classroom.

The functional approach outlined here offers some general strategies for attitude change that should be investigated in future studies. It has been demonstrated by Katz and his colleagues (Katz et al., 1956, 1957; McClintock, 1958; Stotland, Katz, & Patchen, 1959), that different procedures will effect attitude change for each function. In order to change symbolic attitudes from negative to positive, an appeal to the values consistent with the self-concept of individuals and supported by their important reference groups probably will be most effective. For example, a person with negative symbolic attitudes based upon religious ideology might be exposed to new interpretations of biblical references to homosexuality (as outlined, for example, by Boswell, 1980, and McNeill, 1976). Such reinterpretations would be particularly effective if endorsed by prominent religious leaders respected by the individual, and if the individual expected them also to be accepted by her or his close friends and family. At the same time, appeals might emphasize other important values such as justice and individual freedom.

Another way to foster a change from negative to positive symbolic attitudes would be to arrange for positive interactions between the individual and various gay men and lesbians. These interactions should occur under conditions of equal status, common goals, cooperation, and .moderate intimacy (Amir, 1969, 1976). Interactions under these conditions, which might have the effect of transforming symbolic to experiential attitudes, most often occur when close friends or family members of heterosexuals disclose their homosexual orientation. Calls by activists for lesbians and gay men to declare publicly their sexual orientation are based on this premise (one such appeal was made by San Francisco Supervisor Harvey Milk in a tape recording made public after his murder; see Shilts, 1982, p. 374). Even when contact between heterosexual and homosexual persons is to involve strangers (as is likely in a political campaign), more positive attitudes should result when the interactions are carefully structured to meet several criteria: Common group memberships other than sexual orientation should be made salient (e.g., religious, social, ethnic, and political); contact should occur on a one-to-one basis rather than group-to-group; and the lesbian or gay man should violate some commonly held stereotypes or several homosexual persons should be visible so as to demonstrate the diversity of the community (Fiske & Taylor, 1984, chap. 6).

For persons whose attitudes already serve an experiential function, a similar strategy applies. Attitudes that already are favorable should become more so as the individual develops positive relationships with more gay men and lesbians. If the experiential attitudes are negative, they can best be unlearned by inducing incompatible positive affects derived from new, gratifying interactions with homosexual persons, especially loved ones.

Defensive attitudes are the most difficult to change because of their psychodynamic roots. As described in the research of the Katz group (Katz et al., 1956, 1957) such attitudes probably can be influenced only when defensiveness is moderate and only through the arousal of insight into the defensive process. For example, if a man's hostile attitudes are derived from the perception that gay men and lesbians threaten traditional gender roles, and that disruption of those roles threatens his own sense of self, his attitude might change if he is made more aware of its basis. At the same time, he must come to understand that he can tolerate gay men and lesbians without giving up a valued part of himself (viz., his masculinity). Contact with gay men and lesbians might be beneficial if it occurs under conditions that minimize anxiety and that are as pleasant as possible. The problem, of course, is that contact with homosexuals in itself may exacerbate the anxiety of heterosexuals.

This brief discussion offers some testable hypotheses for future research on attitude change. Such research should be a priority for investigators working in this area. Particular attention should be paid to persuasive appeals that can be used practically in large-scale political campaigns.

A METHODOLOGICAL CONSIDERATION

Although a critical review of methods for assessing attitudes toward lesbians and gay men is beyond the scope of this paper, one aspect of assessment is directly related to theoretical considerations. This is the need for explicitly measuring attitudes toward both lesbians and gay men. Despite a recommendation by Morin and Garfinkle (1978), most paper-and-pencil scales have not made this distinction. Attitude scales either mix items concerning lesbians with those relating to gay men (Glassner & Owen, 1976; Hudson & Ricketts, 1980), or the items are worded to refer to "homosexuals" in general (Dunbar, Brown, & Amoroso, 1973; Hansen, 1982a; Henley & Pincus, 1978; Hood, 1973; Larsen et al., 1980; Levitt & Klassen, 1974; Lumby, 1976; Smith, 1971; Weis & Dain, 1979). When respondents are asked to state their attitudes toward "homosexuals," however, it is possible that they are thinking mainly of males. Separate assessment of attitudes toward gay men and lesbians is necessary in order to determine differences in attitudes toward each gender. The perspective articulated in the present paper is intended to be applicable to both females and males. But it may be that attitudes toward lesbians are quite different from those toward gay men because of the fundamentally different social positions of men and women in contemporary society (Rich, 1980). Or it may be, as psychoanalytic theory suggests, that the crucial variable is whether the attitudes are directed at a homosexual person of one's own sex or the opposite sex. Attitude scales should permit empirical investigation of this question.

CONCLUSION

The study of attitudes toward lesbians and gay men is relatively new for the social sciences. In the past few years, however, there has been considerable progress. The present paper has argued for several considerations that will strengthen future research. Most importantly, a general theoretical framework has been proposed for synthesizing extant research according to the psychological functions served by attitudes. I hope that this framework will be viewed as only a first step. It will have served its purpose if it stimulates empirical research and leads to the development of a comprehensive social psychological theory of attitudes toward lesbians and gay men. Such theory would take us beyond the simple and unidimensional concept of "homophobia" and help us to understand both favorable and unfavorable attitudes in their social psychological complexity.

REFERENCES

Adorno, T. W., Frenkel-Brunswik, E., Levinson, D. J., & Sanford, R. N. (1950). *The authoritarian personality.* New York: Harper & Row.

Alston, J. P. (1974). Attitudes toward extramarital and homosexual relations. *Journal for the Scientific Study of Religion, 13,* 479–481.

Altman, D. (1971). *Homosexual: Oppression and liberation.* New York: Outerbridge & Dienstfrey.

Amir, Y. (1969). Contact hypothesis in ethnic relations. *Psychological Bulletin, 71*(5), 319–342.

Amir, Y. (1975). The role of intergroup contact in change of prejudice and intergroup relations. In P. Katz (Ed.), *Towards the elimination of racism.* New York: Pergamon Press.

Bayer, R. (1981). *Homosexuality and American psychiatry: The politics of diagnosis.* New York: Basic Books.

Black, K. N., & Stevenson, M. R. (1984). The relationship of self-reported sex-role characteristics and attitudes toward homosexuality. *Journal of Homosexuality, 10*(1/2), 83–93.

Boswell, J. (1980). *Christianity, social tolerance, and homosexuality.* Chicago: University of Chicago Press.

Bowman, R. (1979). Public attitudes toward homosexuality in New Zealand. *International Review of Modern Sociology, 9,* 229–238.

Breger, L., & Liverant, S. (1961). Homosexual prejudice and perceptual defense. *Journal of Consulting and Clinical Psychology, 25*(5), 459.

Brown, M., & Amoroso, D. (1975). Attitudes toward homosexuality among West Indian male and female college students. *Journal of Social Psychology, 97,* 163–168.

Burd, B. J. (1983). *Differential effects of status and sexual orientation upon evaluation of male and female professional ability.* Unpublished master's thesis, California State University, Sacramento, CA.

Cameron, P., & Ross, K. P. (1981). Social psychological aspects of the Judeo-Christian stance toward homosexuality. *Journal of Psychology and Theology, 9*(1), 40–57.

Carlsen, J. W. (1981). Images of the gay male in contemporary drama. In J. W. Chesebro (Ed.), *Gayspeak: Gay male and lesbian communication.* New York: Pilgrim.

Casas, J. M., Brady, S., & Ponterotto, J. G. (1983). Sexual preference biases in counseling: An information processing approach. *Journal of Counseling Psychology, 30*(2), 139–145.

Chng, C. L. (1980). Adolescent homosexual behavior and the health educator. *Journal of School Health, 50*(9), 517–521.

Churchill, W. (1967). *Homosexual behavior among males: A cross-cultural and cross-species investigation.* New York: Hawthorn.

Conley, J. A., & O'Rourke, T. W. (1973). Attitudes of college students toward selected issues in human sexuality. *Journal of School Health, 43*(5), 286–292.

Cory, D. W. (1951). *The homosexual in America.* New York: Greenberg.

Crew, L. (Ed.). (1978). *The gay academic.* Palm Springs, CA: ETC Publications.

Cuenot, R. G., & Fugita, S. S. (1982). Perceived homosexuality: Measuring heterosexual attitudinal and nonverbal reactions. *Personality and Social Psychology Bulletin, 8*(1), 100–106.

Dannecker, M. (1981). *Theories of homosexuality* (D. Fernbach, Trans.). London: Gay Men's Press. (Original work published 1978)

Davies, C. (1982). Sexual taboos and social boundaries. *American Journal of Sociology, 87*(5), 1032–1063.

Davison, G. C., & Wilson, G. T. (1973). Attitudes of behavior therapists toward homosexuality. *Behavior Therapy, 4,* 686–696.

Dressler, J. (1979). Study of law student attitudes regarding the rights of gay people to be teachers. *Journal of Homosexuality, 4*(4), 315–329.

Dunbar, J., Brown, M., & Amoroso, D. M. (1973). Some correlates of attitudes toward homosexuality. *Journal of Social Psychology, 89,* 271-279.

Dunbar, J., Brown, M., & Vuorinen, S. (1973). Attitudes toward homosexuality among Brazilian and Canadian college students. *Journal of Social Psychology, 90,* 173-183.

Ehrlich, L. G. (1981). The pathogenic secret. In J. W. Chesebro (Ed.), *Gayspeak: Gay male and lesbian communication.* New York: Pilgrim.

Elms, A. C. (1976). *Personality and politics.* New York: Harcourt Brace Jovanovich.

Ferenczi, S. (1956). The nosology of male homosexuality (homoerotism). In E. Jones (Trans.), *Sex in psychoanalysis.* New York: Basic Books. (Original work published 1914)

Fiske, S. T., & Taylor, S. E. (1984). *Social cognition.* Reading, MA: Addison-Wesley.

Fort, J., Steiner, C. M., & Conrad, F. (1971). Attitudes of mental health professionals toward homosexuality and its treatment. *Psychological Reports, 29,* 347-350.

Foucault, M. (1978). *The history of sexuality. Volume 1: An introduction.* New York: Pantheon. (Original work published 1976)

Freedman, M. (1971). *Homosexuality and psychological functioning.* Belmont, CA: Wadsworth.

Fretz, B. R. (1975). Assessing attitudes toward sexual behaviors. *Counseling Psychologist, 5*(1), 100-106.

Freud, S. (1961). *Three essays on the theory of sexuality.* In J. Strachey (Ed. and Trans.), *The standard edition of the complete psychological works of Sigmund Freud.* London: Hogarth Press. (Original work published 1905)

Gallup, G. (1982, November 9). Gallup poll on attitudes about gays. *San Francisco Chronicle,* p. 7.

Garfinkle, E. M., & Morin, S. F. (1978). Psychologists' attitudes toward homosexual psychotherapy clients. *Journal of Social Issues, 34*(3), 101-112.

Gartrell, N., Kraemer, H., & Brodie, H. (1974). Psychiatrists' attitudes toward female homosexuality. *Journal of Nervous and Mental Disease, 159*(2), 141-144.

Glassner, B., & Owen, C. (1976). Variations in attitudes toward homosexuality. *Cornell Journal of Social Relations, 11*(2), 161-176.

Glenn, N. D., & Weaver, C. N. (1979). Attitudes toward premarital, extramarital, and homosexual relations in the U.S. in the 1970s. *Journal of Sex Research, 15*(2), 108-118.

Goode, E. (1981a). Comments on the homosexual role. *Journal of Sex Research, 17*(1), 54-66.

Goode, E. (1981b). The homosexual role: Rejoinder to Omark and Whitam. *Journal of Sex Research, 17*(1), 76-83.

Goodyear, R. K., Abadie, P. D., & Barquest, K. A. (1981). Ascription of negative traits based on sex role and sexual orientation. *Psychological Reports, 49,* 194.

Greenberg, D. F., & Bystryn, M. H. (1982). Christian intolerance of homosexuality. *American Journal of Sociology, 88*(3), 515-548.

Greenberg, J. S. (1975). A study of personality change associated with the conducting of a high school unit on homosexuality. *Journal of School Health, 45*(7), 394-398.

Gross, A. E., Green, S. K., Storck, J. T., & Vanyur, J. M. (1980). Disclosure of sexual orientation and impressions of male and female homosexuals. *Personality and Social Psychology Bulletin, 6*(2), 307-314.

Gurwitz, S., & Marcus, M. (1978). Effects of anticipated interaction, sex, and homosexual stereotypes on first impressions. *Journal of Applied Social Psychology, 8,* 47-56.

Hamilton, D. (Ed.). (1980). *Cognitive processes in stereotyping and intergroup behavior.* Hillsdale, NJ: Lawrence Erlbaum.

Hansen, G. L. (1982a). Measuring prejudice against homosexuality (homosexism) among college students: A new scale. *Journal of Social Psychology, 117,* 233-236.

Hansen, G. L. (1982b). Androgyny, sex-role orientation, and homosexism. *Journal of Psychology, 112,* 39-45.

Hart, M., Roback, H., Tittler, B., Weitz, L., Walston, B., & McKee, E. (1978). Psychological adjustment of nonpatient homosexuals: Critical review of the research literature. *Journal of Clinical Psychiatry, 39*(7), 604-608.

Heinemann, W., Pellander, F., Vogelbusch, A., & Wojtek, B. (1981). Meeting a deviant person: Subjective norms and affective reactions. *European Journal of Social Psychology, 11,* 1-25.

Henley, N. M., & Pincus, F. (1978). Interrelationships of sexist, racist, and antihomosexual attitudes. *Psychological Reports, 42,* 83-90.

Herdt, J. (1981). *Guardians of the flutes: Idioms of masculinity.* New York: McGraw-Hill.

Herek, G. M. (1983). *Individual differences in attitudes toward lesbians and gay men: Social psychological components of sexual ideologies.* Unpublished doctoral dissertation, University of California, Davis, CA.

Herek, G. M. (1984a). Attitudes toward lesbians and gay men: A factor-analytic study. *Journal of Homosexuality, 10*(1/2), 39–51.

Herek, G. M. (1984b). Assessing attitudes toward lesbians and gay men: Scale construction and validation. Manuscript submitted for editorial review.

Herek, G. M. (in press). Primate homosexual behavior in comparative perspective. In T. Maple & R. Nadler (Eds.), *Sexual behavior in the primates.* New York: Academic Press.

Hocquenghem, G. (1978). *Homosexual desire* (D. Dangoor, Trans.), London: Allison & Busby. (Original work published 1972)

Hoffman, M. (1968). *The gay world: Male homosexuality and the social creation of evil.* New York: Basic Books.

Hood, R. W., Jr. (1973). Dogmatism and opinions about mental illness. *Psychological Reports, 32,* 1283–1290.

Hooker, E. (1957). The adjustment of the male overt homosexual. *Journal of Projective Techniques, 21,* 18–31.

Hudson, W. W., & Ricketts, W. A. (1980). A strategy for the measurement of homophobia. *Journal of Homosexuality, 5*(4), 357–372.

Irwin, P., & Thompson, N. L. (1977). Acceptance of the rights of homosexuals: A social profile. *Journal of Homosexuality, 3*(2), 107–121.

James, W. (1890). *Principles of psychology.* New York: Henry Holt & Co.

Karr, R. (1978). Homosexual labeling and the male role. *Journal of Social Issues, 34*(3), 73–83.

Katz, D. (1960). The functional approach to the study of attitudes. *Public Opinion Quarterly, 24,* 163–204.

Katz, D., McClintock, C., & Sarnoff, I. (1957). The measurement of ego defense as related to attitude change. *Journal of Personality, 25,* 465–474.

Katz, D., Sarnoff, I., & McClintock, C. (1956). Ego-defense and attitude change. *Human Relations, 9,* 27–46.

Kinsey, A., Pomeroy, W., Martin, C., & Gebhard, P. (1953). *Sexual behavior in the human female.* Philadelphia: W. B. Saunders.

Kite, M. E. (1984). Sex differences in attitudes toward homosexuals: A meta-analytic review. *Journal of Homosexuality, 10*(1/2), 69–81.

Kitsuse, J. I. (1962). Societal reactions to deviant behavior: Problems of theory and method. *Social Problems, 9*(3), 247–256.

Krulewitz, J. E., & Nash, J. E. (1980). Effects of sex role attitudes and similarity on men's rejection of male homosexuals. *Journal of Personality and Social Psychology, 38*(1), 67–74.

Laner, M. R., & Laner, R. H. (1979). Personal style or sexual preference: Why gay men are disliked. *International Review of Modern Sociology, 9,* 215–228.

Laner, M. R., & Laner, R. H. (1980). Sexual preference or personal style? Why lesbians are disliked. *Journal of Homosexuality, 5*(4), 339–356.

Langer, E. J., & Imber, L. (1980). Role of mindlessness in the perception of deviance. *Journal of Personality and Social Psychology, 39*(3), 360–367.

Larsen, K. S., Cate, R., & Reed, M. (1983). Anti-black attitudes, religious orthodoxy, permissiveness, and sexual information: A study of the attitudes of heterosexuals toward homosexuality. *Journal of Sex Research, 19*(2), 105–118.

Larsen, K. S., Reed, M., & Hoffman, S. (1980). Attitudes of heterosexuals toward homosexuality: A Likert-type scale and construct validity. *Journal of Sex Research, 16*(3), 245–257.

Lehne, G. K. (1976). Homophobia among men. In D. Davis & R. Brannon (Eds.), *The forty-nine percent majority: The male sex role.* Reading, MA: Addison-Wesley.

Levitt, E., & Klassen, A. D., Jr. (1974). Public attitudes toward homosexuality: Part of the 1970 national survey by the Institute for Sex Research. *Journal of Homosexuality, 1*(1), 29–43.

Lief, H. I. (1977). Sexual Survey #4: Current thinking on homosexuality. *Medical Aspects of Human Sexuality, 11,* 110–111.

Lumby, M. (1976). Homophobia: The quest for a valid scale. *Journal of Homosexuality, 2*(1), 39–47.

MacDonald, A. P., Jr. (1974). The importance of sex-role to gay liberation. *Homosexual Counseling Journal, 1*(4), 169–180.

MacDonald, A. P., Jr. (1976). Homophobia: Its roots and meanings. *Homosexual Counseling Journal, 3*(1), 23–33.

MacDonald, A. P., Jr., & Games, R. G. (1974). Some characteristics of those who hold positive and negative attitudes toward homosexuals. *Journal of Homosexuality, 1*(1), 9–27.

MacDonald, A. P., Jr., Huggins, J., Young, S., & Swanson, R. A. (1973). Attitudes toward homosexuality: Preservation of sex morality or the double standard? *Journal of Consulting and Clinical Psychology, 40*(1), 161.

MacDonald, G. (1981). Misrepresentation, liberalism and heterosexual bias in introductory psychology textbooks. *Journal of Homosexuality, 6*(3), 45–60.

Marotta, T. (1981). *The politics of homosexuality.* Boston: Houghton-Mifflin.

Marmor, J. (1980). Overview: The multiple roots of homosexual behavior. In J. Marmor (Ed.), *Homosexual behavior: A modern reappraisal.* New York: Basic Books.

Masters, W. H., & Johnson, V. E. (1979). *Homosexuality in perspective.* Boston: Little, Brown, and Co.

McClintock, C. (1958). Personality syndromes and attitude change. *Journal of Personality, 26,* 479–493.

McConahay, J. B., & Hough, J. C., Jr. (1976). Symbolic racism. *Journal of Social Issues, 32,* 23–45.

McIntosh, M. (1968). The homosexual role. *Social Problems, 16*(2), 182–192.

McNeill, J. J. (1976). *The church and the homosexual.* Kansas City: Sheed Andrews & McMeel.

Mead, G. H. (1934). *Mind, self, and society.* Chicago: University of Chicago Press.

Mieli, M. (1980). *Homosexuality and liberation: Elements of a gay critique* (D. Fernbach, Trans.). London: Gay Men's Press. (Original work published 1977)

Millham, J., San Miguel, C. L., & Kellogg, R. (1976). A factor-analytic conceptualization of attitudes toward male and female homosexuals. *Journal of Homosexuality, 2*(1), 3–10.

Millham, J., & Weinberger, L. E. (1977). Sexual preference, sex role appropriateness, and restriction of social access. *Journal of Homosexuality, 2*(4), 343–357.

Minnigerode, F. (1976). Attitudes toward homosexuality: Feminist attitudes and sexual conservatism. *Sex Roles, 2*(4), 347–352.

Morin, S. F. (1974). Educational programs as a means of changing attitudes toward gay people. *Homosexual Counseling Journal, 1*(4), 160–165.

Morin, S. F. (1977). Heterosexual bias in psychological research on lesbianism and male homosexuality. *American Psychologist, 32,* 629–637.

Morin, S. F., & Garfinkle, E. M. (1978). Male homophobia. *Journal of Social Issues, 34*(1), 29–47.

Morris, P. A. (1973). Doctors' attitudes to homosexuality. *British Journal of Psychiatry, 122,* 435–436.

Mosher, D. L., & O'Grady, K. E. (1979). Homosexual threat, negative attitudes toward masturbation, sex guilt, and males' sexual and affective reactions to explicit sexual films. *Journal of Consulting and Clinical Psychology, 47*(5), 860–873.

Neiderhoffer, A. (1969). *Behind the shield: The police in urban society.* New York: Anchor.

Nelson, J. (1981). Media reaction to the 1979 gay march on Washington. In J. W. Chesebro (Ed.), *Gayspeak: Gay male and lesbian communication.* New York: Pilgrim.

Newsweek poll on homosexuality. (1983, August 8). *Newsweek,* p. 33.

Newton, D. E. (1979). Representations of homosexuality in health science textbooks. *Journal of Homosexuality, 4*(3), 247–254.

Newton, D. E. (1982). A note on the treatment of homosexuality in sex education classes in the secondary school. *Journal of Homosexuality, 8*(1), 97–99.

Nyberg, K. L., & Alston, J. P. (1976). Analysis of public attitudes toward homosexual behavior. *Journal of Homosexuality, 2*(2), 99–107.

Nyberg, K. L., & Alston, J. P. (1977). Homosexual labeling by university youths. *Adolescence, 12*(48), 541–546.

Omark, R. C. (1981). Further comment on the homosexual role: A reply to Goode. *Journal of Sex Research, 17*(1), 73–75.

Pauly, I. B., & Goldstein, S. G. (1970). Physicians' attitudes in treating homosexuals. *Medical Aspects of Human Sexuality, 4,* 26–45.

Pierson, R. (1982, March). Uptight on gay news. *Columbia Journalism Review,* pp. 25–33.

Plummer, K. (1975). *Sexual stigma: An interactionist account.* London: Routledge & Kegan Paul.

Price, J. H. (1982). High school students' attitudes toward homosexuality. *Journal of School Health, 52,* 469–474.

Rich, A. (1980). Compulsory heterosexuality and lesbian existence. *Signs, 5*(4), 631–660.

Rooney, E. A., & Gibbons, D. (1966). Social reactions to "crimes without victims." *Social Problems, 13*(4), 400–410.

Russo, V. (1981). *The celluloid closet: Homosexuality in the movies.* New York: Harper & Row.
San Miguel, C. L., & Millham, J. (1976). The role of cognitive and situational variables in aggression toward homosexuals. *Journal of Homosexuality, 2*(1), 11–27.
Sarnoff, I. (1960). Psychoanalytic theory and social attitudes. *Public Opinion Quarterly, 24*(2), 251–279.
Serdahely, W. J., & Ziemba, G. J. (1984). Changing homophobic attitudes through college sexuality education. *Journal of Homosexuality, 10*(1/2), 109–116.
Shilts, R. (1982). *The mayor of Castro Street: The life and times of Harvey Milk.* New York: St. Martin's.
Siegel, S. A. (1981). Androgyny, sex-role rigidity, and homophobia. In J. W. Chesebro (Ed.), *Gayspeak: Gay male and lesbian communication.* New York: Pilgrim.
Simmons, J. L. (1965). Public stereotypes of deviants. *Social Problems, 13*(2), 223–232.
Simms, S. A. (1981). Gay images on television. In J. W. Chesebro (Ed.). *Gayspeak: Gay male and lesbian communication.* New York: Pilgrim.
Smith, K. T. (1971). Homophobia: A tentative personality profile. *Psychological Reports, 29,* 1091–1094.
Smith, M. B. (1973). Political attitudes. In J. Knutson (Ed.), *Handbook of political psychology.* San Francisco: Jossey-Bass.
Smith, M. B., Bruner, J. S., & White, R. W. (1956). *Opinions and personality.* New York: Wiley.
Snyder, E. E., & Spreitzer, E. (1976). Attitudes of the aged toward nontraditional sexual behavior. *Archives of Sexual Behavior, 5*(3), 249–254.
Snyder, M., & Uranowitz, S. (1978). Reconstructing the past: Some cognitive consequences of person perception. *Journal of Personality and Social Psychology, 36,* 941–950.
Sobel, H. J. (1976). Adolescent attitudes toward homosexuality in relation to self concept and body satisfaction. *Adolescence, 11*(43), 443–453.
Sorenson, R. C. (1973). *Adolescent sexuality in contemporary America.* New York: World.
Staats, G. R. (1978). Stereotype content and social distance: Changing views of homosexuality. *Journal of Homosexuality, 4*(1), 15–27.
Steffensmeier, D., & Steffensmeier, R. (1974). Sex differences in reactions to homosexuals: Research continuities and further developments. *Journal of Sex Research, 10,* 52–67.
Stephan, G. E., & McMullin, D. R. (1982). Tolerance of sexual nonconformity: City size as a situational and early learning determinant. *American Sociological Review, 47,* 411–415.
Storms, M. D. (1978). Attitudes toward homosexuality and femininity in men. *Journal of Homosexuality, 3*(3), 257–263.
Stotland, E., Katz, D., & Patchen, M. (1959). The reduction of prejudice through the arousal of self-insight. *Journal of Personality, 27,* 507–531.
Taylor, A. (1983). Conceptions of femininity and masculinity as a basis for stereotypes of male and female homosexuals. *Journal of Homosexuality, 9*(1), 37–53.
Thompson, G. H., & Fishburn, W. R. (1977). Attitudes toward homosexuality among graduate counseling students. *Counselor Education and Supervision, 17,* 121–130.
Turnbull, D., & Brown, M. (1977). Attitudes toward homosexuality and male and female reactions to homosexual and heterosexual slides. *Canadian Journal of Behavioral Science, 9*(1), 68–80.
Weeks, J. (1977). *Coming out: Homosexual politics in Britain from the nineteenth century to the present.* London: Quartet.
Weinberg, G. (1972). *Society and the healthy homosexual.* New York: St. Martin's.
Weinberger, L. E., & Millham, J. (1979). Attitudinal homophobia and support of traditional sex roles. *Journal of Homosexuality, 4*(3), 237–245.
Weis, C. B., Jr., & Dain, R. N. (1979). Ego development and sex attitudes in heterosexual and homosexual men and women. *Archives of Sexual Behavior, 8*(4), 341–356.
Weissbach, T. A., & Zagon, G. (1975). The effect of deviant group membership upon impressions of personality. *Journal of Social Psychology, 95,* 263–266.
Westermarck, E. (1908). *The origin and development of the moral ideas.* London: MacMillan.
Whitam, F. (1977). The homosexual role: A reconsideration. *Journal of Sex Research, 13*(1), 1–11.
Whitam, F. (1981). A reply to Goode on "The homosexual role." *Journal of Sex Research, 17*(1), 66–72.
Whitam, F. (1983). Culturally invariant properties of male homosexuality: Tentative conclusions from cross-cultural research. *Archives of Sexual Behavior, 12*(3), 207–226.
White, T. A. (1979). Attitudes of psychiatric nurses toward same sex orientations. *Nursing Research, 28*(5), 276–281.

Whitehead, G. I., & Metzger, S. C. (1981). Helping behavior in urban and nonurban settings. *Journal of Social Psychology, 114,* 295–296.

Williams, C. J., & Weinberg, M. S. (1971). *Homosexuals and the military: A study of less than honorable discharge.* New York: Harper & Row.

Williams, F. E. (1936). *Papuans of the trans-fly.* London: Oxford University Press.

Young, M., & Whertvine, J. (1982). Attitudes of heterosexual students toward homosexual behavior. *Psychological Reports, 51,* 673–674.

Misconceptions of Homophobia

John Wayne Plasek, PhD
California State University, Northridge

Janicemarie Allard, PhD
California State University, Los Angeles

ABSTRACT. Recent studies and analyses of social reactions to homosexuality are examined with the goal of linking them to general theories of deviance in the mainstream of sociology and social psychology. Homosexuality as an attitudinal object is classified as person, trait, and characteristic of collectivities and culture. The assumption of homosexuality as a "master status trait" is questioned. Foci of investigation are categorized as cognitive stereotypes, perceptions of threat to others and to valued aspects of society and culture, and the management of homosexuality. Ego-alien and phobic responses are distinguished.

General problems of attitudinal research in the field are identified; chiefly, the overemphasis of cognitive elements and the neglect of affective and behavioral elements. The potential of this imbalance for the reification of homophobia among subjects and for the general public is noted. Other problems include the confounding of cognitive and affective dimensions and the assumption of stability of attitudes in different social settings.

The need for concrete observations of responses to homosexuality in varying social settings and for the study of various types and phases of the disclosure process is specified. We call for grounded empirical observations of reactions to homosexuality within a model of the "social construction of reality" in order to place such studies within the mainstream of sociology and social psychology.

FAILURE TO PARTITION HOMOSEXUALITY AS DIFFERENTIATED OBJECTS OF ATTITUDES

An initial conceptual problem of current attempts to measure attitudes toward homosexuality is the tendency to treat homosexuality as a unitary phenomenon. Investigators fail to recognize important definitional dis-

Dr. Plasek is a professor of sociology at California State University in Northridge and a fellow at the Center for Sex Research. Dr. Allard is an associate professor of sociology at California State University in Los Angeles.

We are grateful for the critical comments of Dr. Clark L. Taylor of the Institute for Advanced Studies of Human Sexuality. Our survey of the existing research was made possible by a grant to the senior author from the California State University Foundation.

Reprint requests should be sent to Dr. Plasek, Department of Sociology, California State University, Northridge, CA 91330.

tinctions pertaining to homosexuality as the object of attitudes. As a step toward clarification, we propose the following analysis of homosexuality as an object of attitudes: (1) homosexuality as a kind of person; (2) homosexuality as a "trait"; and (3) the homosexuality of collectivities and cultural objects.[1] Attitude scales should explore rather than assume respondents' conceptualization of "things homosexual."

The phrasing of many questionnaire items in the attitudinal studies we reviewed imposes upon the respondent the view that "the homosexual" or "homosexuals" constitute a basic kind of person. Examine, for example, the item: "Homosexuals are dangerous as teachers or youth leaders because they try to get sexually involved with children" (Levitt & Klassen, 1974). This item imposes, rather than investigates, the assumption that homosexuality constitutes a "master status trait" (Hughes, 1945) in the minds of respondents. This assumption is shared by such theorists as Gagnon and Simon (1973), who argue that "the homosexual, like most significantly labeled persons (whether the label be positive or negative), has all his acts interpreted through the framework of his homosexuality" (p. 133). That this has not been the case throughout history is attested to by McIntosh's (1968) analysis of the emergence of a homosexual role in eighteenth-century London. It would seem, too, that there are various current social contexts in which statuses other than that of homosexuality are of equal or greater importance to various audiences, for example, the homosexuality of Gore Vidal or Truman Capote. To the extent that respondents do not believe that "homosexuals" are a basic category of social identity or "a kind of person," their responses to such items will be misleading.[2]

A weaker but related assumption common to many existing questionnaire items is the notion of homosexuality as an unspecified "trait." Take for example, the item: "It is easy to tell homosexuals by how they look" (Nyberg & Alston, 1977). Popular language supports the belief that individuals have qualities or traits. It refers to these traits as states of being without specifying whether they are psychological, social, or behavioral and without identifying them as stable or phasic. Such conceptual distinctions, however, are theoretically important.

In the past, it may have been true that only analytical units of "homosexuality" were the individual or the aggregate. Now, in the wake of gay organizational efforts, greater public awareness of gay social enclaves, and the cultural products associated with homosexuality, including movies, plays and the popular arts, it has become important for attitudinal measures to make the related differentiations. Reactions to these phenomena may not always be congruent. For example, an individual may have a neutral response to the existence of "homosexuals," but react negatively to the existence of a gay bar or to a gay parade. These analytical units of homosexuality could represent different dimensions of antihomosexual sentiment. They must be differentiated conceptually and provided for in attitudinal measures.[3]

RESEARCH FOCI

In our survey of empirical studies of antihomosexual attitudes, the dominant mode of investigation was the standard attitudinal scale. These varied from single items to extremely detailed analyses, as seen in the work of Levitt and Klassen (1974), MacDonald and Games (1974), Sobel (1976), and Smith (1971). Other studies included checklists (Simmons, 1965; Rooney & Gibbons, 1966; Steffensmeier & Steffensmeier 1974; Schofield, 1973; Gorer, 1971), open-ended characterizations (Simmons, 1965), semantic differential tests (MacDonald & Games, 1974), experimental laboratory situations (San Miguel & Millham, 1976; Morin, Taylor, & Kleinman, 1975), the labeling and ranking of groups as deviant (Simmons, 1965; Niederhoffer, 1969), and the retrospective analysis of responses to interaction with homosexuals.[4]

Our review of the empirical research yielded three major foci of investigation: (1) cognitive stereotypes of homosexuals; (2) the perception of threat engendered by homosexuals and homosexuality; and (3) opinions concerning the management of homosexuality, including the imposition of social restrictions and the accordance of civil liberties.[5]

Cognitive Stereotypic Characteristics

One of the most common dimensions of attitudinal scales involves the notion that homosexuals may be set apart from heterosexuals on the basis of presumed differences in attitudes, appearance, and behavior. Frequently, negative characteristics include dislike of women, effeminacy, the relative ease with which homosexuals may be identified, promiscuity, sado-masochistic practices, cross-dressing, and the tendency to be either active or passive in sexual behavior.[6]

Less frequently cited are positive characteristics such as creativity, better taste, higher intelligence, virtuosity in certain occupational performances, and heightened sensitivities. These positive traits should not, however, be viewed as necessarily favorable: the stereotype of the American male imposes definite limits on these "valued" characteristics. In other words, a male can have too much sensitivity, creativity, intelligence, for example, thus endorsing the folk notion that "too much of a good thing is a bad thing." Those who assess positive attitudes have not taken this belief into consideration.[7]

Homosexuality Perceived as a Threat

Many items measuring responses to homosexuality may be placed upon a continuum of social and psychological distance from the heterosexual respondent. Those dealing with attitudes toward homosexuality in the intimate sphere, i.e., in relation to the self and the immediate setting, are discussed below in terms of the impingement of homosexuality upon the "life space" of the respondent. Those dealing with the respondent's beliefs and feelings about the consequences of homosexuality for others are considered under the heading "Threat to Others." Finally, attitudes concerning the consequences of homosexuality for "society" and "culture" are considered.[8]

One caveat is in order here: It is appropriate to recognize that respondents, because of differences in cognitive style and political and social concerns, may not uniformly respond to items that fall at different points along the distance continuum. For example, some respondents, when presented with items assessing attitudes toward "society" and "culture," may respond simply in terms of more immediate and personal attitudes toward homosexuality. Ideally, measurement should be sufficiently flexible to allow respondents to cease responding to items when the degree of distance is outside their range of knowledge or experience.

Impingement Into the Life Space. Certain items may be classified as a focus involving *impingement into the respondent's life space.* The life space contains not only the actor but also those who are in close association with him, e.g., children, spouse, close friends, all of whom are seen as extensions of the self. Impingement occurs across a boundary dividing the homosexual "outside" from the presumably heterosexual "inside" and may go in either direction. Examples of inside to outside impingements include the "discovery" that a friend, a child, or a business associate is homosexual. Such intimate impingements are to be distinguished from those involving outside to inside movements, e.g., the willingness of a heterosexual to converse with a known homosexual or the response to a sexual advance by a homosexual.[9] Closely associated are those items that measure exposure to homosexuals: attendance at a party with known homosexuals, friendships with homosexuals, and the like (e.g., Kitsuse, 1962; Blake, 1974).

The nature of such negative responses needs to be clearly delineated. Pattison (1974) has criticized Weinberg's (1972) original conceptualization of homophobia as a classic phobia, arguing that many negative responses are "ego-alien" ("not me") rather than phobic manifestations of fear, anxiety, hostility, and so forth. Such a distinction is crucial and should be incorporated into research instruments.

Threat to Others. Various items assess respondents' fears of presumed attendant consequences of homosexuality. These consequences are outside the respondents' life spaces; they focus upon dangers to others that are attributable to homosexuality. Examples include the belief that homosexuality is associated with child molestation, legalization will lead to the wholesale practice of homosexuality, and that the homosexual is endangering himself by engaging in such activities.[10] Researchers base such items on popular homophobic stereotypes without making a systematic inventory of actual beliefs.[11]

Threat to Other Components of the Culture. Many items in the empirical measurement of antihomosexual attitudes deal with presumed negative consequences of homosexuality for what is generally valued within the general culture, such as the universal desirability of procreation and participation in the nuclear family, the progress of civilization, and masculinity.[12]

A variant of this approach is the notion that homosexuality constitutes a "problem." Items in this category assess respondents' willingness to label homosexuality a problem, without specifying whose problem it is, or they seek responses to the proposition that it is a social problem.[13] Such items seem, at first sight, to be measuring the respondents' cognitive bracketing of homosexuality per se. The status of a phenomenon as a problem, however, always exists within some larger context, i.e., something is a problem to a person, to a community, or in relation to achieving an end. Such contexts are typically not specified. For example, it is common to require response to an item "homosexuality is a social problem," by agreeing or disagreeing. Such a statement is too vague to tap various constructions of homosexuality as a problem.

Items which question the respondents' willingness to label homosexuality as "abnormal" or as a "sickness" also fall in the category of threat to other aspects of the culture. It is the "lack of fit" within the presumed normality that characterizes the presumption that homosexuality is "sick" or "abnormal."[14]

In the category "threat to other aspects of the culture" are items that question the respondents' willingness to label homosexuality (or homosexual behavior) as "immoral."[15] It is assumed that that which is immoral, ipso facto, runs counter to that which is moral, and that that which is moral is part of the general culture.

"Morality" *means* sexual conduct to many respondents;[16] to others, it is taken in its classical sense of "ethics." Thus, immorality equals unconventional, non-normative sexual practice, and homosexuality is tautologically immoral for some respondents. For others, homosexuality is a breach of a broader set of ethical considerations.

A final variant of the category "threat to other aspects of the culture" is found in items which assess the respondents' beliefs concerning the etiology of homosexuality.[17] Such questions assume that homosexuality is something that must be accounted for. It is the problematic and not the normal which requires explanation (Mills, 1940). However, audiences such as physicians, psychiatrists, and sociologists believe that both the normal and the abnormal, the ordinary as well as the exotic, require explanations. Respondents, however, when faced with questions of etiology, are likely led to assume that the phenomenon is abnormal and problematic.

Management/Social Restrictions

Based on the assumption of the problematic nature of homosexuality are items which tap public opinions concerning the management of homosexuality.[18] Some of these items are related to the sickness model. They question the beliefs concerning the appropriate, institutional control of homosexuality. Response categories include incarceration, enforcement or extension of existing laws, psychiatric treatment, and variations on the "live-and-let-live" theme.[19] Although these categories may entail the denial of civil liberties to homosexuals, the punitive nature of such restrictions is problematic. Social restrictions or requirements placed upon those whom respondents perceive as "threats" are not likely to be seen as punitive. Similar restrictions placed on presumable moral transgressions may also be perceived as justifiably punitive. It is appropriate at this point to postulate a continuum of management strategies, upon which existing and emerging forms of moral and social sanctioning can be placed. One way in which such a continuum could be conceptualized would entail a natural "zero" point, representing the respondent's view that nothing should be changed in regard to society's restrictions on homosexuality (see Figure 1). A negative range to the left could represent responses favoring repressive or "therapeutic" measures of control. A range to the right could represent responses favoring the diminution or elimination of existing negative sanctions and the enactment of civil rights legislation. Items in current attitudinal measures that explore the management of homosexuality are not evenly distributed over this continuum. They tend to be skewed to the left. Items around the neutral point are rare.

This bias in the design of instruments is a reflection of their designers'

$- \infty$ $\hfill + \infty$

			0			
eradication	←	more	← no →	less	→	civil
of		repression	change	repression		rights
homosexuality						legislation

Figure 1

Attitudes about changing social restrictions on homosexuality belief in a generally antihomosexual culture and the social science designation of homosexuality as deviance. Such perspectives lead to the assumption that, if a respondent thinks or feels anything, it would be negative. This bias may also indirectly contribute to and crystalize antihomosexual sentiment among respondents. We know from previous studies that a research instrument may have latent functions as an agent of socialization. Few instuments in use make it possible to distinguish the homophile from the indifferent respondent, and some make impossible the distinction between the mildly antihomosexual and the neutral. Items concerning what ought to be done thus reflect and reinforce antihomosexual extremes and fail to tap attitudes at the neutral point on the continuum.

RIGHTS OF HOMOSEXUALS

A related facet of attitudes concerning the management of homosexuality that is often measured is public willingness to accord various civil liberties to homosexuals. The legalization of private homosexual acts between consenting adults, the right of homosexuals to organize for social and political reasons, the non-harassment of homosexual bars and bathhouses, and the right of homosexuals to engage in various occupations and to occupy positions of authority are issues commonly tapped by items in questionnaires.[20] The willingness to accord civil liberties to homosexuals is not, however, to be confused with a generally favorable attitude toward homosexuality. Several studies report that for well-educated, young respondents, favorable attitudes toward civil liberties often go hand in hand with repugnance toward homosexual activities. Such is the case in the findings of Sorenson (1973) and Sobel (1976).

GENERAL PROBLEMS IN THE MEASUREMENT OF ATTITUDES TOWARD HOMOSEXUALITY

In examining questionnaire items used to tap public attitudes toward homosexuality, the following issues have been addressed.

(1) There exists a preponderance of *cognitive* foci. Researchers have been concerned overwhelmingly with how subjects label homosexuality, as bad, sick, sinful, abnormal or immoral. They have been mostly concerned with the general cognitive and evaluative categories within which respondents are willing to place homosexuality. They have been much less concerned with tapping emotional responses toward homosexual objects. Pattison's (1974) distinction between ego-alien and phobic responses has not, to our knowledge, been incorporated in the research.

The research has also failed to recognize behavioral dimensions. A refreshing, albeit only theoretical, exception to this omission is found in the work of Altman (1971). Behavioral instances of antihomosexuality are defined as instances of oppression, which is divided into persecution, discrimination, and tolerance. Persecution is seen as stemming from the illegality of homosexual behavior. Social discrimination is viewed as similar to exploitation, with instances of surcharges for various services (e.g., entertainment and housing) offered to homosexuals. Tolerance is distinguished from acceptance on the basis of the superior status from which the former is extended and the equal status of the latter.

Acceptance, in Altman's view, involves the equality of the heterosexual and homosexual orientation within a pluralistic framework. In his discussion of tolerance, he posits a conflict between affective and cognitive attitudes:

> Most intelligent heterosexuals reject, intellectually, their hostility to homosexuals, while unable to conquer their emotional repugnance. The outward result is tolerance. (p. 42)

He further points to the role of institutions such as the church and psychiatry, which legitimize oppression. He notes the threat that homosexuality poses for the mores of a society organized around the nuclear family and sharply differentiated social sex-roles.

It is probable that negative cognitions of an object will result in its negative treatment. This assumption, however, ignores the importance of situational factors in structuring behavior, attitudes, and sentiments. Most social psychologists contend that people's actions result from an interaction between personal predispositions and situational factors (Magnusson & Endler, 1977). A long line of research attests to the strength of situational factors, for example, Hartshorne and May (1928), La Piere (1934), and Deutscher (1966).

In this failure to tap behavioral dimensions of public attitudes toward homosexuality, social science indirectly provides intellectual support for antihomosexuality. For example, if attitudinal research reveals that a large proportion of the public has negative stereotypes of homosexuality, then the unsophisticated lay audience may infer that there is a general public willingness, attested to by prestigious authorities in the name of "science," to endorse repressive practices. This reasoning might proceed as follows: "If 70 percent of the people think homosexuality is sick, then we can assume that they would be willing to deny homosexuals civil liberties. . . ."

The absence of research on the behavioral aspects of responses toward homosexuality is partly due to the fact that behavioral studies are far more difficult than cognitive studies to design and implement. Behavioral studies require experimental or quasi-experimental designs, with all their cost and care. Fewer subjects can be run. This obstacle insures that the simplest type of research, the written questionnaire which taps cognitive and, less frequently, affective dimensions, will be the prevailing method of inquiry. In future research on public responses toward homosexuality, the major focus should be on what people *do* in relation to homosexuality rather than on what people say. It is ultimately in action, not in words, that a society is libertarian or repressive.

(2) An additional problem, research on public attitudes toward homosexuality confounds cognitive and affective dimensions of attitudes. The lay culture provides for the greater legitimacy of "feelings in response to objective traits of objects" than of "feelings for no reason." If one feels "disgusted," "repelled," or "turned off" by something, then one generally locates the explanation for those feelings in some objective property of the object. Therefore, "cognitive" items may be in many cases artifacts, in a justificatory vein, of basic affective predispositions.

(3) Contemporary studies of attitudes toward homosexuality do not investigate the question of stability of responses in different situations. They imply either an assumed model of stability of attitude or a willingness of the investigators to proceed in the absence of a model of which that attitude forms a part. This problem arises in part because researchers have not conducted "re-tests" of their respondents; most studies are of a "one-shot" nature.

(4) It is naive to assume that individuals respond directly to a physical stimulus. Rather, they respond to a definition of a stimulus, itself a socially constructed consensus. Past studies have assumed that reactions to homosexuality occur in a social vacuum. Here again the measurement situation departs from real situations.

That the individual may respond on the basis of privately held, largely context-independent attitudes may be the case in instances of unexpected disclosure of homosexuality. Where the sexual orientation of a person has been problematic, however, people are likely to "talk" with others in the process of defining appropriate reactions.

Researchers should make use of experimental methods, especially the behavioral laboratory, by involving *groups* of subjects in the study of the *social* process of reactions to homosexuality. At the present time, the preponderance of attitude studies consists of administering a questionnaire to isolated individuals who respond in private. Research designs that include the situational context are needed to counterbalance this trend and to make the study of reactions to homosexuality *social* as well as psychological. There is a tendency for private reactions to be more negative and extreme than public reactions, if previous social psychological studies can be generalized. One of the primary tasks of future research should be to chart variations in attitudes toward homosexuality within the various social contexts in which they occur.

(5) It appears that the antihomosexual items included in most question-naires are drawn from the repertoire of negative stereotypes of the designers rather than from their observations of responses of persons in a variety of settings. Questionnaires are presented as if the construction of their items could be taken for granted. Few authors describe any qualita-tive work such as interviews or participant observation as the basis for the design of their instruments. Nowhere are the origins of items other than previous scales described. All too often the items used are not even made available to the reader. Thus we have no way of assessing the attitudinal portrait elicited by such questionnaires and of comparing it with an atti-tudinal picture that emerged in a natural and spontaneous way.

The systematic failure to tap the culture's patterned responses to homo-sexuality constitutes the single most serious flaw in the existing research. Regardless of the adequacy of sampling (e.g., Levitt & Klassen, 1974) and the sophistication of methodology (e.g., Millham, San Miguel, & Kellogg, 1976), the failure to base the instruments on grounded observa-tions of social reality brings into question the findings of *all* existing studies.

(6) One major outcome of this failure to conduct grounded research is the taking for granted of the respondents' knowledge of the homosexual-ity of another individual. Consider the following items:

a. "It would be upsetting to find I was alone with a homosexual" (Lumby, 1976).
b. "I do not like to associate socially with a person who has a reputa-tion of being homosexual" (Weinberg & Williams, 1974).
c. "Homosexuals should never be allowed to teach or supervise children" (MacDonald, 1976).

Such items do not take into account the problematic nature of respon-dents' knowledge of homosexuality. Homosexuality, unlike other deviant statuses, is not ordinarily observable.[21] Instead, individuals respond to a variety of cues culturally defined as possible indicators of homosexuality. It is usually necessary to respond to others long before their homosexual-ity is revealed or confirmed. Cues forming the bases for suspecting and, in some cases, "confirming" others' homosexuality vary according to subculture, region, sex, context, and other unexplored dimensions. Many such cues apparently pertain to sex-role norms (e.g., effeminacy and lack of involvement with women). Such cues may *erroneously* lead to the label of homosexuality. Ironically, some heterosexual persons may suffer the stigma of societal reactions to homosexuality more frequently than homo-sexuals. Conversely, homosexuals often have considerable power to manipulate such cues to conceal their sexual orientation.[22]

Past studies have not investigated the process of social determination of the individual's homosexuality wherein cues are perceived and debated and behavior is closely scrutinized. Questionnaire items fail to place knowledge of homosexuality upon a continuum. Instead, research subjects are presented with a "known homosexual" toward whom their reactions are measured.[23] The nature of the identification process, however, may bear significantly upon the nature of reactions toward homosexuality.

The practice in questionnaires of treating homosexuality as "given," we believe, reveals that items are constructed in a vacuum without observing spontaneous reactions occurring in real situations. Perhaps this reflects a tendency on the part of researchers to ignore the fact that social interaction is a complex process, one which can be captured only after long periods of observation. The task for research, therefore, is to specify conditions under which identification of homosexuality is made, to determine the nature of previous knowledge, and to assess the attitudinal impact of variations within these two areas.

CONCLUSION

The observation of societal reactions to homosexuality constitutes a potentially productive arena in which unanswered questions in the sociology of deviance might be pursued. Such investigation can be based on the sensitizing notions of Berger and Luckman (1967) concerning the social construction of reality as an incorporating framework. This theoretical perspective has captured the sociological imagination, but has been ignored in empirical studies.

Our review of research on homophobia reveals that studies of societal reactions to homosexuality, like studies of homosexuality in general, have failed to interest the mainstream of sociology, even in the general area of deviance theory. These studies are "one-shot" endeavors and methodologically weak. They appear in specialized journals, read by counselors and those engaged in "gay research."

Since the advent of Gay Liberation in 1969, a network of "gay researchers" has emerged whose work so far has not had any general sociological impact. This failure may be due to the fact that their research stems from a political commitment and is addressed to political goals. Even the behavioral studies tend to examine the extremes of negative responses, such as the denial of employment, because these are of political and humane concern.

There remains, too, the professional stigma associated with a sustained research interest in the topic of homosexuals: "If you're *that* interested in them, you must be one!" That stigma still keeps many competent researchers away.

It is now appropriate for researchers to reformulate "from the ground up" the conceptualizations of social reactions to homosexuality based upon the interplay of responses between labelers and the labeled, the characteristics of subculture and self-identity, and the management strategies, both personal and collective, of the labeled. In other words, all processes in the manufacturing of a stigmatized class with political interests must be considered. Investigators should try to observe and record the process by which a stigmatized identity is proposed, and identify a set of particularistic and highly variable cues by which it is signified and which becomes consensually refined and crystallized. Researchers should try to detail the forms of collaboration in which stigmatized "insiders" and stigmatizing "outsiders" assign themselves territory and talk.

Formulations of social processes seem necessary in order to rescue the study of societal reactions to homosexuality from manufactured categories. Only through studies of such processes in situ can we discover the attitudinal links between cognitive, affective, and behavioral aspects of homosexuality.

NOTES

1. As sociologists we argue for the necessity of viewing reactions to homosexuality as a social phenomenon structuring the nature of social relationships, and as a cultural phenomenon influencing the goals and values of actors in pertinent situations.

2. One gratifying exception to this tendency is an item in the ATHS Scale, "Homosexuals are pretty much all alike (agree or disagree)." See MacDonald (1973), MacDonald and Games (1974), and MacDonald (1976).

3. Reference is made to homosexuality as a "lifestyle." This notion should be explored as an object of attitudes, too, although its conceptualization still seems to be vague.

Related to this failure to partition the objects of attitudes is the relative weakness of most studies in selecting and describing respondents. Although some studies do take account of basic demographic variables such as age, sex, religion, and socioeconomic status, most fail to ascertain the sexual orientation of the respondent and very few consider a potentially critical variable, "extent and nature of personal contact with homosexuals." Thus, biased samples may produce questionable findings and vital information may have been omitted.

4. Tests of validity, reliability, scalability, and so on, were often absent. Notable exceptions are found in the work of Levitt and Klassen (1974), Blake (1974), Lumby (1976), Millham, San Miguel, and Kellogg (1976). Plummer (1975) criticizes all such modes of investigation: "Such studies of attitudes toward homosexuality cannot be taken as a very reliable guide to either what people actually believe or what they would do in a concrete situation. They may even become part of the global reified notion of 'societal reaction' which precipitates a self-fulfilling prophecy. . . ." (p. 104). He advocates the study of concrete social reactions to homosexuality, as in the investigations of Gerrassi (1966), Gallo et al. (1966) and Williams and Weinberg (1971).

5. Attempts to delineate research foci were rare. A notable exception is the work of Blake (1974). His dimensions are similar to ours: value judgments of homosexual acts as they contradict social institutions, social expectations for personal interaction with persons identified as homosexuals and proscribed for homosexuals in social contexts, and descriptive attributes of homosexuals.

6. See, for example, MacDonald (1976), MacDonald and Games (1974), MacDonald, Huggins, Young, and Swanson (1973), Rooney and Gibbons (1966), Steffensmeier and Steffensmeier (1974), Simmons (1965), Levitt and Klassen (1974), Weinberg and Williams (1974), Blake (1974),

Millham, San Miguel, and Kellogg (1976). As early as 1957, Evelyn Hooker found that psychiatrists could *not* identify homosexuals within a matched sample of heterosexuals and homosexuals on the basis of Rorschach analyses.

7. See, for example, MacDonald (1976), MacDonald and Games (1974), MacDonald et al. (1973), Simmons (1965), Weinberg and Williams (1974), and Millham, San Miguel, and Kellogg (1976).

8. These three types of threat are amenable to techniques of social distance scaling. Relations between exposure and interaction and the respondents' boundary definitions might be explored.

9. Examples of items measuring impingement on the life space from inside to outside may be found in the works of MacDonald et al. (1973), MacDonald and Games (1974), MacDonald (1976), Sorenson (1973), Kitsuse (1962), Blake (1974), Millham, San Miguel, and Kellogg (1976). Items measuring outside to inside threats may be found in the works of the above writers and that of Levitt and Klassen (1974) and Smith (in Weinberg, 1972).

10. See, for example, MacDonald (1973), MacDonald and Games (1974), MacDonald (1976), Rooney and Gibbons (1966), Levitt and Klassen (1974), Blake (1974), Millham, San Miguel, and Kellogg (1976).

11. By rationales, we intend to indicate that such beliefs are not causes of antihomosexual attitudes, but are cognitive devices "shoring up" affective elements of antihomosexuality.

12. Items measuring the threat of homosexuality to other components of the culture may be found in the works of MacDonald (1973), MacDonald and Games (1974), MacDonald (1976), Levitt and Klassen (1974), Weinberg and Williams (1974), Smith (in Weinberg, 1972), and Millham, San Miguel, and Kellogg (1976).

13. Homosexuality as a problem is assessed by Schofield (1970) and Levitt and Klassen (1974).

14. A great deal of research includes the assessment of homosexuality as abnormal or sick. See, for example, MacDonald et al. (1973), MacDonald and Games (1974), MacDonald (1966), Sorenson (1973), Rooney and Gibbons (1966), Steffensmeier and Steffensmeier (1974), Schofield (1970), Gorer (1971), Simmons (1965), Levitt and Klassen (1974), Smith (in Weinberg, 1972), Sobel (1976), Weinberg and Williams (1974), Blake (1974), Millham, San Miguel, and Kellogg (1976).

15. See, for example, MacDonald et al. (1973), MacDonald and Games (1974), MacDonald (1976), Sorenson (1973), Sobel (1976), Gorer (1971), Oberholtzer (1971), Simmons (1965), Levitt and Klassen (1974), Nyberg and Alston (1976), Weinberg and Williams (1974), Blake (1974), Millham, San Miguel, and Kellogg (1976).

16. Among some segments of the population, sex is not directly referred to but obliquely euphemized. One common "euphemism" for sexual conduct is "morality."

17. Measurements of etiology are found in the works of Levitt and Klassen (1974), Smith (in Weinberg, 1972), Weinberg and Williams (1974), Blake (1974), Millham, San Miguel, and Kellogg (1976).

18. See Emerson and Messinger (1977).

19. See, for example, MacDonald et al. (1973), MacDonald and Games (1974), MacDonald (1976), Levitt and Klassen (1974), Smith (in Weinberg, 1972), Sorenson (1973), Sobel (1976), Blake (1974), Gorer (1971), Schofield (1973), Millham, San Miguel, and Kellogg (1976). For a more specialized set of rights concerning academic life, see Crew (1978).

20. Attitudes toward homosexuals who teach children, however, is confounded with the dimension of "threat." Assessments concerning civil liberties may be found in the work of MacDonald et al. (1973), MacDonald and Games (1974), MacDonald (1976), Levitt and Klassen (1974), Sobel (1976), Blake (1974), Smith (in Weinberg, 1972), Millham, San Miguel, and Kellogg (1976), National Opinion Research Center (1982).

21. We are ignoring instances of direct "disclosure" (e.g., a member being solicited for homosexual activities, admissions, etc.). These constitute a limited portion of the conditions under which societal reactions are generated.

22. That this manipulation of cues is varied, and not simply a matter of concealment, is attested to by the report that lower class homosexuals may "flaunt" their sexuality within their occupational contexts, as a means of overcoming their even more devalued lower-class status (Farrell & Morrione, 1974).

23. Whether the "known" homosexual engages in sexual activities and the subculture on a lifelong, permanent basis; as a "stage" of development; or in the episodic, intermittent manner is not explored. We assume that the researchers envisage the first type. We would argue that societal responses vary considerably by type.

36HOMOPHOBIA: AN OVERVIEW

REFERENCES

Altman, D. (1971). *Homosexual: Oppression and liberation.* New York: Outerbridge & Dienstfrey.
Berger, P. L., & Luckman, T. (1967). *The social construction of reality.* London: Penguin Press.
Blake, D. M. (1974). *Measuring attitudes towards homosexuals: A brief scale for educational and evaluative purposes.* Unpublished master's thesis, University of Iowa, Iowa City, IA.
The consenting adult homosexual and the law: An empirical study of enforcement and administration in L. A. County. (1966). *UCLA Law Review, 13,* 643–832.
Crew, L. (Ed.). (1978). *The gay academic.* Palm Springs, CA: ETC Publications.
Deutscher, I. (1966). Words and deeds: Social science and social policy. *Social Problems, 13,* 235–254.
Emerson, R., & Messinger, S. (1977). The micro-politics of trouble. *Social Problems, 25*(2), 121–134.
Farrell, L., & Morrione, T. J. (1974). Social interaction and stereotypic responses to homosexuals. *Archives of Sexual Behavior, 3,* 425–442.
Gagnon, J. H., & Simon, W. (1973). *Sexual conduct: The social sources of human sexuality.* Chicago: Aldine Press.
Gallo, J. J., et al. (1966). The consenting adult homosexual and the law. *UCLA Law Review, 13,* 686–742.
Gerassi, J. (1966). *Boys of Boise: Furor, vice and folly in an American city.* New York: Macmillan.
Gorer, G. (1971). *Sex and marriage in England today.* London: Thomas Nelson & Sons.
Hartshorne, H., & May, N. (1928). *Studies in the nature of character* (Vol. 1). New York: Macmillan.
Hooker, E. (1957). The adjustment of the male overt homosexual. *Journal of Projective Techniques, 21,* 18–31.
Hughes, E. (1945). Dilemmas and contradictions of status. *American Journal of Sociology, 50*(5), 253–259.
Kitsuse, J. I. (1962). Societal reaction to deviant behavior: Problems of theory and method. *Social Problems, 9*(3), 247–256.
La Piere, R. T. (1934). Attitudes versus actions. *Social Forces, 13*(2), 230–237.
Levitt, E., & Klassen, A. D., Jr. (1974). Public attitudes towards homosexuals: Part of the 1970 national survey by the Institute for Sex Research. *Journal of Homosexuality, 1*(1), 29–47.
Lumby, M. E. (1976). Homophobia: The quest for a valid scale. *Journal of Homosexuality, 2*(1), 39–47.
MacDonald, A. P., Jr. (1976). Homophobia: Its roots and meanings. *Homosexual Counseling Journal, 3*(1), 23–33.
MacDonald, A. P., Jr., & Games, R. G. (1974). Some characteristics of those who hold positive and negative attitudes toward homosexuals. *Journal of Homosexuality, 1*(1), 9–27.
MacDonald, A. P., Jr., Huggins, J., Young, S., & Swanson, R. A. (1973). Attitudes toward homosexuality: Preservation of sex morality or the double standard? *Journal of Consulting and Clinical Psychology, 40*(1), 161.
Magnusson, D., & Endler, N. (Eds.). (1977). *Personality at the crossroads: Current issues in interactional psychology.* Hillsdale, NJ: Lawrence Erlbaum.
McIntosh, M. (1968). The homosexual role. *Social Problems, 16*(2), 182–192.
Millham, J., San Miguel, C. L., & Kellogg, R. (1976). A factor-analytic conceptualization of attitudes towards male and female homosexuals. *Journal of Homosexuality, 2*(1), 3–10.
Mills, C. W. (1940). Situated actions and vocabularies of motives. *The American Sociological Review, 6,* 904–913.
Morin, S. F., Taylor, K. E., & Kleinman, S. J. (1975, September). *Attitudes toward homosexuality and social distance.* Paper presented at the 83rd Annual Meeting of the American Psychological Association, Chicago, IL.
National Opinion Research Center. (1982). *General social surveys, 1972–1982.* Chicago: Author.
Niederhoffer, A. (1969). *Behind the shield: The police in urban society.* New York: Anchor.
Nyberg, K. L., & Alston, J. P. (1976). Analysis of public attitudes toward homosexual behavior. *Journal of Homosexuality, 2*(2), 99–107.
Nyberg, K. L., & Alston, J. P. (1977). Homosexual labeling by university youths. *Adolescence, 12*(48), 542–546.

Oberholtzer, W. (Ed.). (1971). *Is gay good? Ethics, theology, and homosexuality.* Philadelphia: Westminster Press.

Pattison, E. M. (1974). Confusing concepts about the concept of homosexuality. *Psychiatry, 37*(4), 340–347.

Plummer, K. (1975). *Sexual stigma: An interactionist account.* London: Routledge & Kegan Paul.

Rooney, E. A., & Gibbons, D. C. (1966). Social reactions to "crime without victims." *Social Problems, 13*(4), 400–410.

San Miguel, C. L., & Millham, J. (1976). The role of cognitive and situational variables in aggression towards homosexuals. *Journal of Homosexuality, 2*(1), 11–27.

Schofield, M. (1973). *Sexual behavior of young adults.* London: Penguin Press.

Simmons, J. L. (1965). Public stereotypes of deviants. *Social Problems, 13*(2), 223–232.

Smith, K. T. (1971). Homophobia: A tentative personality profile. *Psychological Reports, 29,* 1091–1094.

Sobel, H. J. (1976). Adolescent attitudes towards homosexuality in relation to self concept and body satisfaction. *Adolescence, 11*(43), 443–453.

Sorenson, R. C. (1973). *Adolescent sexuality in contemporary America.* New York: World.

Steffensmeier, D., & Steffensmeier, R. (1974). Sex differences in reactions to homosexuals: Research continuities and further developments. *Journal of Sex Research, 10,* 52–67.

Weinberg, G. (1972). *Society and the healthy homosexual.* New York: St. Martin's Press.

Weinberg, M., & Williams, C. (1974). *Male homosexuals.* New York: Oxford Press.

Williams, C. J., & Weinberg, M. S. (1971). *Homosexuals and the military: A study of less than honorable discharge.* New York: Harper & Row.

Attitudes Toward Lesbians and Gay Men: A Factor-Analytic Study

Gregory M. Herek, PhD
Yale University

ABSTRACT. This paper reports a series of factor analyses of responses to attitude statements about lesbians and gay men. Using a common factor model with oblique rotation, a bipolar "Condemnation-Tolerance" factor was observed repeatedly in four separate samples of undergraduates. The factor accounts for 35–45% of the total common variance in responses, and is similar for male and female respondents and for questionnaires concerning both lesbians and gay men. A "Beliefs" factor accounts for another 5% of the total variance. It is argued that scales assessing attitudes toward lesbians and gay men should restrict their content to items loading highly on the Condemnation-Tolerance factor.

As prejudice against lesbians and gay men becomes more widely recognized as a social issue, its accurate assessment becomes more important for social scientists. In the last decade, an unprecedented amount of research has been directed toward developing reliable and valid scales for measuring attitudes toward lesbians and gay men (e.g., Hudson & Ricketts, 1980; Larsen, Reed, & Hoffman, 1980; MacDonald & Games, 1974). The typical procedure for constructing such scales is to collect a large pool of statements about lesbians and gay men and, using various scaling procedures, to select from this pool a small subset of items that constitutes the final scale (Edwards, 1957). An important problem encountered in this process is that of discovering the interrelationships among responses, and the extent to which such relationships can be summarized in terms of a few dimensions or factors. This is a significant issue

I wish to thank Stephen L. Franzoi, Dean K. Simonton, Walter W. Hudson, Carol Corcoran, David DeVoe, Karen Ebeling, Steve Hinkle, Martin Rogers, Alan Zonderman, Valerie Cook, and Martin Wong for their assistance with this project. An earlier version of this paper was presented at the meeting of the Western Psychological Association in Honolulu, HI in 1980. The research was partially supported by a grant from the University of California, Davis. Reprints may be obtained by writing to the author, Department of Psychology, Yale University, Box 11A Yale Station, New Haven, CT 06520.

39

in attitude scale construction because the existence of different factors and their degree of interrelatedness will affect scoring procedures. Additionally, empirical study of such factors is important in its own right.

Factor analysis is the most appropriate method for addressing the question of dimensionality because it permits the distillation of the variance within a large set of variables to a small set of underlying patterns (see Rummel, 1970; Thorndike, 1978). Two previous studies of attitudes toward lesbians and gay men have used factor-analytic techniques, but each suffers from methodological shortcomings.

Mosher and O'Grady (1979) obtained responses from 104 males to their Homosexual Threat Inventory (HTI) for a principal-factor analysis. Communalities were estimated (the estimation method was not specified in the published report), followed by iteration. It is difficult to evaluate this analysis because so few details are given about the results. For example, the authors reported only the proportion of explained variance for each factor, but not the proportion of total variance. Consequently, the reader cannot know whether the smaller factors account for a sufficient proportion of variance even to warrant interpretation. Aside from this, several other criticisms are relevant.

First, no rationale was provided for the use of an orthogonal (varimax) rotation. The authors assumed that scores on one factor generally would be uncorrelated with scores on another factor, but that both would tap "homosexual threat." In a later section of this paper, I shall argue against this assumption. Another problem is that the complexity of several scale items is high, i.e., they have high loadings on more than one factor. All three of the statements with loadings greater than .30 on Factor 3 ("Lack of Tolerance for Homosexuality") have similarly high loadings on Factor 2 ("Fear and Denial of Personal Homosexual Tendencies"). Of the two remaining items that load higher than .30 on Factor 2, one has an even higher loading on Factor 1 ("Hostility Toward Homosexuals to Bolster Hypermasculine Identity"). There appears to be only one unique item for Factor 2 and none for Factor 3. Consequently, it is difficult or impossible to interpret the underlying factors of the HTI.

In addition to these shortcomings, the scale items themselves are of poor quality. Many carry double meanings, are offensively worded, or both (e.g., "I've never been able to understand why anyone would fuck a man in the ass when you could have better sex with a woman"; or "I'd rather be dead than queer"; or "I could never bring myself to suck another man's cock"). The statements are intended to tap male respondents' feelings of personal threat from homosexuals, but it is likely that many men simply are offended by the locker-room language so pervasive in the questionnaire. In summary, Mosher and O'Grady's factor analysis does not provide a great deal of insight for empirical or theoretical perspectives on prejudice against gay men and lesbians.

In the only other factor-analytic study previously reported, Millham, San Miguel, and Kellogg (1976) used varimax rotation to extract six orthogonal (uncorrelated) factors from responses to their Homosexuality Attitude Scale (HAS). Since differing proportions of explained variance were associated with comparable factors for lesbian and male homosexual targets, Millham and his colleagues concluded that the cognitive patterning of attitudes toward lesbians differs from that of attitudes toward male homosexuals.

Although it has several strong points (for example, the use of separate item-pools for lesbian and gay male targets and the large sample size), there also are some problems with the analysis. First, dichotomous (true-false) responses were obtained to the questionnaire items. Such a procedure tends to produce interitem correlations that either are artificially limited in size or are inflated (Comrey, 1978). Either result affects the factor solution. A better alternative would have been to use continuous measures (e.g., Likert scales with a range of several points). A second limitation is the use of unit values (i.e., equal to 1) in the diagonal of the correlation matrix. The solution from such a procedure is likely to be distorted, even when followed by iteration to stability (it is not reports whether such iteration was carried out). The risk is even higher when, as in this study, dichotomous responses are used (Comrey, 1978, p. 652).

Another problem is that three of the six factors may be low level factors ("Preference for Male over Female Homosexuals," "Preference for Female over Male Homosexuals," and "Cross-Sexed Mannerisms"). They account for a small proportion of the variance and consist of pairs of highly correlated items that measure very similar phenomena. Analyses with different samples and a different item pool are needed to test whether these factors are spurious products of the particular items included in the original questionnaire.

Perhaps the greatest flaw in the analysis by Millham's group is their assumption that the factors should be uncorrelated, as indicated by the use of varimax rotation. They provide no rationale for using this rotational technique, yet their decision has important implications. If factor scores are assumed to be uncorrelated, it means that many individuals could express completely positive views about lesbians or gay men on one factor (say, that they are not dangerous and pose no threat to society) but that this will bear no relation to their views on some other factor (say, that they pose a personal threat).

Such an assumption is unwarranted, however. It has been argued on epistemological grounds that the world cannot realistically be treated as though the basic functional unities represented by factors are uncorrelated (Rummel, 1970, p. 388). Since the different dimensions of attitudes toward lesbians and gay men are most probably interrelated to some degree, the factor solution should indicate the magnitude of the relationships. At the least, orthogonality should be demonstrated empirically rather than assumed.

Millham's research group itself has cast doubts upon the orthogonality of their factors. Weinberger and Millham (1979) conducted a second-order factor analysis (with varimax rotation) using the factors from the HAS scale and factors from a questionnaire about sex roles. Although the interscale correlations were not reported, it is clear that the three lesbian factors and the three male homosexual factors that account for the bulk of the variance in the HAS are related. Each loads on the first higher order factor at a level greater than .60. The three low-level factors loaded on their own small factors (whose share of the total variance is not reported).

In contrast to the varimax procedure, oblique rotation (of which orthogonal rotation is a subset) permits empirical assessment of interfactor relatedness by calculating factor correlations. It will indicate if the factors truly are unrelated, but it also will permit them to be correlated if that is a better solution. The research reported in the present paper used a factor-analytic procedure with oblique rotation to ascertain the number of factors accounting for a significant proportion of the variance in attitudes toward lesbians and gay men, and the extent to which they are intercorrelated.

METHOD

In the analyses reported in the present paper, the Pearson product-moment correlation matrix for the data was computed first with the SPSS PEARSON CORR subprogram (Nie, Hull, Jenkins, Steinbrenner, & Bent, 1975). The matrix then was analyzed with the SPSS FACTOR subprogram with "PA2" factoring, an *R*-type analysis based upon a respondents-by-items matrix that produces a principal-factors solution. Communalities were estimated by squared multiple correlations, followed by iteration (see Rummel, 1970, pp. 314–320, for a discussion of the merits of this method for estimating communalities). The PA2 procedure produces orthogonal factors which are allowed to become correlated if an oblique rotation is used. This procedure was followed with a direct oblimin rotational criterion and with *delta* set equal to zero for the rotation. In an initial analysis, all factors with eigenvalues greater than one were extracted in order to obtain an initial set of factors for interpretation. Substantively uninterpretable factors and those accounting for a very small proportion of the variance were excluded from subsequent analyses. Throughout this paper, the percentage of total common variance associated with each factor after rotation is reported, rather than the proportion of explained variance, since this percentage more accurately indicates the relative importance of each factor.

Preliminary Analyses

Exploratory factor analyses were conducted with three separate samples of undergraduates at the University of Nebraska at Omaha. In the first study, the Attitudes Toward Homosexuality Scale (ATHS-Form G), developed by MacDonald, Huggins, Young, and Swanson (1973), was administered to 72 respondents (40 females, 32 males). The ATHS-Form G consists of 28 statements about homosexuals and homosexuality (lesbians and gay men are not differentiated). Students responded to each item using a five-point Likert scale ranging from *strongly agree* to *strongly disagree.*

The results suggest that the ATHS is not a unidimensional instrument. A large factor, accounting for 43% of the total common variance, consisted of items expressing moral condemnation of homosexuality and advocating repression of homosexuals (items 2,4,6,7,12,14,15,16,17,19, 20,21,22,23,25,26). Two smaller factors also emerged that were substantively interpretable. Items loading highly on one factor denied any similarities between heterosexual and homosexual relationships (6% of the total common variance; items 3,5,13,18). Items on the other factor expressed feelings of personal revulsion or threat concerning homosexuality (5% of the total common variance; items 1,9,10,11,27). Correlations among the factors ranged from $-.25$ to $.53$.

The results underscore the importance of careful factor-analytic study prior to developing an attitude scale. It appears that the ATHS actually consists of several subscales, which should be considered in scoring. Researchers using the ATHS should investigate this possibility through additional factor analyses with larger samples and, if the results reported here are replicated, should consider revising the ATHS scoring procedure. It might be desirable, for example, to eliminate the items associated with the smaller factors and thereby produce a shorter, unidimensional scale.

The finding of greatest interest for the present study, however, does not pertain to the ATHS, as such. Instead, the results raise the question of whether these three factors are stable dimensions of attitudes toward homosexuality, or merely artifacts of the particular items used or idiosyncrasies of the sample. To investigate this issue, a larger pool of items was assembled. In addition to ATHS items, the new questionnaire also included statements used by Levitt and Klassen (1974) and Smith (1971), as well as some newly constructed items. Forty-seven items about "homosexuals" were used (lesbians were not differentiated from gay men). The questionnaire was administered to 104 undergraduates at the University of Nebraska at Omaha (57 females, 47 males). As before, students responded to each item on a 5-point Likert scale.

Four interpretable factors emerged from the first analysis. In subsequent solutions, a major bipolar factor emerged repeatedly, consisting of items indicating general tolerance or general condemnation for homosexuality. It accounted for a large proportion of the total common variance (42% with either a 3-factor solution or a 4-factor solution) and most of the explained variance (83% with a 3-factor solution, 77% with a 4-factor solution). Some smaller factors consisting of items expressing stereotypical beliefs about homosexuals also emerged, the largest accounting for 5% of the total common variance in each solution. Another small factor (3.5% of the total common variance) included statements expressing a desire to avoid contact with homosexuals and to keep them away from children. The smaller factors correlated with the Condemnation-Tolerance factor at levels ranging from .34 to .59.

Subsequently, a 59-item revised questionnaire was developed from items with high loadings on single factors from the previous analysis, and from newly constructed items. As before, lesbians and gay men were not differentiated. This questionnaire was administered to a new sample of 130 undergraduates at the University of Nebraska at Omaha (66 females, 64 males).

Once again, responses were subjected to several analyses with oblique rotation. Results were similar to those obtained earlier. The bipolar Condemnation-Tolerance factor again accounted for much of the total common variance (e.g., 36% for a 3-factor solution, 39% for a 4-factor solution). The second factor usually consisted of items expressing stereotypical beliefs about homosexuals and accounted for roughly 5% of the total common variance. In one instance (with a 4-factor solution), however, the stereotypical statements were divided between the third and fourth factors, which accounted for 3.7% and 2.6% of the total common variance, respectively. The second factor in this solution consisted of items juxtaposing homosexual and heterosexual relationships (e.g., items concerning romantic love between gays or lesbians, lesbians and gays as parents or as children). It was similar to the second and third factors obtained previously with the ATHS-Form G. The smaller factors were not correlated with each other, but were correlated with the general factor at levels ranging from .30 to .50.

Subsequent Factor Analysis

The results suggest the presence of a fairly stable Condemnation-Tolerance factor that accounts for between 35% and 45% of the total common variance in attitudes toward lesbians and gay men. A Beliefs factor also is present that accounts for approximately 5% of the total common variance. Other smaller factors also may be present.

Several shortcomings can be noted about the methods used to obtain the data, however. First, the analyses were conducted with very small samples. Although the minimally acceptable ratio of cases to variables in factor analysis remains a matter of research taste, it should be as large as possible (Rummel, 1970). Comrey (1978) argues that at least 200 cases should be analyzed. All three samples were too small by this criterion. Second, the items of Millham et al. (1976) were not included in the questionnaire (this phase of the research was under way at the time their article was published), so it is difficult to compare these results directly to theirs.

Finally, the questionnaires did not differentiate lesbians from gay men. In light of the considerable evidence that negative attitudes toward lesbians and gay men are associated with traditional sex role attitudes (MacDonald & Games, 1974; Minnigerode, 1976; Weinberger & Millham, 1979), the effects of gender are of central importance in this area of research. In particular, the possibility of an interaction effect between sex of respondent and sex of target should be examined in order to test the often-advanced hypothesis that many people are hostile toward homosexuals because they fear their own unarticulated homoerotic impulses (Cory, 1951; Ferenczi, 1914/1956; MacDonald, 1976; Marmor, 1980; Weinberg, 1972). Such an assertion suggests that homosexuals of one's same sex will be a source of particular anxiety to insecure individuals. Millham et al. (1976) reported findings that supported this proposition, but their analysis is problematic for reasons already detailed. It remains for a careful factor-analytic study to resolve this question empirically.

Based upon these considerations, another questionnaire was constructed, administered to a larger sample, and factor analyzed. Items from the previously analyzed questionnaires were included, along with some newly constructed items. Additionally, the items comprising the six factors reported by Millham et al. (1976) were included as marker variables to permit a comparison of results. The complete questionnaire consisted of 66 statements and was administered in two forms: one in which all items referred to lesbians (lesbian target) and one in which all items referred to gay men (gay male target). Each questionnaire employed a 9-point Likert scale ranging from *strongly agree* to *strongly disagree.* This expanded interval scale allowed greater response variation than in the preliminary study (which used a 5-point scale) and the Millham et al. study (which used a 2-point, true-false scale).

The two questionnaires were distributed randomly to separate samples of volunteers in introductory psychology classes at the University of California at Davis ($N = 635$), California State University at Sacramento ($N = 74$), California State University at Chico ($N = 93$), and Miami University in Oxford, Ohio ($N = 147$). Forty-three of the returned questionnaires were missing one or more responses and were omitted from the analysis. This left a total of 437 students who completed the lesbian target questionnaire (276 females, 161 males) and a separate group of 469 respondents who completed the gay male target questionnaire (282 females, 187 males).

In order to compare the factor structures for each sex and according to sex of target, responses from males and females first were analyzed separately for each of the two versions of the questionnaire. This procedure resulted in four data sets—lesbian target responses for females and for males, and gay male target responses for females and for males. Each data set was submitted to an SPSS PA2 analysis, using oblique rotation with *delta* set at zero. (This value had yielded the most interpretable results in the preliminary studies.)

RESULTS

The results were very similar to those obtained with previous samples. This was in spite of the different geographic locales of the samples, and the span of three years separating the two parts of the research. Each set of responses yielded two interpretable factors. The smaller factor was similar for all four groups, accounting for less than 6% of the total common variance. As in previous analyses, the items loading on this factor were statements of beliefs about lesbians and gay men, rather than of attitudes toward them. Included were statements such as "Male homosexuals tend to be very feminine"; "Most lesbians are generally afraid of men"; "Male homosexuals are more likely to seduce young people than are heterosexuals"; and "Most lesbians have unusually strong sex drives."

For all four groups, a Condemnation-Tolerance factor accounts for a large proportion of the total common variance: 32.5% for male responses to the lesbian target, 34.9% for female responses to this target, 35.1% for male responses to the gay male target, and 37% for female responses. Correlations between this factor and the Beliefs factor ranged from .36 to .48 for the four groups. The item-loadings on the Condemnation-Tolerance factor were compared among groups using a coefficient of congruence (Harman, 1967, p. 269) on the factor pattern matrices. The coefficient of congruence is a measure of the degree of similarity between two different factor matrices or vectors of factor loadings. The statistic ϕ can range in value from +1.00 to −1.00, and can be interpreted in a manner similar to a correlation coefficient. Values greater than .85 usually are considered to indicate a high degree of similarity between factors.

When female and male respondents were compared, there was no difference between them for either the lesbian target ($\phi = .97$) or the gay male target ($\phi = .98$). Female and male responses therefore were combined and new factor pattern matrices were computed, one for each target. When the two vectors of loadings were compared, $\phi = .92$. This indicates that the Condemnation-Tolerance factor is highly similar for attitudes toward lesbians and gay men, and directly contradicts a conclusion of Millham et al. (1976). It suggests that the cognitive organization of attitudes toward the two target groups is qualitatively alike, and that it is possible to use the same pool of questionnaire items to assess attitudes toward both. The items and their loadings on the Condemnation-Tolerance factor are listed in Appendix A.

Comparison With Previous Research

Since the items used by Millham et al. (1976) were included as marker variables in the present research, it is possible to compare results from the two studies. Although oblique rotation yielded results clearly different from those reported earlier by Millham and his associates, it seemed possible that a varimax rotation might more closely replicate their findings. For this reason, SPSS PA2 analyses with varimax rotation were conducted for the lesbian and gay male targets. Following the procedure of Millham et al., female and male responses were combined for each target.

For the gay male target, a major factor emerged consistently that accounted for approximately 39% of the total common variance. All items from Millham's Moral Reprobation and Personal Anxiety factors, and three of the six items from the Repressive-Dangerous factor loaded on this factor at a level greater than .30. Smaller factors, accounting for less than 4% of the total common variance corresponded to the Repressive Dangerous, Personal Anxiety, and Cross-Sexed Mannerisms factors. Items expressing preference for either lesbians or gay men did not load on any factor at a level greater than .30. Similar results were obtained for the lesbian target, except that a Repressive-Dangerous factor emerged that accounted for 5% of the total common variance.

Although this analysis used a procedure similar to Millham's, the results differed considerably. The large factor, which corresponds to the previously observed Condemnation-Tolerance factor, includes most of the items on the major factors obtained by Millham et al. (1976). It appears that the Cross-Sexed Mannerisms factor accounts for very little of the total variance, and the factors indicating preference for either gay males or lesbians may have been artifacts of the earlier questionnaire or sample. Millham and his colleagues did not conduct a second analysis with a different sample, so their research does not answer this question. Since the present study employed several samples and included respondents from different geographic areas, the results can be generalized more safely than can the findings of the Millham group.

DISCUSSION

The results of the present study indicate that a single bipolar factor accounts for a large portion of the variance in the cognitive organization of attitudes toward homosexuality among the college students sampled. The same factor emerged for both male and female respondents, and for attitudes toward both lesbians and gay men. It was obtained with both orthogonal and oblique rotations, although the latter method best represents the interfactor correlations observed during analysis. These findings are significant for two reasons.

First, they point to the appropriateness of a unidimensional scale for assessing attitudes toward homosexual persons, and provide an item pool for constructing such an instrument. Scales designed to assess general attitudes toward homosexuality should include only items loading on the Condemnation-Tolerance factor. (The item pool in Appendix A can be expanded through additional factor analyses with newly constructed items.) The minor factors reported in this paper account for such small proportions of variance that their inclusion in a global attitude scale would not be justified. Additionally, the most frequently observed smaller factor concerns beliefs about lesbians and gay men rather than attitudes toward them, so items loading on it would not be appropriate for an attitude scale for this reason as well (Fishbein & Ajzen, 1975).

A second implication of the results presented in this paper is that the same item pool can be used for assessing attitudes toward both lesbians and gay men, and for both female and male respondents. This does not deny the existence of gender differences in attitudes, of course, but it means that they do not take the form of different attitude factors for each sex. Instead, sex differences will be manifested in the mean attitude scores obtained by males and by females on a scale constructed from the items in Appendix A. Using a unidimensional attitude scale constructed from those items, for example, Herek (1984) observed consistently more negative attitudes (indicated by higher mean scale scores) among heterosexual males than among heterosexual females, especially for attitudes toward gay men.

The Condemnation-Tolerance factor described in this paper includes items that characterize homosexuality as unnatural, disgusting, perverse, and sinful; as a danger to society and requiring negative social sanctions; and as a source of personal anxiety to the individual respondent, consequently leading to avoidance of gay men and lesbians. In short, this factor summarizes the personal and cultural attitudes that have been described variously as *homoerotophobia* (Churchill, 1967), *homosexphobia* (Levitt & Klassen, 1974), and, most popularly, *homophobia* (MacDonald, 1976; Morin & Garfinkle, 1978; Weinberg, 1972).

While these terms convey a shared meaning for lesbians, gay men, their friends, and their political supporters, they are eschewed in the present discussion because of their allusion to a clinical entity sharing characteristics of other phobias. Such a conceptualization may be attractive to some because it shifts the stigma of psychological dysfunction or maladjustment from homosexual persons to those who are hostile toward them. It cannot be considered an appropriate characterization, however, until it has been shown that "homophobic" individuals manifest physical and psychological responses comparable to other phobic reactions. For example, homophobics should manifest physiological fear responses when exposed to homosexual persons just as other phobics do when confronted with the objects of their fears, but this reaction has not been observed among many persons expressing hostile attitudes toward homosexuality (see Shields & Harriman, 1984).

Despite the nascent state of research in this area, it seems clear that hostility toward lesbians and gay men is motivated by a variety of factors in addition to simple fear (e.g., Hudson & Ricketts, 1980; MacDonald, 1976; Weinberg, 1972). For example, one person's negative attitudes may result from a need for acceptance by members of a valued social group, while a second person may hold similar attitudes primarily as a defense against unconscious conflicts, and a third person simply may be expressing negative social stereotypes. In other words, attitudes toward lesbians and gay men probably serve different functions for different individuals (Katz, 1960; Smith, 1973; Smith, Bruner, & White, 1956). Future research should be directed toward uncovering the major functions and understanding their antecedents in order to provide a foundation for a theoretical model explaining the multiple origins of prejudice against lesbians and gay men. Such a model is sorely needed by social scientists and others working to eliminate this prejudice.

REFERENCES

Churchill, W. (1967). *Homosexual behavior among males.* New York: Hawthorn.

Comrey, A. L. (1978). Common methodological problems in factor-analytic studies. *Journal of Consulting and Clinical Psychology, 46*(4), 648–659.

Cory, D. W. (1951). *The homosexual in America.* New York: Greenberg.

Edwards, A. L. (1957). *Techniques of attitude scale construction.* New York: Appleton-Century-Crofts.

Ferenczi, S. (1956). The nosology of male homosexuality (homoerotism). In E. Jones (Ed. and Trans.), *Sex in psychoanalysis.* New York: Dover (Original work published 1914)

Fishbein, M., & Ajzen, I. (1975). *Belief, attitude, intention, and behavior.* Reading, MA: Addison-Wesley.

Harman, H. H. (1967). *Modern factor analysis.* (2nd ed.). Chicago: University of Chicago Press.

Herek, G. (1984). *Assessing attitudes toward lesbians and gay men: Scale construction and validation.* Manuscript submitted for publication.

Hudson, W. W., & Ricketts, W. A. (1980). A strategy for the measurement of homophobia. *Journal of Homosexuality, 5*(4), 357–373.

Katz, D. (1960). The functional approach to the study of attitudes. *Public Opinion Quarterly, 24,* 163–204.

Larsen, K. S., Reed, M., & Hoffman, S. (1980). Attitudes of heterosexuals toward homosexuality: A Likert-type scale and construct validity. *Journal of Sex Research, 16*(3), 245–257.

Levitt, E. E., & Klassen, A. D. (1974). Public attitudes toward homosexuality: Part of the 1970 national survey by the Institute for Sex Research. *Journal of Homosexuality, 1*(1), 29–43.

MacDonald, A. P., Jr. (1976). Homophobia: Its roots and meanings. *Homosexual Counseling Journal, 3*(1), 23–33.

MacDonald, A. P., Jr., & Games, R. G. (1974). Some characteristics of those who hold positive and negative attitudes toward homosexuals. *Journal of Homosexuality, 1*(1), 9–27.

MacDonald, A. P., Jr., Huggins, J., Young, S., & Swanson, R. A. (1973). Attitudes toward homosexuality: Preservation of sex morality or the double standard? *Journal of Consulting and Clinical Psychology, 40*(1), 161.

Marmor, J. (1980). *Homosexual behavior: A modern reappraisal.* New York: Basic Books.

Millham, J., San Miguel, C. L., & Kellogg, R. (1976). A factor-analytic conceptualization of attitudes toward male and female homosexuals. *Journal of Homosexuality, 2*(1), 3–10.

Millham, J., & Weinberger, L. E. (1977). Sexual preference, sex role appropriateness, and restriction of social access. *Journal of Homosexuality, 2*(4), 343–357.

Minnigerode, F. A. (1976). Attitudes toward homosexuality: Feminist attitudes and sexual conservatism. *Sex Roles, 2*(4), 347–352.

Mosher, D. L., & O'Grady, K. E. (1979). Homosexual threat, negative attitudes toward masturbation, sex guilt, and males' sexual and affective reactions to explicit sexual films. *Journal of Consulting and Clinical Psychology, 47*(5), 860–873.

Morin, S. F., & Garfinkle, E. M. (1978). Male homophobia. *Journal of Social Issues, 34*(1), 29–47.

Nie, N. H., Hull, C. H., Jenkins, J. G., Steinbrenner, K., & Bent, D. H. (1975). *Statistical Package for the Social Sciences* (2nd ed.). New York: McGraw-Hill.

Rummel, R. J. (1970). *Applied factor analysis.* Evanston, IL: Northwestern University Press.

Shields, S. A., & Harriman, R. E. (1984). Fear of male homosexuality: Cardiac responses of low and high homonegative males. *Journal of Homosexuality, 10*(1/2), 53–67.

Smith, M. B. (1973). Political attitudes. In J. Knutson (Ed.), *Handbook of political psychology.* San Francisco: Jossey-Bass.

Smith, M. B., Bruner, J. S., & White, R. W. (1956). *Opinions and personality.* New York: Wiley.

Smith, K. T. (1971). Homophobia: A tentative personality profile. *Psychological Reports, 29,* 1091–1094.

Thorndike, R. M. (1978). *Correlational procedures for research.* New York: Garden Press.

Weinberg, G. (1972). *Society and the healthy homosexual.* New York: St. Martin's.

Weinberger, L. E., & Millham, J. (1979). Attitudinal homophobia and support of traditional sex roles. *Journal of Homosexuality, 4*(3), 237–245.

APPENDIX A:
ITEMS LOADING ON THE
CONDEMNATION-TOLERANCE FACTOR

Items are phrased for the lesbian target; for the gay male target, substitute the words "male homosexual" for "lesbian." Factor pattern loadings for lesbian target and gay male target, respectively, are in parentheses. Item numbers correspond to original questionnaire.

1. The growing number of lesbians indicates a decline in American morals. (.522, .787)
2. Laws regulating lesbian behavior should be loosened. ($-.671$, $-.761$)
4. Lesbian couples should be allowed to adopt children the same as heterosexual couples. ($-.592$, $-.558$)
5. Lesbians are sick. (.529, .685)

6. I would *not* be too upset if I learned that my daughter were a lesbian. (−.586, −.664)
7. Homosexual behavior between two women is just plain wrong. (.703, .832)
8. Some of this country's most valuable female citizens have probably been lesbians. (−.357, −.468)
10. Lesbians should *not* be allowed to hold responsible positions. (.386, .620)
11. It would be very easy for me to have a conversation with a woman I know to be a lesbian. (−.599, −.539)
12. By its nature, sex between two lesbians can only be animalistic pleasure. (.398, .595)
15. Lesbians should be required to undergo psychotherapy. (.399, .653)
16. I would be nervous if a lesbian sat next to me on a bus. (.468, .521)
17. Female homosexuality is a sin. (.725, .841)
18. Female homosexuality is merely a different kind of lifestyle that should *not* be condemned. (−.756, −.923)
20. There is an element of homosexuality in all men and women. (−.461, −.470)
21. Just as in other species, female homosexuality is a natural expression of sexuality in human women. (−.660, −.737)
23. I would like to have lesbian friends. (−.709, −.661)
24. Lesbian couples should be allowed to dance together in public places the same as heterosexuals. (−.582, −.683)
27. I would *not* like to have lesbian friends. (.683, .704)
28. Practicing lesbians should *not* be allowed to be members of churches or synagogues. (.481, .503)
29. I think lesbians are disgusting. (.771, .757)
30. Female homosexuality is a threat to many of our basic social institutions. (.501, .715)
32. Laws against homosexuality are necessary to keep down the number of lesbians in the population. (.384, .596)
34. Lesbians should *not* be allowed to teach school. (.542, .729)
36. Bars that cater solely to lesbians should be placed in one specific and known part of town. (.397, .495)
37. If my sister (or best female friend, if you do not have a sister) told me she were a lesbian, it would distress me greatly. (.715, .654)
38. If a woman has homosexual feelings, she should do everything she can to overcome them. (.658, .841)
44. Female homosexuality is detrimental to society because it breaks down the natural divisions between the sexes. (.531, .689)
45. Female homosexuality is a perversion. (.760, .820)
46. Lesbians just don't fit into our society. (.647, .762)
47. Lesbians should be allowed to teach young children. (−.494, −.637)
53. I would *not* change my feelings toward a female friend if I learned that she were a lesbian. (−.652, −.616)
54. Many lesbians are very moral and ethical people. (−.462, −.565)
56. Female homosexuality in itself is no problem, but what society makes of it can be a problem. (−.694, −.843)
57. A woman's homosexuality should *not* be a cause for job discrimination in any situation. (−.571, −.603)
59. Female homosexuality is an inferior form of sexuality. (.464, .710)
61. The idea of lesbian marriages seems ridiculous to me. (.626, .771)
64. If I learned my daughter were a lesbian, I would suggest she seek psychiatric help. (.503, .663)

Fear of Male Homosexuality: Cardiac Responses of Low and High Homonegative Males

Stephanie A. Shields, PhD
Robert E. Harriman, BA
University of California, Davis

ABSTRACT. Males with high negative attitudes toward male homosexuality are often referred to in research as homophobics, yet it is unknown whether high homonegative males actually exhibit physiological responses characteristic of phobics. In a series of studies, heart rate was monitored in males with high or low negative attitudes toward male homosexuality as they viewed slides of landscapes and slides depicting explicit sexual activity. If high homonegativity is equivalent to homophobia, high homonegative males should exhibit heart rate acceleration to slides of male-male sexual activity, but, like low homonegative males, deceleration to all other slide types. Significant group effects were obtained only in the pilot study. Examination of individual response patterns in the pilot study and the two subsequent studies showed that high homonegative attitudes were necessary but not sufficient for heart rate acceleration to male-male slides. Results confirm the existence of the phobic type of heart rate acceleratory pattern among some, but not all, high homonegative males.

The degree to which people express negative attitudes about homosexuality varies greatly. In some cases fear appears to be a significant component of negative attitudes. For example, males who are especially rejecting of male homosexuality tend to view male homosexuals as personally dangerous and threatening (Steffensmeier & Steffensmeier, 1974). The idea that negative attitudes toward male homosexuality are associated

A portion of the results were presented at the 1982 meeting of the Western Psychological Association, Sacramento, CA. The authors wish to express their special thanks to Gregory M. Herek for his assistance in this project. Dr. Shields is an Assistant Professor of Psychology at the University of California at Davis. Mr. Harriman is a mental health counselor at the Yolo County Community Care Continuum in Davis. Reprints may be obtained by writing Dr. Shields, Department of Psychology, University of California, Davis, CA 95616.

with fear has led researchers and the lay public to label homonegative attitudes "homophobic" (Herek, 1984; Morin & Garfinkle, 1978; Weinberg, 1972). The primary component of homophobia is an irrational, persistent fear or dread of homosexuals (Morin & Garfinkle, 1978). Because the term phobia should be reserved for the expression of a particular kind of fear, Hudson and Ricketts (1980) suggest that the label *homophobia* is appropriate to use in only certain cases, and furthermore, that homonegativism alone may not account for or predict the existence of homophobia. Until now there has been no empirical research that has examined the phobic constituents of homophobia or whether, in fact, it is appropriate to label any type of homonegativism as homophobic.

Cardiac response patterns can be used as indicators of fearfulness. Sokolov (1963) identified two response patterns associated with stimulus value. The defensive response (DR) involves simultaneous heart rate acceleration and constriction of blood vessels in the scalp; the orienting response involves heart rate deceleration and vasodilation. The heart rate component of the DR is reliably elicited by fear-provoking or aversive stimuli, whereas a heart rate orienting response (OR) occurs in the presence of novel or interesting stimuli, regardless of content (Fredrikson, 1981; Hare, 1973; Hare & Blevings, 1975; Raskin, Kotses, & Bever, 1969). Significant vasoconstrictive and vasodilative effects have not been consistently reported (Hare & Blevings, 1975). Hare (1973) found that spider phobics responded to slides of spiders with a DR, while nonfearful subjects responded to the same slides with an OR. Klorman and his associates (Klorman, Wiensenfeld, & Austin, 1975) reported that subjects categorized by questionnaires as high or low in fear of mutilation showed different cardiac responses to slides of mutilation victims. High fear subjects showed components of the DR while low fear subjects showed components of the OR. Thus one can discriminate between fearful and nonfearful subjects on the basis of the type of cardiac response pattern exhibited in specific stimulus situations.

Attitudinal and cardiac measures were used in the present research to examine the relationship between homonegativism and homophobia. Attitude measures were used to preselect males with high and low negative attitudes toward male homosexuality. Only males were studied because the incidence of the DR was expected to be greater in a male population as attitudinal research has shown that males typically have more negative attitudes toward male homosexuality than do females (Herek, 1983a; Turnbull & Brown, 1977). Cardiac responses of high and low homonegative groups were compared by measuring heart rate and cephalic vasomotor activity as subjects viewed slides with and without sexual content. If strongly held negative attitudes regarding homosexuality are, in fact, symptomatic of homophobia, then males scoring high on a measure of negative attitudes should exhibit cardiac defensive responses, while males with less negative attitudes should exhibit orienting responses when viewing slides of two males engaged in explicit sexual activity. No differences in the groups' heart rate responses should occur when slides of neutral scenes or other types of sexual activity are shown.

PILOT STUDY

Subjects

A 43-item Sexual Attitudes Questionnaire, intended to tap fear of male homosexuality, was devised. The questionnaire was composed of 17 items from the "Attitudes Toward Male Homosexuality Scale (Form M)" of MacDonald and Games (1974). These items were masked by an additional 26 items pertaining to sexual behavior unrelated to male homosexuality. Subjects rated each item on a 9-point Likert scale expressing their degree of agreement with the statement. Possible scores on the male homosexuality items ranged from 17 (low homonegativity) to 153 (high homonegativity). The questionnaire was administered to a large mixed-sex group of undergraduate volunteers in a single testing session. Before they began the session, subjects were informed that some would be invited to participate in the second part of the experiment which would involve viewing slides of explicit sexual activity.

Two groups of male subjects were selected on the basis of questionnaire responses (mean age = 20 years). The five male subjects scoring lowest in negative attitudes toward male homosexuality (mean score = 25) were assigned to the Low Homonegative (LH) group, while the five highest scoring (mean score = 125) were assigned to the High Homonegative (HH) group.

Materials and Apparatus

Because methodology was nearly identical in the three studies reported here, materials and procedure of the pilot study are described in detail. Stimuli were six colored slides of landscape scenes (neutral slides) and six colored slides of explicit sexual activity between two persons: two slides of male and female partners (male-female), two slides of female partners (female-female), and two slides of male partners (male-male). Photos for sexual slides were taken from material obtained at local adult bookstores. Two raters matched the sexual slides for kind of sexual activity across sexual slide types. Gender of the sexual partners was judged by the two raters to be unambiguous in all slides. Blank slides, which lightly illuminated the screen, separated stimulus slides. Slides were projected upon a screen about 2.5 m from the subject and cast an image approximately 45 × 65 cm.

Physiological responses were recorded on a Beckman R-611 Dyno-graph. A Beckman chest respiration belt placed around the chest and a Type 9853A coupler were used to record respiration. (Respiration was recorded solely to identify artifact in the other measures.) Heart rate was obtained from a Standard Lead II configuration and a Beckman Type 9857 cardiotachometer coupler. Vasomotor activity was recorded with a Beckman photocell pulse transducer secured to the middle of the forehead with a single wrap of an elastic band and a Beckman Type 9853A coupler.

Procedure

Subjects were contacted by telephone and asked to participate in the second part of the study. Each subject was seen individually by a single male experimenter who was unaware of the subject's performance on the questionnaire. The subject sat upright in a comfortable recliner in a sound-dampened, air-conditioned, dimly lit room which contained the projection equipment. The physiological recording equipment was located in an adjacent room. After the electrodes and transducer had been attached, the experimenter left the room; the subject was alone for the re-mainder of the experiment. After a 10-min rest period, a tape-recorded male voice described the experimental procedure. Slide presentation began about 30 seconds after the taped message ended. A neutral slide was shown at the beginning of the presentation and between each of the sexual slides. Each slide was shown for 10 s, with the interval between slides randomly varied between 25 s and 35 s. Although subjects were told that order of slide presentation would be random, all viewed slides in the same order: male-female, female-female, male-male, male-female, female-female, male-male. Subjects were debriefed following the slide presentation to insure that they suffered no negative consequences from participation. No subject reported experiencing any discomfort during the experiment.

Results and Discussion

To determine whether groups differed in resting heart rate, mean heart rate for the 5-s period prior to the presentation of the first neutral slide and each of the sexual slides was calculated. Group differences in mean heart rate were nonsignificant, $t(8) = .98$.

Heart rate responses to slide types were determined for each subject by expressing the mean heart rate during each of the ten 1-s periods follow-ing slide onset as a deviation from the mean heart rate during the 5-s period prior to slide onset. Mean second-by-second changes in heart rate for each group to male-male slides and neutral slides are illustrated in

Figure 1. Responses of both groups to the neutral, male-female, and female-female slides were similar and indicative of an OR. The groups differed in response to the male-male slides, with the HH group showing heart rate acceleration indicative of a DR and the LH group showing the OR deceleration pattern.

Group responses to the four slide types were tested in a 2 (Group) $\times$ 4 (Slide), repeated-measures analysis of variance. Individual subject scores were expressed as a sum of change-scores. Main effects of Group were

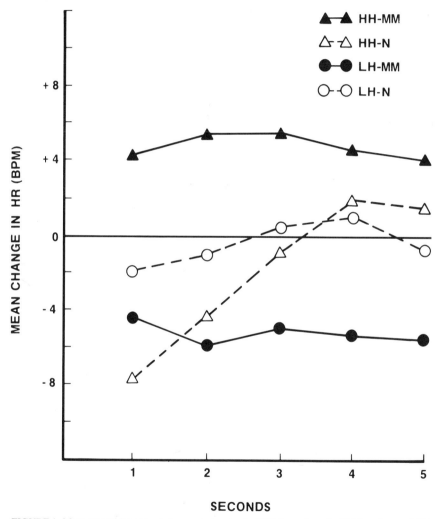

SECONDS

FIGURE 1. Mean second-by-second changes in heart rate (HR) for male-male (MM) and neutral (N) slides for high homonegative (HH) and low homonegative (LH) subjects in pilot study.

significant, $F(1,4) = 19.5$, $p < .05$, as was the Group $\times$ Slide interaction, $F(3,12) = 3.9$, $p < .05$. Post hoc F tests for simple effects showed that the significance of the interaction was due to differences between HH and LH subjects in response to male-male slides, $F(1,20 = 15.5$, $p < .01$. HH males exhibited acceleration; LH males, deceleration. The groups did not differ significantly in their responses to any other slide type.

To determine whether groups differed in resting vasomotor amplitude, mean amplitude for the five pulses prior to the presentation of the first neutral slide and each of the sexual slides was calculated. Group differences in mean amplitude were nonsignificant, $t(7) = 1.8$.

Vasomotor responses for each subject were determined by expressing the mean pulse amplitude during each of the ten 1-s periods following slide onset as a percent change from the mean pulse amplitude during the 5-s period prior to slide onset. A 2 (Group) $\times$ 4 (Slide), repeated-measures analysis of variance was performed using the sum of percent change for each slide type as the dependent measure. The main effect of Group was significant, $F(1,3) = 9.1$, $p < .025$. Though the LH group showed less vasoconstriction than the HH group, effects for individual slides were nonsignificant.

That the DR was not observed in the vasomotor data is consistent with similar research on other phobic populations. The vasoconstrictive component of the DR has not been consistently observed. Some investigators have found that it discriminates between phobic and nonphobic subjects (Hare, 1972; Hare & Blevings, 1975); others believe it is not a legitimate indicator of the DR (Raskin, Kotses, & Bever, 1969). Because it appeared to have limited applicability to the study of defensive responses to sexual stimuli, vasomotor activity was not analyzed in the subsequent studies.

Group differences were reflected in individual heart rate response patterns. The DR was defined as occurring during the slide presentation period when heart rate change from the preslide period was greater than zero for three or more consecutive seconds. All LH subjects decelerated to the male-male slides, whereas three of the five HH subjects accelerated.

Overall, results paralleled those of other studies in which phobic stimuli elicited the DR, in that it was possible to differentiate between HH and LH groups on the basis of their heart rate responses to male-male slides. The LH group exhibited an OR to male-male slides, whereas a majority of the HH group exhibited a DR to this slide type. Both groups showed an OR to all other slide types.

Though the results showed a DR only in high homonegative males, the small sample size suggested the need for replication. In addition, two limitations in the study required correction. Information regarding participants' sexual orientation had not been obtained and the reliability and validity of the scale that was used for subject selection had not been established.

STUDY 2

Subjects

The Attitudes Toward Lesbians and Gay Men Scale (ATLG; Herek, 1983a, 1984a) the Kinsey scale of orientation of sexual behavior (Kinsey, Pomeroy, & Martin, 1948), the Trait subscale of the Spielberger State-Trait Anxiety Inventory (STAI, Form X-2; Spielberger, Gorsuch, & Lushene, 1970), and the sexual knowledge portion of the Sex Knowledge and Attitudes Test (SKAT; Lief & Reed, 1972) were administered to 54 male and 85 female undergraduates. Scores on the ten-item Attitudes Toward Gay Men subscale of the ATLG were used to select ten heterosexual males (i.e., men who had indicated on the Kinsey scale that their sexual behavior had been exclusively heterosexual) expressing high negative attitudes toward homosexuality and ten expressing low negative attitudes for the laboratory portion of the study. Mean score on the ATLG subscale was 34.4 for LH and 68.8 for HH; the mean for all males who responded to the questionnaire was 56.5, which was not significantly different from the scale norm (Herek, 1983a) for male college students (58.1). Mean age of HH subjects was 18.5 years, and for LH subjects 19 years. As in the first study, subjects were contacted by telephone.

Procedure

The stimuli, physiological recording apparatus, and laboratory procedures were unchanged from the pilot study except the presentation order of the sexual slides was randomized. As in the pilot study, a neutral slide preceded the presentation of each sexual slide and the last slide shown was also a neutral slide. It was predicted that HH males would respond with the DR whereas LH males would respond with the OR to male-male slides.

Results and Discussion

HH and LH subjects' responses to the STAI and SKAT were compared via *t* tests for independent groups and showed no significant differences.

The procedure for quantifying physiological responses, including definition of OR and DR, was identical to that used in the pilot study.

Resting heart rate was computed as in the pilot study and groups were compared via *t* test; the group difference was nonsignificant.

Contrary to predictions, when group data were analyzed, no DR was evident in the HH males' responses to male-male slides. Differences in group responses to slide type were tested in a 2 (Group) × 4 (Slide), repeated-measures analysis of variance. Individual scores were expressed as a sum of difference scores for the first 7 s after slide onset plus 100 to eliminate the effects of sign differences. Main effects of Group and of Slide were nonsignificant, as was the Group × Slide interaction. The composition of each group was then examined more closely. In the pilot study HH males had all scored at least one standard deviation above the group mean on the Homophobia Scale, but in the present study, the HH group was far less negative. Six of the ten HH subjects had scores on the Gay subscale less than one standard deviation above the norm. It may be that the DR is characteristic only of extreme homonegativity. The content of different scales for assessment of attitudes toward homosexuality used in the pilot study and this study may also account for sample discrepancies.

In order to determine whether the attitude scales could be considered comparable, both were administered to another undergraduate sample of men and women. Factor analysis of the combined scales (principal components with varimax rotation) resulted in a single factor solution accounting for 48% of the variance. All but six of the 27 items loaded on the first factor, suggesting that the same dimensions of attitudes toward homosexuality are tapped by both scales. In addition, internal consistency of the Sexual Attitude Questionnaire was computed and a Chronbach's α coefficient of .92 was obtained for the scale. Although the scale had been constructed ad hoc for use in the pilot study, it nevertheless successfully measured attitudes toward homosexuality in a manner comparable to a validated scale.

Individual response patterns were examined to see if any subject, whether HH or LH, responded with the DR at any time. Data for all four slide types were complete for 14 of the 20 subjects tested (9 HH and 5 LH). (Equipment difficulties resulted in incomplete data for six subjects.) No LH subject accelerated to male-male slides; two accelerated to other slide types. Four HH subjects accelerated to male-male slides; but two also accelerated to other slide types. When Gay subscale scores of HH males exhibiting the DR were compared to those who did not exhibit the DR, the difference was nonsignificant. These results must be interpreted with great caution, however, as sample sizes were quite small.

These results suggest that homonegativity is necessary, but not sufficient, to evoke homophobic patterns of cardiac response. For male-male slides, the heart rate acceleration associated with phobic reactions was never observed among LH subjects, but was present in nearly half of the

HH subjects. Because the DR was observed, albeit inconsistently, something other than degree of negativism must account for the presence of the effect.

STUDY 3

For a number of years social psychologists have investigated attitudes from the standpoint of the functions served for the individual holding those attitudes (Katz, 1960). Like attitudes toward other social principles and groups, attitudes toward homosexuality may serve one of several functions for the individual (Herek, 1984; Morin & Garfinkle, 1978). Specifically, they may reflect conformity to one's peer group, previous experience with the attitude object as reinforcing or punishing, or a defensive reaction to unconscious conflicts. Operating from the psychodynamic perspective, one should expect to see unconscious conflicts expressed in statements which reflect the individual's inability to deal directly with the source of his/her discomfort. These statements will reflect the operation of strategies for dealing with the conflict (ego defense mechanisms), and typically contain strong affective language and suggest a tendency to view the conflict as symptomatic of others rather than oneself. This form of ego-defensive strategy does characterize the verbal response patterns of some males who hold negative attitudes toward homosexuality (Herek, 1983b). Phobic responses are fear reactions out of proportion to the threat posed, and so represent the evaluation of reality in terms of highly subjective criteria independent of the objective facts of one's situation. Thus, phobic responses, because of their highly subjective frame of reference, should be more common among individuals who exhibit an ego-defensive basis for their attitudes toward homosexuality than among those for whom attitudes have a more objective foundation.

In the present study, men whose attitudes toward male homosexuality appeared to be ego-defensively based were contrasted with men for whom attitudes involved other, more objectively based functions, such as social conformity, previous experience with gay men, lack of information about homosexuality, or conflicting religious values. Ego-defensive subjects, when presented with male-male slides, should be more likely to exhibit a DR than men whose attitudes do not reflect an intrapsychic conflict regarding male homosexuality. Functions of homonegative attitudes for subjects were identified via content analysis of essays on attitudes toward homosexuality (Herek, 1983b). Respondents were asked to write brief essays explaining their reactions to male homosexuals and lesbians. Essays were coded for thematic patterns indicating various attitude functions. It was predicted that knowledge of the function of negative attitudes would enable identification of those HH males most likely to exhibit the DR.

Subjects

The ATLG and the Kinsey scale of orientation of sexual behavior were administered to mixed-sex groups of undergraduates ($N = 248$). Twenty exclusively heterosexual males (mean age 19 years) expressing high negative attitudes toward homosexuality were selected for the laboratory portion of the study. Only HH subjects were included because in both the pilot study and Study 2 all LH subjects exhibited the OR to male-male slides, establishing that defensive responses should only be observed in HH subjects. As before, subjects were contacted by telephone.

Procedure

The stimuli, physiological recording apparatus, and laboratory procedures were unchanged from Study 2, except that the number of each type of sexual slide shown was increased to three.

Results and Discussion

The procedure for quantifying physiological responses, including definition of OR and DR, was identical to that used in the two previous studies. Resting heart rate was computed as in the pilot study; group differences were nonsignificant, $t(12) = .32$.

Each subject's difference scores for each slide type were summed over the first 7 s after slide onset. In order to eliminate the effects of sign differences, 100 was added to each sum. Group differences were then tested in a 2 (Group) $\times$ 4 (Slide), repeated-measures analysis of variance. No significant effects were obtained, indicating that Ego-defensive and Non–ego-defensive groups did not differ in response to any slide type.

Individual response patterns were then examined. Of the 14 subjects for whom data were complete, for all slide types, seven were Ego-defensive and seven were Non–ego-defensive. None of the Ego-defensive and four of the Non–ego-defensive showed the DR to the male-male slides. Only one Ego-defensive subject exhibited acceleration to any slide type (female-female). As in Study 2, there was no relationship between degree of homonegativity and occurrence of the DR, nor was there any evidence that acceleration to the male-male slide was indicative of general aversion to sexual slides.

GENERAL DISCUSSION

Results of the three studies reported here confirm the existence of a cardiac defensive response (heart rate acceleration) among some high homonegative males who are presented with slides of two males engaging in sexual activity. Although high homonegativity alone was not a reliable indicator of the DR's occurrence, the defensive response to male-male slides was never observed in LH males. Figure 2 shows patterns representative of the OR and DR in two subjects. The OR is characterized by constant deceleration or minimal acceleration followed by deceleration. The DR, in contrast, shows an acceleratory pattern.

There were a few instances of heart rate acceleration to slide types other than male-male in both LH and HH groups. In order to rule out the

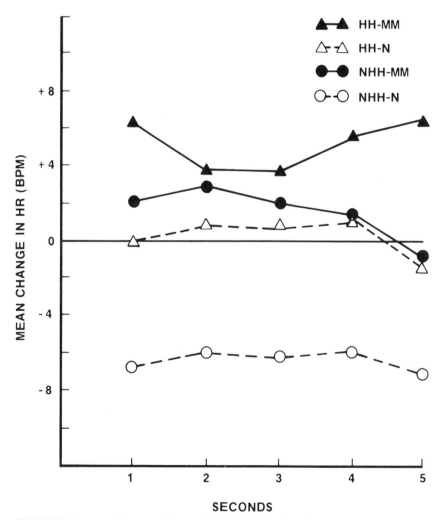

FIGURE 2. Mean second-by-second change in heart rate (HR) for male-male (MM) and Neutral (N) slides for a Study 2 high homonegative (HH) subject and a Study 3 Non-ego-defensive high homonegative (NHH) subject.

possibility that HH subjects were more likely to respond with the DR generally, post hoc analysis of the relationship between homonegativity (High versus Low) and occurrence of the DR (Yes versus No) was completed for each slide type across all subjects (HH = 28 and LH = 10). Fisher's exact test (two-tailed) was computed for each 2 × 2 contingency table and only for the male-male slides was there a significant association between homonegativity and occurrence of the DR ($p < .04$).

HH males who exhibited the DR to male-male slides were compared to other HH males to determine what other measured aspects of personality correlate with the presence of the DR. Turnbull and Brown (1977) have suggested that homophobia is but one facet of an individual's general sexual conservatism. The DR to male-male slides was not related to general sex phobia reaction, i.e., a DR to at least one other type of sexual slide in addition to the male-male slides. Presence of the DR to male-male slides was also unrelated to scores on a sex knowledge questionnaire (Study 2). Further indication of the specific nature of the DR to male stimuli is the fact that no HH subject exhibited the DR to female-female slides even though scores on the Gay subscale of Herek's test are highly correlated with scores on the Lesbian subscale (Herek, 1983a). Subjects who exhibited the DR also did not differ from other subjects in level of trait anxiety (Study 2) suggesting that they were not simply more prone to react adversely to novel stimuli.

When the functions served by HH attitudes were examined in Study 3, ego-defensiveness was ruled out as the basis for the DR. None of the HH males who expressed an ego-defensive function as the basis of their negative attitudes exhibited the DR to male slides. Contrary to predictions, the DR was instead found in a subgroup of HH subjects who justified their negative attitudes with references to non–ego-defensive functions.

Because results were contrary to predicted patterns, it would be valuable to determine whether the DR pattern could be predicted with greater precision from knowledge of other characteristics in addition to attitude functions. Subjects who participated in Study 3 were involved in a larger study of attitudes toward homosexuality (Herek, 1983b). Post hoc analyses on some of the measures which appeared to have the most bearing on homophobia were used to obtain additional information regarding personality characteristics of the HH participants. Non–ego-defensive men who have responded with the DR were compared with Non–ego-defensive men who have responded with the OR and with Ego-defensive men (all of whom had exhibited the OR) on several personality inventories. Because of the very small sample size, directions of difference, rather than tests of significance, are reported here. The three groups did not differ in the amount of contact they reported they had had with gay men and lesbians, although the DR group had higher (more negative) scores on the gay men subscale of the ATLG. The DR group had higher scores on the Attitudes Toward Women Scale (Spence, Helmreich, & Stapp, 1973), a measure of gender role attitudes, indicating a more traditional conception of the social dimensions of gender than the other two groups. The DR group had higher scores on the Traditional Family Ideology Scale (Levinson & Huffman, 1955), indicating more traditional views on authority and gender-roles. The DR group had higher scores on two of the subscales of the Defense Mechanisms Inventory (Gleser & Ihilevich, 1969) which indicate tendencies to externalize personal conflicts, a characteristic of the authoritarian personality; this group also had lower scores on the subscale indicating a tendency to employ reaction formation as a defense. In summary, the DR group, in contrast to other HH males, was more negative in attitudes toward gay males, more authoritarian and more traditional in sex-role values, and more prone to project negative attributes as an ego-defensive strategy. It must also be noted that HH males exhibiting the OR were, in turn, more authoritarian and traditional than LH males. These results suggest that future laboratory studies should test the proposition that the male most likely to exhibit the DR is one who not only holds strong negative attitudes toward gay men, but also is more extreme in his adherence to traditional gender-role ideology and moral standards.

Homophobia has also been considered in terms of its social functions (Lehne, 1976). Morin and Garfinkle (1978) reviewed the literature on homophobia and concluded that male homophobia serves to keep heterosexual men within the traditionally defined role: If males are encouraged to abhor same-sex contact, they will be more likely to maintain culturally approved heterosexual standards. Thus, homophobia may be fostered by socialization pressures to conform to sex-coded roles. Tripp (1975) described an even broader function of homophobia in suggesting that sexual orientation is not only maintained, but is initiated by the formation of strong aversion reactions. That is, sexual interest is directed toward discriminative choices and is repelled from all other alternatives. In this view homophobia could be considered the logical and ineluctable consequence of heterosexual preference. Homophobia emerges as a consequence of rigid adherence to the traditional male role; men who do not adhere to the role are seen as deviant by traditional heterosexual men. The fear response of the HH men in this study could be explained in terms of fear of deviance. Rigid heterosexual men would not want to lose their identity as traditional males by being deviant viewers of gay pornography and a DR is elicited by the fear of being labeled homosexual.

The present research demonstrated a strong affective component in the homonegativism of some, but not all, strongly homonegative males. Male homophobics responded to slides of male sexual partners in the same way as spider phobics respond to slides of spiders. Yet spider phobia and homophobia are by no means identical. The great difference between the unreasonable fear of spiders (or mutilation, snakes, etc.) and fear of homosexuality lies in the assignment of responsibility for such acquired pathologies. Whereas spider phobics typically accept responsibility for their fear and even seek treatment, homophobics do not. To the homophobic it is homosexual men who are "sick."

Although negative attitudes were not always predictive of the occurrence of the DR, the fact that the DR was found at all is striking in that subjects were drawn from a normal college population at a fairly liberal university. Although negative attitudes of HH males were strong, they may not reflect the degree of fear manifest in subjects who experience more extreme forms of homophobia. The results of this study support the view that homophobia is an emotional reaction to male-directed male sexuality, but it is not equivalent to the expression of homonegative attitudes alone.

Practically, the similarity between responses of homophobic subjects and subjects in other phobia studies suggests a way to help homophobics overcome their fear. Morin and Garfinkle (1978) describe how education and familiarization with the gay lifestyle can be enough to destroy stereotypes and change the negative attitudes of some men. The results of the present research suggest that the strategies for changing negative attitudes toward homosexuality may differ with the function served by the attitude. Education alone may be sufficient to effect an attitude change in some who have strong negative attitudes, but others who exhibit the homophobic pattern in addition to negative attitudes may require education and desensitization to overcome their fear. The traditional male role prevents men from expressing "feminine" emotions and from touching and embracing other men—whether they be lovers, family, or friends. By combining education and desensitization, male homophobics might find relief from their fear and, as a result, lead fuller emotional lives uninhibited by the constraints of the rigid male role.

REFERENCES

Fredrikson, M. (1981). Orienting and defensive reactions to phobic and conditioned stimuli in phobics and normals. *Psychophysiology, 18,* 456–465.
Gleser, G. C. & Ihilevich, D. (1969). An objective instrument for measuring defense mechanisms. *Journal of Consulting and Clinical Psychology, 33,* 51–60.
Hare, R. D. (1972). Cardiovascular components of orienting and defensive responses. *Psychophysiology, 9,* 606–614.
Hare, R. D. (1973). Orienting and defensive responses to visual stimuli. *Psychophysiology, 10,* 453–464.
Hare, R. D. & Blevings, G. (1975). Defensive responses to phobic stimuli. *Biological Psychology, 3,* 1–13.
Herek, G. M. (1983a). *Assessing attitudes toward lesbians and gay men: Scale construction and validation.* Unpublished manuscript.

Herek, G. M. (1983b). *Individual differences in attitudes toward lesbians and gay men: The social psychology of sexual ideology.* Unpublished doctoral dissertation, University of California, Davis.

Herek, G. M. (1984). Attitudes toward lesbians and gay men: A factor analytic study. *Journal of Homosexuality, 10*(1/2), 39–51.

Hudson, W. W. & Ricketts, W. A. (1980). A strategy for the measurement of homophobia. *Journal of Homosexuality, 5*(4), 357–372.

Katz, D. (1960). The functional approach to the study of attitudes. *Public Opinion Quarterly, 24,* 163–204.

Kinsey, A., Pomeroy, W. & Martin, C. (1948). *Sexual behavior in the human male.* Philadelphia: W. B. Saunders.

Klorman, R., Wiensenfeld, A. R., & Austin, M. L. (1975). Autonomic responses to affective visual stimuli. *Psychophysiology, 12,* 553–550.

Lehne, G. H. (1976). Homophobia among men. In D. David & R. Brannon (Eds.), *The forty-nine percent majority: The male sex role.* New York: Addison Wesley.

Levinson, D. J. & Huffman, P. E. (1955). Traditional family ideology and its relation to personality. *Journal of Personality, 23,* 251–273.

Lief, H. I. & Reed, D. M. (1972). *Sex Knowledge and Attitude Test (S.K.A.T.), (2nd ed.).* Center for the Study of Sex Education Medicine, University of Pennsylvania.

MacDonald, A. P., Jr. & Games, R. G. (1974). Some characteristics of those who hold positive and negative attitudes toward homosexuals. *Journal of Homosexuality, 1,* 9–27.

Morin, S. F. & Garfinkle, E. M. (1978). Male homophobia. *Journal of Social Issues, 34,* 29–47.

Raskin, D. C., Kotses, H., & Bever, J. (1969). Cephalic vasomotor and heart rate measures of orienting and defensive reflexes. *Psychophysiology, 6,* 149–159.

Sokolov, E. (1963). *Perception and the conditioned reflex.* New York: Macmillan.

Spielberger, C. D., Gorsuch, R. L., & Lushene, R. E. (1970). *STAI Manual.* Palo Alto, CA: Consulting Psychologists Press.

Spence, J. T., Helmreich, R., & Stapp, J. (1973). A short version of the Attitudes Toward Women Scale (AWS). *Bulletin of the Psychonomic Society, 2,* 219–220.

Steffensmeier, D. & Steffensmeier, R. (1974). Sex differences in reactions to homosexuals: Research continuities and further developments. *Journal of Sex Research, 10,* 52–67.

Tripp, C. A. (1975). *The homosexual matrix.* New York: McGraw-Hill.

Turnbull, D. & Brown, M. (1977). Attitudes toward homosexuality and male and female reactions to homosexual and heterosexual slides. *Canadian Journal of Behavioral Science, 9,* 68–80.

Weinberg, G. (1972). *Society and the healthy homosexual.* Garden City, NY: Anchor Books.

Sex Differences in Attitudes Toward Homosexuals: A Meta-Analytic Review

Mary E. Kite, MS
Purdue University

ABSTRACT. Sex differences in attitudes toward homosexuality were examined using Glass's d as an estimator of effect size. There was a small mean effect ($d = .207$) indicating that males have more negative attitudes than females toward homosexuals. However, this effect was found to decrease in magnitude when sample size was controlled for, with larger studies being less likely to have a sex difference. Year of publication was also found to be related to the effect sizes with more recent studies tending to show a larger effect size. Sex of target is also discussed as a potentially important variable.

Research on attitudes toward homosexuals and, in particular, those who hold negative attitudes toward this group has rapidly increased in the past decade. This attitude research has focused on the reasons one might hold negative attitudes, the personality characteristics of those who hold negative attitudes, and reactions of heterosexuals to homosexuals.

Much of the research on this topic has focused on the personality characteristics of those who hold negative attitudes toward homosexuals. It has been shown that people who hold negative attitudes toward homosexuals are likely to support the maintenance of traditional sex roles (MacDonald, 1974), are more likely to stereotype the sexes than those who hold positive attitudes (Dunbar, Brown, & Amoroso, 1973), and favor preserving the double standard between men and women (MacDonald, 1974; MacDonald, Huggins, Young, & Swanson, 1973). Furthermore, a person who holds negative attitudes toward homosexuals is

Special thanks to Alice Eagly for her valuable assistance throughout this project and to Kay Deaux for comments on an earlier version of this manuscript. Requests for reprints should be addressed to Mary E. Kite, Department of Psychological Sciences, Purdue University, West Lafayette, IN 47907.

69

less likely to know a homosexual (Hansen, 1982; Kite, 1983), may see homosexuals as sick and dangerous (Steffensmeier & Steffensmeier, 1974), and may be status conscious, authoritarian and sexually rigid (Smith, 1971). Irwin and Thompson (1975, cited in Henley & Pincus, 1978) reported that Protestants and Roman Catholics are less tolerant of homosexuals than are Jews, members of other religions and nonaffiliates. Finally, other studies suggest that an individual who holds negative attitudes toward homosexuals is likely to hold negative attitudes toward other minorities and underrepresented groups as well. Minnergerode (1976) and Henley and Pincus (1978), for example, reported a strong positive correlation between attitudes toward women and attitudes toward homosexuals. Henley and Pincus also reported that negative attitudes toward homosexuals are positively correlated with negative attitudes toward blacks.

Measurement of attitudes toward homosexuality has been varied both in content and format, with measures ranging from one-item questions to fully developed scales. Further, the scales often vary in sex of target with no sex specified in some scales (e.g., Price, 1982; Smith, 1971), questions about males and females not distinguished in others (e.g., Dressler, 1979; Nyberg & Alston, 1977a), or some scales using only a male or a female target (e.g., Millham, San Miguel, & Kellogg, 1976; Sobel, 1976). In addition, although instruments have improved, many early studies using questionnaires that were vague and ambiguously worded and which often had no reported reliability. The questionnaires measuring attitudes toward homosexuality vary almost from study to study.

Despite a general tendency to focus on males, several studies have looked at sex differences in attitudes toward homosexuals. Results on this issue are unclear, however, with some studies finding that males hold more negative attitudes than females (e.g., Nyberg & Alston, 1977b; Price, 1982; Weis & Dain, 1979), some finding that the negativity of the attitude depends on the sex of the homosexual target (e.g., Karr, 1978; Millham, San Miguel, & Kellogg, 1976; Millham & Weinberger, 1977), and others finding no sex differences (e.g., Glenn & Weaver, 1979; MacDonald, 1974; Smith, 1971). This is the question that this paper will address meta-analytically. The conflicting results of independent studies on this issue are difficult to understand using the traditional reviewing process, which tends to rely on statistical significance for drawing conclusions about a series of studies. This method, sometimes referred to as vote-counting (Light & Smith, 1971), is problematic because statistical significance or insignificance provides little information about the strength or importance of a relationship (see Glass, McGaw, & Smith, 1981 for a discussion of this topic). Thus, simply examining the studies that report these varied results does not reveal whether there is a sex difference, and, if there is, what variables might affect the magnitude of this difference.

Although there is uncertainty surrounding this issue, many authors focus exclusively on males in their research (e.g., Karr, 1978; Sobel, 1976) or have used the results of those studies finding a sex difference as justification for selecting only male subjects (e.g., Kite, 1983a; Kruelwitz & Nash, 1980). Further, authors often do not report specific information on sex differences even though they use both male and female subjects (e.g., Glenn & Weaver, 1979; Leitner & Cado, 1982; Smith, 1971).

The traditional method of reviewing articles in order to integrate findings and reach some conclusion about their results is rapidly being replaced by the use of meta-analytic techniques. This process of statistically combining results of independent studies was brought to the attention of psychologists mainly by Glass in 1976.

The past few years have seen an increasing number of articles using this technique as well as a number of articles on the fundamental statistical issues underlying meta-analysis (e.g., Hedges, 1981, 1982a; Rosenthal & Rubin, 1979, 1982). The present investigation makes use of Glass's estimator of effect sizes, the d statistic, in order to examine meta-analytically whether there are sex differences in attitudes toward homosexuality, and, if so, the magnitude of this difference.

INDEPENDENT VARIABLES

Several independent variables will be examined in this study in order to determine if they are influencing the effect sizes obtained. Independent variables can account for a great deal of the variance among effect sizes. Variables that will be examined in this paper are sex of author, sex of target, type of question, sample size, and year of publication. Table 1 contains information about individual study characteristics.

Sex of Author

Sex of author has been shown to have an effect in other areas of research. For example, Eagly and Carli (1978), in their meta-analysis on social influence, found that authors were more likely to report findings that are socially desirable for members of their own sex. Results such as these bring to our attention how biases can effect results of research. Although no sex-of-author differences are expected in this analysis, sex of author will be examined as a potentially important variable. The majority of the authors in this area of research are male, as can be seen in Table 1.

Table 1
Study Characteristics

Study	Year	Number of Subjects* Total	Male	Female	Sex of Author Senior**	Percent Male***	Item N	Mean Effect Size
A	1979	100	50	50	1	1	--	.3592
B	1982	278	148	130	1	1	22	.6179
C	1977	535	310	225	1	1	1	.2889
D	1974	373	168	105	1	3	10	.0409
E	1979	4158	1926	2232	1	1	3	0.0000
F	1980	70	38	32	1	1	20	.9972
G	1982	143	--	--	1	1	15	.2472
H	1983	1240	467	595	2	2	22	-.0683
I	1980	249	116	133	1	1	7	.4113
J	1971	130	--	--	1	1	9	0.0000
K	1982	40	20	20	1	3	10	0.0000
L	1978	96	48	48	2	2	3	.3397
M	1983	366	154	212	1	1	26	.3240
N	1974	197	94	103	1	1	13	0.0000
O	1977	267	117	150	1	3	1	.3095
P	1978	1504	701	803	1	1	3	.0895
Q	1977	1197	570	627	1	1	1	-.0156
R	1974	197	94	103	1	1	--	.1580
S	1980	190	100	90	2	1	--	.2889
T	1976	795	--	--	1	1	38	.1102
U	1980	300	99	201	1	1	--	.1102
V	1979	267	117	150	1	3	38	.1500
W	1978	80	40	40	2	3	2	.3588
X	1978	211	119	92	2	3	--	-.0041

* When number of males and females was unknown, the total N was evenly split for purposes of anlaysis.

**For Senior Author: 1=male 2=female

***For percent male author: 1=greater than 50% male, 2=less than 50% male, 3= 50% male, 50% female

Sex of Target

Some studies have found a Sex of Subject × Sex of Target interaction; Millham and Weinberger (1977) and Millham, San Miguel, and Kellogg (1976), for example, found that males were more negative toward homosexuals when the target was a male homosexual; when the target was a lesbian, females were more negative.

Other studies have reported only a main effect for sex of target. Herek (in press) and Garfinkle & Morin (1978) found that males are more negative than females regardless of sex of target. Although many studies do not examine sex of target, results of these studies suggest that, if there is a sex difference in attitudes toward homosexuals, it may depend upon the sex of the homosexual target.

Type of Questionnaire

Morin and Garfinkle (1978) suggest that a sex difference occurs only when the questions deal with personal threat or anxiety as opposed to more general beliefs about homosexuals. Thus, the type of question used in each study will be analyzed to determine if there is support for this hypothesis.

The number of items used as a measure of attitude toward homosexuality will also be examined. This is a more straightforward measure of how the instrument might affect the results. It would be reasonable to expect that a longer questionnaire would tap more dimensions of attitudes toward homosexuals than a one-item questionnaire, increasing the likelihood of detecting a sex difference if there is one. For example, Levitt and Klassen (1974), who do not report a sex difference, simply asked subjects how wrong they felt homosexuality was. Millham, San Miguel, and Kellogg (1976), who do find a sex difference, asked a variety of questions about the subjects' beliefs and attitudes toward homosexuality. Other things being equal, a longer questionnaire would be expected to have a higher reliability than an instrument with only a few questions (e.g., Anastasi, 1982; Nunnally, 1978).

Sample Size

Sample sizes for the studies in this area vary from 40 to over 4,000. Because Glass's estimator of effect size is independent of sample size, this variable will be examined as a predictor of outcome. It is difficult to tell from the research reports how samples were selected. However, a larger sample would be expected to be more representative of the population even if random selection were used in all cases (e.g., Hays, 1981) and should be a better indicator of whether there is a sex difference.

Year of Publication

Finally, year of publication will be examined. As life situations of males and females become increasingly similar, one might expect gender differences in attitudes to lessen. Such changes in attitudes over time would be reflected in the dates the articles were published. No differences due to attitude change are predicted, though, as no research has reported such changes. However, it should be noted that most research in this area was conducted within the past fifteen years, a limited sample for detecting such differences.

Year of publication might also influence the effect sizes because study quality in general is improving over time. Further, more reliable measures have been published and recent studies are likely to use a measure with established reliability. Reliable measures would be expected to tap a sex difference if there is one, thus, these more recent studies would be more likely to find any sex differences.

METHOD

Sample of Studies

An attempt was made to retrieve all studies that examined sex differences in attitudes toward homosexuals. The search was begun with a computerized literature search from the following data bases: Social Science Search, 1972–1983; Sociological Abstracts, 1963–1983; ERIC, 1966–1983; Psychological Abstracts, 1967–1983; Pre-psych, 1981–February, 1983. Keywords used in the computer search were "attitudes" and "homosexuals." In addition, bibliographies of located studies were checked and major sex journals were hand-searched to locate any studies not found by the computer search.

Restrictions on the studies were that subjects be predominately heterosexual, that the subjects be predominately native English speakers, and that the subjects be at least high school age. Dissertations were eliminated from this study. It was necessary to discard two studies because, although the authors reported that there was a significant sex difference, the information provided could not be used for computing an effect size (Cuenot & Fugita, 1982; Young & Whertvine, 1982).

Effect Sizes

For each study, an attempt was made to compute an effect size directly with the d statistic. This statistic is the ratio of the difference between group means to the standard deviation of the group (Glass, McGaw, & Smith, 1981), defined in this meta-analysis as the pooled estimate from the male and female group. The sign of the d was set as positive when males held a more negative attitude than females and negative when females were found to hold a more negative attitude than males. A zero would reflect no difference between the sexes.

When the appropriate information was available, group means and standard deviations were used to compute the effect size for the study. When not retrievable, F or t statistics were used to estimate the effect size. In cases where it was simply reported that there were no sex differences, the effect size was recorded as zero.

There were several studies that reported results on more than one dependent measure. In these cases, the effect sizes were averaged over dependent measures. In cases where results for gay male and lesbian targets were reported separately, the effect sizes were computed separately and then averaged. The separate effect sizes were retained for analysis of sex of target differences.

Hedges (1982a) has shown that when sample sizes are small (e.g., the control group sample size is less than 20), Glass's d is a biased estimator of effect sizes. Although Glass's estimator should be unbiased in this meta-analysis, the corrected effect sizes were computed and are used in the analyses reported in this paper.

This meta-analysis is based on 24 independent studies. The effect sizes are reported in Table 1. As can be seen, 16 studies have effect sizes indicating that males are more negative toward homosexuals, five studies simply report no sex differences (recorded as $d = 0$) and three studies have a small negative effect size, indicating that females in that study tended to be more negative toward homosexuals. These effect sizes, when applicable, are averaged across sex of target. In most cases, however, sex of target is either male, male and female but not analyzed separately, or unspecified. The mean effect size was found to be .207 with a standard deviation of .243. The median effect size is .202.

The mean effect size was also computed on only those studies for which the actual effect size could be recovered. Thus, those studies for which the effect size was reported as $d = 0$ were eliminated from this analysis, because in these cases zero is only an estimate of the actual effect size in that study, including those studies in the sample biases the results in the feminine direction. Excluding these studies, however, biases the results in the masculine direction. The mean effect size for the group without the estimated effect sizes is .262 with a standard deviation of .25. As 16 of the studies reported a positive effect size and only three reported a negative effect size, the true effect size, if available, would be expected to be positive. Thus, the effect size computed with all studies is a more conservative estimate of the effect size.

Ninety-five percent confidence intervals were computed around each effect size and around the mean effect size. The interval around the mean, computed for all studies, is .105 to .310. As this confidence interval does not include zero, it can be concluded that the mean effect size is significant. Although the effect is small, it indicates that men have more negative attitudes toward homosexuals than do women.

Homogeneity Test

Hedges (1982b) has stated that although a pooled estimate of an effect size provides a summary of the results of a series of independent studies, this pooled estimate can be misleading when the effect sizes are not homogeneous. He provides a statistical test for whether experiments have the same effect size. If effect sizes are homogeneous across groups, the test statistic *(Hb)* is distributed as a central chi-square with $(p - 1)$ degrees of freedom.

The effect sizes in this study were subjected to Hedge's statistical test. *Hb* was found to be 78.93, which is significant ($p < .001$, $df = .24$). Therefore, the hypothesis that these studies are homogeneous is rejected.

ANALYSIS OF INDEPENDENT VARIABLES

Variables examined here that might account for some of this heterogeneity are sex of author, sex of target, sample size, type of questionnaire and year of publication.

Sex of Author

Sex of author was examined in two ways: sex of senior author and proportion of male authorship. Sex of senior author was correlated with the effect sizes and found to be not significant ($r = .23$). However, the number of male senior authors was greatly disproportionate (20 male authors vs. four female authors). Therefore, total study authorship was divided into three categories—greater than fifty percent male, less than fifty percent male, and equal numbers of male and female authors. Although the mean effect size for the predominately male author group was higher (.24 compared to .13 for the predominately female group and .14 for the equal split group), this difference was not significant ($F < 1$). It should be noted, however, that even with this categorization the majority of the studies had predominately male authorship. It is possible that more female researchers would make this difference more pronounced.

Sex of Target

To examine sex of target, studies were coded on whether the targets were male, both male and female, or simply "homosexual." Results of analysis of this variable were not significant ($F < 1$).

The above analysis is problematic as few studies provide information about sex differences analyzed by target. Since the effect sizes often had to be computed for both male and female targets combined, it is not possible to analyze by sex of target for those studies. Because of the grouping of male and female targets into one category, it is unlikely that the above analysis would uncover any sex of target differences. However, effect sizes were computed by sex of target when possible. These effect sizes are shown in Table 2. The mean effect size for male targets was computed

Table 2

Effect Sizes for Male Homosexual and Lesbian Targets

Study	Effect Size	
	Homosexual Male	Lesbian
H	.03635	.07388
L	.33967	------
M	.24321	.13929
O	.35730	-.18233
R	.19160	.12431
T	.41784	-.19747
Mean Effect Size	.22600	.07050

as .226 with a standard deviation of .15. The mean effect size for female targets was .070 with a standard deviation of .15. These results suggest that males are more negative toward male homosexuals than female subjects are but that there is little sex difference in attitudes toward lesbians. These results must be interpreted with caution as the number of studies reporting this information is small. Because of this small sample, no statistical test was performed. If the information were available, this variable might account for much of the variance.

Black and Stevenson (1983) have reported that when sex of target is not specified, 75% of all males and 41% of all females reported thinking only of males while completing the questionnaire. Further, 53% of the females and 25% of the males reported thinking of both males and females. Six percent of the females, and none of the males, reported thinking of females only. If this pattern holds for other groups and other questionnaires, one would expect that almost all subjects were thinking, at least in part, of males. This lends support to the hypothesis that males are more negative than females toward homosexuals only when the target is (or is perceived to be) male.

Sample Size

Sample size had a marginally significant negative correlation with the effect sizes ($r = -.33$, $p < .057$), suggesting that as sample sizes increase, effect sizes decrease. The sex difference seems to diminish as the sample pool becomes larger, which would suggest that the obtained sex differences are being heavily influenced by sampling error or subject selection. Most studies used a college population but it is difficult to tell how subjects were selected for participation, making it difficult to determine whether this is having an impact.

Because of this finding, effect sizes were weighted by sample size. When weighted by total N, the mean effect size is .084, much smaller than when sample size is not taken into account. Also, as the study with the largest sample size simply reported no sex difference, the weighted effect sizes, and the correlation between sample size and effect size, were computed for only those studies for which the actual effect size could be recovered. This weighted mean effect size is .134; the correlation between sample size and the effect sizes increases and is significant ($r = -.55$, $p < .008$).

As sample size has a major influence on the size of the effect, results from studies with small or homogeneous samples should be interpreted with caution as differences obtained may be due to sampling bias.

Year of Publication

There was also a marginally significant correlation between year of publication and the effect sizes ($r = .23$, $p = .06$). This might suggest that the sex difference in attitudes toward homosexuals is increasing over time. However, as mentioned earlier, it might also suggest that the more recent studies used more reliable measures or were otherwise better designed. Almost all of the studies included in this paper were correlational studies, using paper and pencil measures. However, the quality of the instruments used varied a great deal, with quality tending to increase as the area has become better developed.

Type of Question

Scale questions used to assess attitudes toward homosexuality were classified into two groups, as suggested by Morin and Garfinkle (1978). These were predominately general questions about homosexuality (i.e., I believe homosexuality is wrong) or predominately personal anxiety questions (i.e., I would not want to be close to a homosexual). There were no significant differences between these groups ($F = .19$), failing to support Morin and Garfinkle's hypothesis.

Number of questions used in the dependent measures was also examined. This variable was not significant ($r = .14$). Although this correlation is positive, suggesting a tendency for studies using more questions to obtain larger effect sizes, this variable is not extremely important.

CONCLUSIONS

There is a small sex difference in attitudes toward homosexuals, with males having a more negative attitude than females toward homosexuals. As effect sizes for sex difference research tend to be small (e.g., Eagly & Carli, 1978; Hall, 1978; Hyde, 1981), the size of this effect is not unusual. However, this research showed that much of this difference can be accounted for by sample size, year of publication and possibly sex of target. It is important for researchers to take these findings into consideration both when interpreting the present research and designing future studies.

Sample size is an important consideration. Researchers should use as large an N as possible and should try to select an unbiased sample. The smallest sample size included in this meta-analysis was 40; the largest was over 4,000. It is difficult to predict the optimum sample size as many variables need to be taken into account, including type of research being conducted and number of dependent measures and confidence in the random selection of subjects. Individual researchers will need to assess what is sufficient for their purpose.

Several reliable instruments are available for measuring attitudes toward homosexuals. The larger effect sizes found in more recent years might be due to the use of more reliable instruments or better study design in recent years. In light of the findings for year of publication and effect size, the correlation between number of items and year of publication was examined. However, this was found to be not significant, suggesting that it does not necessarily depend on using longer scales. When designing a study, researchers should select an instrument on the basis of its reported reliability and other relevant statistics. It would be useful if the instruments used in this area of research could become more standardized, making comparisons across studies easier to interpret.

Finally, as noted earlier, there is a tendency to concentrate on male subjects and male targets in homosexuality research. Those studies that do use both male and female targets and subjects tend to collapse across these two variables rather than reporting separate results. The present findings suggest that although males are more negative toward homosexuals, the difference may be dependent upon a Sex of Target × Sex of Subject interaction. Researchers should be aware of this possibility and should control for sex of homosexual target or use it as a variable in their studies. Reporting sex of target differences in more detail would allow this variable to be examined in a more systematic way.

It is important that researchers in this area recognize that sex differences in attitudes toward homosexuals are not as pervasive as some studies would suggest. By being aware of the variables influencing this difference, the research in this area can be improved and new knowledge can be gained.

REFERENCES

Anastasi, A. (1982). *Psychological Testing* (5th ed.) New York: Macmillan.

Black, K. N., & Stevenson, M. R. (1983). *Factors affecting attitudes toward lesbians and male homosexuals.* Paper presented at the Association for Women in Psychology, Seattle, WA.

Cuenot, R. G., & Fugita, S. S. (1982). Perceived homosexuality: Measuring heterosexual attitudinal and non-verbal reactions. *Personality and Social Psychology Bulletin, 8*(1), 100–106.

Dressler, J. (1979). Study of law student attitudes regarding the rights of gay people to be teachers. *Journal of Homosexuality, 4*(4), 315–329.

Dunbar, J., Brown, M., & Amoroso, D. (1973). Some correlates of attitudes toward homosexuality. *Journal of Social Psychology, 89,* 271–279.

Eagly, A. H., & Carli, L. L. (1978). Sex of researchers and sex-typed communications as determinants of sex differences in influenceability: A meta-analysis of social influence studies. *Psychological Bulletin, 90,* 1–20.

Garfinkle, E., & Morin, S. F. (1978). Psychologist's attitudes toward homosexual psychotherapy clients. *Journal of Social Issues, 34*(3), 101–111.

Glass, G. V. (1976). Primary, secondary and meta-analysis of research. *Educational Researcher, 5,* 3–8.

Glass, G. V., McGaw, B., & Smith, M. L. (1981). *Meta-analysis in Social Research.* Beverly Hills, CA: Sage Publications, Inc.

Glenn, N. D., & Weaver, C. N. (1979). Attitudes toward premarital, extramarital and homosexual relations in the U.S. in the 1970s. *The Journal of Sex Research, 15*(2), 108–118.

Hall, J. A. (1978). Gender effects in decoding nonverbal cues. *Psychological Bulletin, 85,* 845–875.

Hansen, G. L. (1982). Measuring prejudice against homosexuality (homosexism) among college students: A new scale. *The Journal of Social Psychology, 117,* 233–236.

Hays, W. (1981). *Statistics* (3rd ed.). New York: Holt, Rinehart & Winston.

Hedges, L. V. (1981). Distribution theory for Glass's estimator of effect size and related estimators. *Journal of Educational Statistics, 6,* 107–128.

Hedges, L. V. (1982a). Estimation of effect size from a series of independent studies. *Psychological Bulletin, 92,* 490–499.

Hedges, L. V. (1982b). Fitting categorical models to effect sizes from a series of experiments. *Journal of Educational Statistics, 7,* 119–137.

Henley, N. M., & Pincus, F. (1978). Interrelationship of sexist, racist, and antihomosexual attitudes. *Psychological Reports, 42,* 83–90.

Herek, G. (1983). Assessing attitudes toward lesbians and gay men: Scale construction and validation. Unpublished manuscript.

Hyde, J. W. (1981). How large are cognitive gender differences? A meta-analysis using w^2 and d. *American Psychologist, 36,* 892–901.

Irwin, P., & Thompson, N. L. (1975). Toleration of homosexuality: A social profile. Paper presented at Eastern Psychological Association.

Irwin, P., & Thompson, N. L. (1977). Acceptance of the rights of homosexuals: A social profile. *Journal of Homosexuality, 3*(2), 107–121.

Karr, R. G. (1978). Homosexual labeling and the male role. *Journal of Social Issues, 34*(3), 73–83.

Kite, M. E. (1983a). High versus low homophobics: The effects of expected interaction. Study in progress, Purdue University.

Kite, M. E. (1983b). The measurement of attitudes toward homosexuals. Unpublished data, Purdue University.

Kruelwitz, J. E., & Nash, J. E. (1980). Effects of sex role attitudes and similarity on men's rejection of male homosexuals. *Journal of Personality and Social Psychology, 38*(1), 215–228.

Leitner, L. M., & Cado, S. (1982). Personal constructs and homosexual stress. *Journal of Personality and Social Psychology, 43*(4), 869–872.

Levitt, E., & Klassen, A. (1974). Public attitudes toward homosexuality: Part of the 1970 national survey by the Institute for Sex Research. *Journal of Homosexuality, 1,* 29–43.

Light, R. J., & Smith, P. V. (1971). Accumulating evidence: Procedures for resolving contradictions among different research studies. *Harvard Educational Review, 41,* 429–471.

MacDonald, A. P. (1974). The importance of sex-role to the gay liberation. *Homosexual Counseling Journal, 1*(4), 169–180.

MacDonald, A. P., Huggins, J., Young, S., & Swanson, R. A. (1973). Attitudes toward homosexuality: Preservation of sex morality or the double standard. *Journal of Consulting and Clinical Psychology, 40,* 161.

Millham, J., San Miguel, C. L., & Kellogg, R. (1976). A factor-analytic conceptualization of attitudes toward male and female homosexuals. *Journal of Homosexuality, 2*(1), 3–10.

Millham, J., & Weinberger, L. E. (1977). Sexual preference, sex role appropriateness, and restriction of social access. *Journal of Homosexuality, 2*(4), 343–356.

Minnergerode, F. A. (1976). Attitudes toward homosexuality: Feminist attitudes and social conservatism. *Sex Roles, 1,* 160–165.

Morin, S. F., & Garfinkle, E. M. (1978). Male homophobia. *Journal of Social Issues, 34*(1), 29–47.

Nunnally, J. C. (1978). *Psychometric Theory* (2nd ed.). New York: McGraw-Hill, 225–255.

Nyberg, K. L., & Alston, J. P. (1977a). Analysis of public attitudes toward homosexual behavior. *Journal of Homosexuality, 2*(2), 99–107.

Nyberg, K. L., & Alston, J. P. (1977b). Homosexual labeling by university youths. *Adolescence, 12*(48), 541–556.

Price, J. H. (1982). High school students' attitudes toward homosexuality. *The Journal of School Health, 52*(8), 469–473.

Rosenthal, R., & Rubin, D. B. (1979). Comparing significance levels of independent studies. *Psychological Bulletin, 86,* 1165–1168.

Rosenthal, R., & Rubin, D. B. (1982). Comparing effect sizes of independent studies. *Psychological Bulletin, 92,* 500–504.

Smith, K. T. (1971). Homophobia: A tentative personality profile. *Psychological Reports, 29,* 1091–1094.

Sobel, H. (1976). Adolescent attitudes toward homosexuality in relation to self concept and body satisfaction. *Adolescence, XI*(43), 443–453.

Steffensmeier, D., & Steffensmeier, R. (1974). Sex differences in reactions to homosexuals: Research continuities and further developments. *The Journal of Sex Research, 10*(1), 52–67.

Weis, C. B., & Dain, R. N. (1979). Ego development and sex attitudes in heterosexual and homosexual men and women. *Archives of Sexual Behavior, 8*(4), 341–355.

Young, M., & Whertvine, J. (1982). Attitudes of heterosexual students toward homosexual behavior. *Psychological Reports, 51,* 673–674.

The Relationship of Self-Reported Sex-Role Characteristics and Attitudes Toward Homosexuality

Kathryn N. Black, PhD
Michael R. Stevenson, PhD (cand.)
Purdue University

ABSTRACT. The present study investigated the relationship between self-reported sex-role characteristics and attitudes toward homosexuality using the Bem Sex Role Inventory, the Personal Attributes Questionnaire and the Attitudes toward Homosexuality Scale. Relationships occur for both males and females who are exhibiting greater amounts of cross-sex traits. Females with more instrumental characteristics were more accepting while males with more expressive characteristics were more rejecting. These findings are discussed in relation to those of Weinberger and Millham (1979) who also investigated this relationship, as well as to research investigating the relationship between attitudes toward homosexuality and attitudes toward sex roles and feminism.

A number of studies have shown that those persons who do not support equality between the sexes and who believe that males and females should maintain separate and traditional sex roles are more negative in their attitudes toward homosexuality (MacDonald, Huggins, Young, & Swanson, 1973; MacDonald & Games, 1974; Morin & Garfinkle, 1978; Smith, Resick, & Kilpatrick, 1980; Weinberger & Millham, 1979).

One might suspect that those persons who are traditionally sex typed in their characteristics would also be less accepting of homosexuality. Weinberger and Millham (1979) investigated attitudes toward homosexuality as influenced both by beliefs about equality and subjects' masculinity/femininity as assessed by the Bem Sex Role Inventory (BSRI).

Requests for reprints should be sent to Kathryn N. Black, Associate Professor of Psychological Sciences, Purdue University, West Lafayette, IN 47907. Michael R. Stevenson is a graduate instructor who will complete his doctoral studies in 1984.

83

They found that masculine males, feminine females, and androgynous individuals were more negative than were masculine females, feminine males, and the undifferentiated. They interpreted these findings in a framework making use of the idea that those who perceive themselves as deviant will react less negatively to other deviants than those who do not perceive themselves as deviant (Freedman & Doob, 1968). Weinberger and Millham (1979) suggested that androgynous persons, a category generally reported to exhibit more positive behavior, are "fence straddlers" who may choose to adopt majority attitudes to lessen their experience of deviance.

The present study further investigated the relationship between self-reported sex-role characteristics and attitudes toward homosexuality. This study not only used the Bem Sex Role Inventory but also the Personal Attributes Questionnaire, another widely used measure that yields scores labeled masculinity and femininity.

METHOD

One hundred forty-one undergraduates at a large, public, midwestern university volunteered to participate in this experiment in order to satisfy part of a research participation requirement for introductory psychology. In order to have an homogeneous sample, data are reported here for only Caucasian subjects between the ages of 17 and 23. There were 62 males and 65 females. The modal age was 18 years; 57% were freshmen. Homosexuals were asked not to fill out the attitudes toward homosexuality measure. It was possible for them to do this with anonymity since all subjects were offered the option of refusing to answer any part of the questionnaire.

This sample is somewhat unusual in that approximately one third of the subjects came from families whose parents were divorced, one third came from families where at least one parent was deceased, and the remaining third were from intact families. Subjects with these characteristics were originally solicited in order to assess the importance of parental marital status as a predictor of attitudes toward homosexuality. However, there were no significant differences among these groups on any of the dependent measures employed in this study and therefore no reason to believe that parental marital status affected the results reported here.

Measures

The Attitudes Toward Homosexuality Scale (ATH) was adapted from items developed and reported by Millham, San Miguel, and Kellogg (1976). It consisted of the 20 items listed in Table 1. The 20 items

Table 1. Items included in the attitudes toward homosexuality scale

MR   1. The growing number of homosexuals indicates a decline in
           American morals. (disagree)

MR/RD   2. Laws regulating homosexual behavior should be loosened.
           (agree)

MR/PA   3. Homosexuals are sick. (disagree)

MR   4. There is nothing particularly wrong with homosexual behavior.
           (agree)

RD   5. Homosexuals are no more likely to commit crime (nonsexual)
           than are heterosexuals. (agree)

PA   6. It would be very easy for me to have a conversation with
           someone I know to be a homosexual. (agree)

RD   7. Homosexuals should be required to undergo psychotherapy.
           (disagree)

MR   8. Homosexuality is a sin. (disagree)

MR   9. Just as in other species, homosexuality is a natural
           expression of sexuality in humans. (agree)

PA   10. I would like to have homosexual friends. (agree)

PA   11. I won't associate with known homosexuals if I can help it.
           (disagree)

MR/PA 12. I do not think homosexuals are disgusting. (agree)

RD   13. Homosexuals do not use physical injury as a usual part of
           their sexual behavior. (agree)

RD   14. Homosexuals should be made to take examinations for VD
           regularly. (disagree)

RD   15. Bars that cater solely to homosexuals should be placed in
           one specific and known part of town. (disagree)

PA   16. If a family member or best friend told me that they were
           homosexual, it would distress me greatly. (disagree)

RD   17. Homosexuals should be required to register with the police
           department where they live. (disagree)

RD   18. Homosexuals are no more likely to try to seduce young people
           than are heterosexuals. (agree)

MR/PA 19. Homosexuality is a perversion. (disagree)

PA   20. Homosexuals have as much right as heterosexuals to teach
           young children. (agree)

selected fell into three areas which Millham et al. (1976) labeled personal anxiety in the presence of homosexuals (PA); ideas of moral reprobation (MR); and belief of the need for repression of homosexual behavior and that homosexuals are dangerous (RD). In adapting the scale for use in this study, the following changes were made. Items were stated so that there were equal numbers of positive and negative statements about homosexuals, thus controlling for a possible agreement bias. Although the original scale allowed only agree and disagree responses, we allowed subjects to indicate one of three responses; agree, uncertain or undecided, and disagree. This allowed for increased variability in scores, and we believe allowed the subjects to indicate more accurately their attitudes. In addition, items were phrased to refer to homosexuals in general rather than specifying lesbians or male homosexuals. However, at the end of the questionnaire, subjects were asked to report whether they were thinking primarily of male homosexuals, female homosexuals, or about both equally while filling out the questionnaire.

Scoring the scale resulted in three separate scores: an acceptance score, a rejection score, and an undecided score. Each score could range from 0 to 20. The acceptance score was the number of responses given by the subjects in accord with the response listed in parentheses in Table 1. The rejection score was the number of rejecting responses given by the subjects. The undecided score was the number of undecided/uncertain responses given by the subjects. The acceptance score and rejection score were broken down into subscale scores for Personal Anxiety (PA), Moral Reprobation (MR) and Repressive Dangerous (RD). Items corresponding with these subscales are indicated in Table 1.

Two measures of sex role attributes were used. The 30-item form of the Bem Sex Role Inventory (BSRI) (Bem, 1981) consists of 10 masculine, 10 feminine and 10 neutral items. Subjects were asked to rate themselves on a 7-point Likert-type scale on each of the items. A 16-item form of the Personal Attributes Questionnaire (PAQ) (Spence, Helmreich, & Stapp 1974) was also used. On the PAQ, subjects were asked to rate themselves on eight masculine and eight feminine items, each of which is presented on a 5-point Likert-type scale. This form of the PAQ differed from the traditional "short form" in that only those items used in classifying subjects by sex type were administered.

Masculine and feminine items on both of these scales are personality characteristics that have been found to be judged as more desirable for one sex than the other. For example, "independent" appears on both measures as a masculine item, while "understanding" appears on both scales as a feminine item. We will refer to the scores as M scores and F scores as we agree with those who suggest that these are primarily measures of instrumentality and expressiveness, one aspect of stereotypic masculinity and femininity.

RESULTS

No significant differences were found between the sexes for either the total scores or the subscales of the ATH. Undecided responses were used on the average about one quarter of the time by all subjects. Table 2, therefore, shows mean scores, for the sexes combined, for accept and reject totals and subscale scores.

Related *t* tests on the accept and reject scores for the subscales showed that subjects were more rejecting than accepting ($p < .001$) on the PA and MR items but more accepting with respect to RD items. Not surprisingly then, comparisons among subtest scores found that both PA and MR scores were significantly different from RD scores with subjects responding in a more accepting fashion on items on the repressive-dangerous scale. Scores on the RD and MR subscale did not differ.

The majority of males, 73%, reported that "homosexual" for them referred to males. The remainder used the term to refer to both male and female homosexuals. In contrast, 37% of females reported that they were thinking primarily of males, while 62% indicated that they were thinking of both sexes about equally. One subject indicated that she was thinking primarily of female homosexuals. These findings are consistent with those reported by Black and Stevenson (1983) using the same scale in a larger sample.

Analyses of variance of mean ATH scores broken down by the sex of the homosexual referent group revealed no significant differences for females. In this sample, then, females who used the term "homosexual" to refer to males did not differ in their attitudes from those who used the term to refer to both males and females. However, for male subjects, those who used "homosexual" to refer to males were significantly ($p < .005$) more rejecting and less accepting than those who used the term to refer to both male and female homosexuals. For males who were thinking primarily of male homosexuals, the mean accept and reject scores were 5.22 and 9.69, respectively. For those who were thinking of both male and female homosexuals while completing the scale, the mean accept and reject scores were 9.12 and 5.71, respectively.

Table 2. Means and Standard Deviation of ATH Scores

N = 127

	Accept	Reject
Total	6.91 (5.10)	8.01 (5.00)
PA	2.17 (2.40)	4.12 (2.67)
MR	2.19 (2.50)	4.01 (2.38)
RD	3.76 (2.19)	1.65 (1.58)

The median scores used for classification into sex-role categories were those obtained from this sample. The BSRI M median was 5.0 and the F median was 5.7. Each point on the BSRI scale was labeled; a 5 on the scale indicated "often true" and 6 indicated "usually true." The PAQ M median was 3.1 and the F median was 3.3. These scores are close to the midpoint of the PAQ 5-point scale which is labeled only at the ends.

As has been reported elsewhere, the two M scales were highly correlated (.77 for males and .59 for females) as were the feminine scales (.73 for males and .77 for females). Table 3 gives, for the sexes separately, the correlation of the BSRI and PAQ M and F scores with both accept and reject scores on the ATH. Sample sizes vary slightly as PAQ scores were not available for one female and four males who did not fill out this questionnaire.

Correlations were computed separately for the two male subgroups who were thinking either of males only or both sexes. These correlations were highly similar to those for the entire group. Therefore, only data for the whole sample are reported here. The correlations between M and F scores and ATH subscales were also examined and were similar to those for the total scores.

The correlations presented in Table 3 show that those males who had higher F scores on the PAQ tended to be less accepting and more rejecting of homosexuality. In contrast, those females who have higher M scores as measured by both the PAQ and the BSRI are more accepting of homosexuality.

Using the median split method, both the BSRI and the PAQ scores were used to classify subjects into four categories: masculine, feminine, androg-

Table 3. Correlations between ATH Scores and Measures of Sex Role Characteristics

Males	BSRI N = 62		PAQ N = 58	
	M	F	M	F
Accept	.0837 p = .259	-.1965 p = .063	.0086 p = .474	-.3454 p = .004
Reject	-.0196 p = .440	.1887 p = .071	.0662 p = .311	.4080 p = .001
Females	N = 64		N = 63	
Accept	.2985 p = .008	-.0441 p = .365	.4053 p = .001	-.1106 p = .194
Reject	-.1931 p = .063	.1997 p = .057	-.2717 p = .016	.2330 p = .033

ynous, and undifferentiated. Analyses of variance were computed, separately for the sexes, comparing ATH total scores and subscores among the four classifications. The Student Newman-Keuls ($p < .05$) procedure was used to test for simple effects. Since there were significant differences in the ATH scores of males who use "homosexual" to refer to males and those who use the term to refer to both males and females, two-way analyses of variance were computed for ATH scores by sex of referent and sex-role category. No significant interactions were found between sex of referent and sex-role category. Table 4 shows the means and standard deviations for males of the total ATH scores as well as those subscales for which significant differences associated with sex-role classification were found. These analyses showed that the groups classified by the PAQ differed for the total reject score and the PA and MR reject subscales. Significant simple effects were found only for the MR reject score with androgynous males more rejecting than undifferentiated males.

Since no difference due to referent group was found for females, one-way analyses of variance were done for the females investigating differences among the four sex-role categories. Table 5 shows the means and standard deviation for the total ATH scores plus those subscales for which significant differences were found. Simple effects tests showed that BSRI categorized, masculine females were more accepting of homosexuality than undifferentiated females on the PA and MR subscales. Further, PAQ classified androgynous females were more accepting than feminine females on the RD subscale. In line with the reported correlations for males, inspection of the subgroup scores shows that those groups with higher femininity scores (i.e., androgynous and feminine) are more rejecting. Consistent with the significant correlations, examination of the scores for females shows that those subgroups with high M scores (i.e., androgynous and masculine) are most accepting.

DISCUSSION

This study has found that there are relationships between scores on self-report scales designed to measure stereotyped sex-role characteristics and attitudes toward homosexuality. Relationships occur for both males and females who are exhibiting greater amounts of cross-sex traits, but in opposite directions as females with more instrumental characteristics are more accepting, while males with more expressive characteristics are more rejecting. Since Weinberger and Millham (1979) did not analyze separately for the sexes, it is difficult directly to compare our findings with theirs. However, it does appear that both studies found that females categorized as masculine tend to be more accepting while those categorized as feminine are less accepting. However, findings concerning the

Table 4. Means and Standard Deviations by Sex Role Classification for Males

ATH Scale	Sex Role Measure	Androgynous	Masculine	Feminine	Undifferentiated	F Value	P Value
Accept	BSRI	4.93 (5.59) n = 15	7.11 (4.58) n = 19	6.36 (5.54) n = 11	6.53 (4.69) n = 17	0.25	.857
Reject	BSRI	10.53 (5.50) n = 15	7.84 (3.83) n = 19	8.36 (5.66) n = 11	7.88 (5.29) n = 17	0.56	.645
Accept	PAQ	5.89 (5.66) n = 18	6.79 (5.06) n = 14	4.70 (2.63) n = 10	7.10 (5.29) n = 20	0.74	.536
Reject	PAQ	10.00 (5.36) n = 18	7.57 (4.31) n = 14	10.90 (3.75) n = 10	6.90 (5.21) n = 20	2.77	.050*
PA Reject	PAQ	4.94 (2.71) n = 18	4.50 (2.34) n = 14	5.40 (1.78) n = 10	3.00 (2.70) n = 20	3.69	.017**
MR Reject	PAQ	5.22 (3.04) n = 18	3.86 (2.90) n = 14	4.90 (1.91) n = 10	2.85 (2.64) n = 20	2.92	.042**

Student

* Newman-Keuls nonsignificant at (.05)

** Student Newman-Keuls significant. And. > Undif.

Table 5. Means and Standard Deviation by Sex Role Classification for Females

ATH Scale	Sex Role Measure	Androgynous	Masculine	Feminine	Undifferentiated	F Value	P Value
Accept	BSRI	8.26 (5.59) n = 19	10.50 (6.04) n = 10	7.00 (5.09) n = 21	5.20 (2.98) n = 15	2.46	.07
Reject	BSRI	7.26 (5.06) n = 19	5.20 (6.37) n = 10	8.38 (5.05) n = 21	7.93 (3.39) n = 15	1.15	.32
Accept	PAQ	9.05 (5.25) n = 19	9.27 (6.08) n = 11	4.89 (3.83) n = 18	7.35 (4.99) n = 17	2.73	.05*
Reject	PAQ	6.74 (4.88) n = 19	6.64 (5.75) n = 11	9.83 (4.34) n = 18	6.29 (4.67) n = 17	2.02	.12
PA Accept	BSRI	2.84 (3.17) n = 19	4.10 (2.42) n = 10	2.33 (2.31) n = 21	1.00 (1.20) n = 15	3.50	.02**
PA Accept	PAQ	3.16 (2.89) n = 19	3.64 (2.91) n = 11	1.33 (1.88) n = 18	2.06 (2.19) n = 17	2.74	.05*
PA Reject	PAQ	3.26 (2.66) n = 19	2.91 (2.81) n = 11	5.44 (2.23) n = 18	3.82 (2.79) n = 17	3.00	.04*
RD Accept	PAQ	4.53 (1.50) n = 19	4.45 (2.21) n = 11	2.83 (1.79) n = 18	4.12 (2.20) n = 17	2.94	.04**
MR Accept	PAQ	2.21 (2.92) n = 19	4.00 (2.83) n = 10	2.24 (2.59) n = 21	0.93 (1.03) n = 15	3.07	.03**

*   Student Newman-Keuls nonsignificant at (.05)

** Student Newman-Keuls significant at (.05)

PA Accept undifferentiated < Masculine.

RD Accept feminine < androgynous.

MR Accept undifferentiated < Masculine.

androgynous and undifferentiated are in opposition, as we found the androgynous female more accepting and the undifferentiated less so. Our findings concerning androgynous and undifferentiated males are like those of Weinberger and Millham; however, we found that masculine categorized males were less rejecting of homosexuality than those with cross sex-typed characteristics.

The findings for females might be explained in a system using the concept of deviancy. Females who are high in stereotypical masculine traits (instrumentality) have demonstrated their willingness to go against societal norms; perhaps, then, they are more able to accept behaviors of others that are not normative. This explanation does not work for males, however, since those males who are stereotypically deviant are more rejecting; one might suggest that these males have become sensitive to any suggestions that they are not masculine and that their negative reaction to homosexuality is a defensive one. Such explanations are clearly ad hoc, and perhaps it would be more appropriate to conclude that two studies have found a relationship between self-reported sex-role characteristics and attitudes toward homosexuality; however, since the findings agree only in part, it appears that the relationship is a complex one, and its exact nature needs further research.

Other research with the ATH does support the conclusion that those who support traditional sex roles will be rejecting of homosexuality (Villwock & Black, 1983). The finding that the relationship between sex roles and homosexuality is different than that between measures of attitudes toward feminism and homosexuality should not be surprising as these measures do not appear to be highly correlated with sex role measures. Spence and Helmreich (1978) reported on the relationship between the Attitude Toward Women Scale (AWS) and the PAQ. Of the four correlations which result from a consideration of the relationship between M and F scores and the AWS for the sexes separately, only two were significant, and these were of a magnitude of .11 and .16.

It should also be noted that our findings would have been different if we had used only one of the sex role measures. Specifically, while both measures showed relationships for females, for the males only the PAQ consistently produced significant results. Another possible difficulty is that we are continuing to see changes in sex role norms and accepted behavior for males and females. Such changes may mean that the relationship between sex role measures and attitudes will change.

It is also important to note that attitudes toward homosexuality are also in flux. Our data show that in this sample, subjects were less likely to give a rejecting response to those items on the RD scales than on the other scales. These items appear to be more closely related to factual information than items on the other scales. One might hypothesize that as more factual information becomes available to the general public, attitudes as measured by these items will change. Attitudes related to moral prejudice against homosexuality and personal anxiety about homosexuality may be more difficult to change.

Finally, it should be pointed out that while the BSRI and PAQ are presently the most widely used measures of sex-role characteristics, they measure only one aspect of sex-role stereotypes. It is possible that measures of other aspects of sex roles, such as occupational choice, specific behaviors, or style of dress, may show a different relationship with attitudes toward homosexuality.

REFERENCES

Bem, S. (1981). *Bem Sex-Role Inventory Professional Manual.* Consulting Psychologist Press.

Black, K. N., & Stevenson, M. R. (1983). Some factors which result in a more positive attitude towards homosexuality. Manuscript submitted for publication.

Freedman, J. L., & Doob, H. N. (1968). *Deviancy: The Psychology of being different.* New York: Academic Press.

MacDonald, A. P., & Games, R. G. (1974). Some characteristics of those who hold positive and negative attitudes toward homosexuals. *Journal of Homosexuality, 1*(1), 9–27.

MacDonald, A. P., Huggins, J., Young, S., & Swanson, R. A. (1973). Attitudes toward homosexuality: Preservation of sex morality or the double standard. *Journal of Consulting and Clinical Psychology, 40*, 161.

Millham, J., San Miguel, C. C., & Kellogg, R. A. (1976). Factor analytic conceptualization of attitudes toward male and female homosexuals. *Journal of Homosexuality, 2*(1), 3–10.

Morin, S. F., & Garfinkle, E. M. (1978). Male homophobia. *Journal of Social Issues, 34*, 29–47.

Smith, A. D., Resick, P. H., & Kilpatrick, D. G. (1980). Relationships among gender, sex-role attitudes, sexual attitudes, thoughts, and behaviors. *Psychological Reports, 46*, 359–367.

Spence, J. T., & Helmreich, R. L. (1978). *Masculinity and femininity: Their psychological dimensions, correlates, and antecedents.* Austin, TX: University of Texas Press.

Spence, J. T., Helmreich, R. L., & Stapp, J. (1974). The Personal Attributes Questionnaire: A measure of sex-role stereotypes and masculinity-femininity. *JSAS Catalog of Selected Documents in Psychology, 4*, 127.

Villwock, D. N., & Black, K. N. (1983). The effect of ''feeling different'' upon attitudes toward deviant groups. Unpublished manuscript.

Weinberger, L. E., & Millham, J. (1979). Attitudinal homophobia and support of traditional sex roles. *Journal of Homosexuality, 4*(3), 237–246.

The Relationships Among Sexual Beliefs, Attitudes, Experience, and Homophobia

Joseph E. Aguero, PhD
Laura Bloch, BS
Purdue University

Donn Byrne, PhD
State University of New York at Albany

ABSTRACT. Male and female subjects were given a series of questionnaires to assess their attitudes, behaviors, and experiences in relation to homosexuality. The findings indicated the presence of two systems, one dealing with affective orientation and the other with general beliefs (learned problem or physiological problem) about the origins of homosexuality. It was found that the greatest dislike toward homosexuals existed in those subjects who responded with negative affect *and* believed that homosexuality was a learned problem. Avoidance of social situations where homosexuals are present was evidenced in subjects who responded with negative affect and believed homosexuality was due to genetic factors.

Society's general attitude toward sexual behaviors has undergone change during the last 25 years (Byrne, 1977). There are reasons to believe that the greatest degree of change involves a more open-minded attitude from society in general vis-à-vis sexual behavior. Recently, one particular variation of sexual behavior, homosexuality, has been a hotly debated issue and the center of attention in newscasts and newspapers.

Homosexuals were rated as the third most dangerous people in the United States in a public opinion survey conducted during the 1960s. They were outranked only by communists and atheists (Wilson, Strong, Clarke, & Johns, 1977) with 82% of the men and 58% of the women agreeing on that ranking. As recently as 1974, the majority of people surveyed were reluctant to give homosexuals the right to have private homosexual relationships (Levitt & Klassen, 1974). Kinsey's (Kinsey,

Joseph E. Aguero is Assistant Professor in the Psychology Department, University of Wisconsin-Fox Valley, Menasha, WI 54952. Laura Bloch is an accounting officer with private industry in Detroit, MI. Donn Byrne is Professor of Psychology at the State University of New York, Albany. Reprint requests should be addressed to Dr. Aguero at the above address.

Pomeroy, & Martin, 1948) survey indicated that about 38% of the men and 13% of the women surveyed had had at least one homosexual experience to the point of orgasm. How can these two sets of percentages be reconciled? For women, the percentages are not in disagreement, but for men, it *could* mean that many who had had a homosexual experience hated it.

The previously cited surveys also indicate a higher degree of dislike for homosexuals by the male population. One factor which has been advanced in order to describe this high percentage of dislike in males is the concept of male homophobia (Morin & Garfinkle, 1978):

> From a cultural perspective homophobia is defined as any belief system which supports negative myths and stereotypes about homosexual people. More specifically, it can be used to describe: (a) belief systems which hold that discrimination on the basis of sexual orientation is justifiable; (b) the use of language or slang, e.g., "queer," which is offensive to gay people; and/or (c) any belief system which does not value homosexual life styles equally with heterosexual life styles (p. 30)

One important aspect of homophobia is the actual *fear reaction* exhibited by heterosexual males who are classified as homophobic. Experiments which have measured penile volume changes in responses to erotic slides have indicated that in homophobic males there is a statistically significant increase in volume when viewing pictures of nude, adult females *and* decreases of penile volume when viewing pictures of nude males (Freund, Langevin, Gibiri, & Zajac, 1973; Langevin, Stanford, & Block, 1975).

If one accepts the existence of homophobia in heterosexual males, and given that phobic reactions are likely to be the result of learning or experience, the next logical step would be to assess the possible personality systems that can influence the negative attitudes generated by homophobic reactions. Byrne's (1977) model of the sexual behavior sequence contains two possible constructs that might help to explain the mechanisms involved in homophobic reactions. These constructs are the belief systems and attitudinal or affect systems.

BELIEF SYSTEMS AND ATTITUDES

Two major belief systems about homosexuality can be said to operate exclusively of each other. One, a heterosexual person may believe that homosexuality is largely determined by learning and personal choice. Basically, these people are likely to believe that a person can become a homosexual if he/she does not watch his/her step. Heterosexual people with negative attitudes toward homosexuality would view any self-deviation from the heterosexual role stereotype as highly threatening since such deviations may indicate that they themselves may be sliding toward the "other" undesirable group. Consequently, the homosexuality of others tends to be viewed as a highly threatening situation given the fact that homosexuals may have a high degree of similarity (if one excludes sexual preferences) to heterosexual individuals. That is, the more normal a homosexual appears to be the more threat that is perceived by heterosexuals who believe homosexuality is learned. Those with positive attitudes are likely to feel attraction toward, or at least disregard, the homosexual component when making like-dislike judgments about a person known to be homosexual.

The second set of beliefs is the view that homosexuality is a physiological (or genetic) disorder. This belief produces attitudes toward homosexuality that are basically similar to attitudes toward the handicapped. If one has negative attitudes the tendency would be to feel sorry for (pity) the homosexuals and their plight. Positive attitudes, on the other hand, are likely to produce patronizing feelings such as "helping" the poor homosexual "cope" with his burden. The increased perceived similarity of homosexuals mentioned in the preceding paragraph is not threatening to this group of heterosexuals mainly because they would be inclined to see it as success by the homosexual group at attaining some semblance of normality. Similar attitudes would be attitudes toward a handicapped person who succeeds (i.e., gets a college degree) against odds set by nature. It is important to note that it is not that the person becomes normal, but that the person is able to function in a world of normal people.

Another related attitudinal system is that of affective responses (see Fisher, Byrne, & White, 1983), labeled *erotophobia* (negative affect to sexual arousal) and *erotophilia* (positive affect to sexual arousal). This system, together with evaluations of homosexuality, interacts with the belief component (learned vs. genetic) to determine such instrumental acts as approach-avoidance, expression of like-dislike, and the forming of friendships with homosexuals or the forming of anti-gay groups such as Anita Bryant's "Save Our Children" society. Byrne's (1977) model of the sexual behavior sequence as adapted to the concept of homophobia is presented in Figure 1.

PREVIOUS EXPERIENCE

The effects of previous contact with homosexuals (whether social or interactive) should produce a stronger effect on those heterosexually oriented people who believe that homosexuality is learned. The net effect of experience is likely to result in a polarization of attitudes; those with positive attitudes will become more positive because they would tend to see homosexuality as a variation in a theme and homosexuals as people

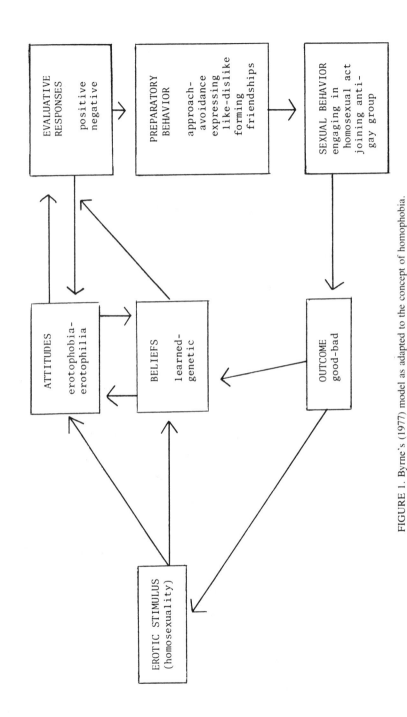

FIGURE 1. Byrne's (1977) model as adapted to the concept of homophobia.

with similar qualities as themselves; and those with negative attitudes will become more negative still because of stronger perceived similarities.

PURPOSE OF THE STUDY

The purpose of this study was to determine if the hypothesized groups (learning vs. physiological) exist and show the expected patterns of attitudes. A questionnaire to assess the general beliefs and attitudes was constructed for this purpose together with a hypothetical homosexual case in order to obtain mean ratings on the like-dislike and pity-patronizing scales.

The Sexual Opinion Survey (SOS; Fisher et al., 1983) is included to test the validity of the assertion of Morin and Garfinkle (1978) that homophobics tend to have a more restrictive sex role and are likely to show negative feelings to unusual sexual behaviors. Using the Fisher et al. terminology, homophobic males would be likely to be at the lower end of the SOS scale; that is, erotophobes.

Survey questionnaires that probe into the experience and behaviors of the subjects are included for two reasons. First, it is important to determine the incidence of heterosexual and homosexual behaviors in the two groups; that is, a measure of the relationship among beliefs, attitudes, and experience. Second, these surveys will also yield basic demographic data which not only are important for the interpretation of the findings from this survey but also serve as reference points for future research.

METHOD

Subjects

Subjects were 476 (255 females and 221 males) undergraduate students at Purdue University who participated in order to fulfill the experimental requirement for a course in introductory psychology. Participation was completely anonymous, and subjects were given the option of leaving with full credit prior to the start of the experiment. Subjects were also required to read and sign a 24-hour advanced consent form which explained the procedures of the experiment.

Questionnaires

The questionnaire given to each subject consisted of six sections. Section 1 dealt with questions about the subjects' background (i.e., sex, age, religion, etc.). Section 2 consisted of the Sexual Opinion Survey (SOS). Section 3 inquired about the sexual behaviors of the subjects (i.e., number of times per month that the subjects practiced specific behaviors such as kissing, masturbation, sexual fantasies, intercourse, etc., and whether with an opposite sex or same sex partner). Section 4 consisted of a series of questions designed to tap into the attitudes and beliefs about homosexuality. Section 5 inquired as to the subjects' previous experiences with homosexuals, and presented the subjects with a hypothetical case of a friend admitting his/her homosexuality to the subjects. Subjects were asked to respond by indicating their feelings on a 7-point scale on the following variables: dislike, pity, respect, annoyance, amusement, and superiority. Section 6 consisted of an experimental feedback questionnaire designed to assess the subjects' reactions to participation in sexual research.

Procedure

The questionnaires were distributed to same sex groups. Subjects were seated with two empty seats in between each subject, and in only every other row of seats in order to insure complete anonymity. Prior to the distribution of questionnaires the subjects were reminded that they were free to leave with full credit for the experiment. Only five subjects opted to leave at any time during the experimental sessions. At the end of the experimental session the subjects were given a written and an oral debriefing explaining the purpose of the study. The experimenter provided an opportunity for the subjects to request (by filling out a request form) a preprint of the results of the experiment. Approximately 178 subjects requested copies of the results.

RESULTS AND DISCUSSION

Demographic Data

Table 1 shows the general characteristics of the sample. In general, male subjects were roughly two-thirds of a year older than female subjects. Males and females also differed in that males had, on the average, higher scores in the SOS questionnaire than female subjects, indicating a more liberal sexual attitude. The groups did not differ significantly in general background.

Table 2 shows the various sexual experiences and behaviors of the sample. Males reported a higher number of fantasies dealing with bestiality, having sex outdoors, incest, homosexuality, having sex with a stranger, power over another person, and romantic love. Females reported a higher number of fantasies dealing with someone else having power over the female subject. Males also reported a higher incidence of masturbation alone while females reported a higher incidence of kissing opposite sex

Table 1. Demographic characteristics of the sample

VARIABLE	----TOTAL SAMPLE----			------MALES ONLY-----			--FEMALES ONLY--		
	N[1]	MEAN	STD DEV	N	MEAN	STD DEV	N	MEAN	STD DEV
Age	477	19.20	1.63	221	19.60	1.39	255	18.91	1.39
Class[2]	475	1.68	.82	219	2.02	.87	255	1.38	.63
Back-ground[3]	477	2.66	1.30	221	2.62	1.31	255	2.69	1.29
SOS[4]	476	88.83	26.72	216	96.90	16.38	255	80.49	22.12

[1] male and female N do not add up to total N due to blank responses.

[2] freshman=1, graduate student=5

[3] rural area=1, large urban metro=5

[4] lowest limit (erotophobe)=21, highest limit (erotophile)=147

Table 2. Sexual experiences of the sample (average number of occurences per month).

VARIABLE	----MALES ONLY----			----FEMALES ONLY----		
	N	MEAN	STD DEV	N	MEAN	STD DEV
FANTASIES						
rape	212	1.12	2.98	238	.98	3.08
bestiality	209	.31	1.76	235	.02	.13
sex outdoors	215	4.87	10.68	245	2.98	5.35
under someone's power	211	2.67	10.00	241	3.42	5.10
incest	211	.81	2.80	234	.15	.80
homosexuality	210	.70	3.99	237	.28	1.21
sex with a stranger	214	5.36	10.86	240	1.75	4.54
power over someone	214	4.30	8.76	239	2.13	3.64
romantic love	218	14.53	17.88	251	12.64	14.45
MASTURBATION						
alone	215	7.61	9.80	237	2.11	4.04
with opposite sex	210	2.76	8.43	240	1.95	4.11
with same sex	206	.08	.61	234	.09	1.02
KISSING						
with opposite sex	217	27.64	31.92	244	33.39	34.73
with same sex	206	.01	.10	234	.18	1.31
PETTING						
with opposite sex	212	13.92	20.64	248	14.19	20.89
with same sex	203	.05	.26	232	.09	.95
ORAL SEX						
to opposite sex	210	3.79	8.45	243	3.24	5.17
to same sex	205	.12	.82	234	.03	.40
by opposite sex	209	3.89	9.07	240	3.25	5.14
by same sex	206	.13	.84	234	.08	.77
INTERCOURSE						
with opposite sex	213	5.83	10.50	244	6.52	12.23
with same sex	205	.05	.35	234	.05	.55
group sex	206	.17	1.19	234	.04	.27

persons. Incidence of oral sex and intercourse did not differ significantly for the male and female samples.

Belief Systems and Attitudes

A factor analysis was performed on subjects' responses to the questionnaire dealing with attitudes and beliefs about homosexuality. In order to avoid confounding the data, 42 experimental booklets were discarded because subjects had marked either "primarily homosexual" or "exclusively homosexual" in the sexual orientation question. The factor analysis indicated the presence of three general factors. The first factor included most items dealing with affective responses and accounted for 68% of the variance in the sample. The second factor consisted of three responses which dealt with the ability to change (unlearn) from a homosexual role to a heterosexual role, and thus, beliefs that homosexuality is learned. The second factor accounted for 25% of the variance. The third factor included questions that appear to deal with affect, but it only accounted for less than 5% of the variance and was disregarded. The correlation between factor 1 and 2 was low ($r = .18$), and there was a moderate correlation between factors 1 and 3 ($r = .39$).

By performing a median split for each sex on SOS scores, the affective factor scores, and the learned factor scores, eight groups of subjects were generated in order to test the hypotheses. A between-groups analysis of variance was performed for each dependent variable. The results indicated that the highest degree of dislike was experienced by those subjects who had high scores on the affect factor (high scores indicated negative affect) and who also believed that homosexuality was a learned problem ($F[1,452] = 10.19$, $p < .01$; see Table 3).

Figure 2 shows the relationship between SOS scores and the learned-genetic factor relationship. Erotophobes appear to have an equally high degree of dislike toward homosexuals regardless of whether they think it is a learned or genetic problem, while erotophiles had higher dislike *only* when they believed that homosexuality was a learned problem. These data extend strong support to Morin and Garfinkle's (1978) notion that homophobics tend to have a more restricted sex role. The data also qualify the hypothesis that a higher degree of dislike will be experienced when there is both a negative emotional reaction to unusual sexual behaviors and a belief that homosexuality is acquired; it is only true of those subjects who score high on the SOS scores (erotophiles).

Sexual Experience and Attitudes

The mean responses to the question "During the last four years, have you ever had a sexual experience with a member of the same sex?" in-

Table 3. The Homophobic Scale.

Affective Factor

1. I would feel uncomfortable if I were in a public restroom at the same
    time as a homosexual.

2. I would feel uncomfortable if I were sitting next to a homosexual on a bus.

3. I would feel uncomfortable if I were living next door to a homosexual.

4. Homosexuals should not be allowed to vote.

5. I would not work for a company that hires homosexuals.

6. If I were to notice two strangers engaged in homosexual behavior in a
    public restroom I would be likely to report them to the police.

7. Homosexuals should not be allowed to run for public office.

8. A person's homosexual inclination should not be a cause for dismissal from
    a job, provided that his or her code of conduct conforms to expected
    norms (negative loading).

Beliefs Factor

1. Homosexuality is most likely based on a genetic factor.

2. Homosexuals cannot help being the way they are.

3. No amount of therapy can change homosexual preference.

dicated that very low levels of experience were reported by homophobics (all erotophobes and those erotophiles who believed that homosexuality is a learned problem), but statistically significant higher levels of experience were reported by erotophiles with genetic beliefs. One conclusion would be that the erotophiles with genetic beliefs, who are heterosexually oriented, may occasionally engage in homosexual *acts* for "kicks" without fear of "catching it" (homosexuality) since they believe it is a genetic problem. The same relationship holds in the mean responses to the question "having felt sexually attracted to a member of the same sex," with the only difference being that means were, on the average, higher for the reported attraction than for the actual behavior.

The mean responses to the question "Have you ever been in a social situation where homosexuals have been present?" indicated, however, that those subjects with negative affect toward homosexuality tend to avoid homosexuals more if they think homosexuality is a *genetic* problem ($F[1,452] = 7.55$, $p < .01$). This finding was especially true of erotophiles. Figure 3 shows the relationship between the affective component and the genetic component across the SOS scales. From these data it would appear that erotophiles with negative affect avoid social situations in which homosexuals are present, and perhaps this represents a desire to avoid being counted as members of the "outcast" group.

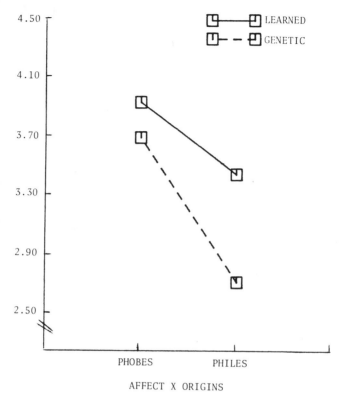

AFFECT X ORIGINS

FIGURE 2. The relationship of the SOS and genetic-learned beliefs on dislike toward a friend who admits to his/her homosexuality.

Sex Differences

On the average, males showed a higher degree of dislike toward the hypothetical homosexual than females ($F[1,452] = 17.71$, $p < .01$) and more annoyance also ($F[1,452] = 3.84$, $p < .01$). The only significant interaction involving sex of subject was noted in the "superiority" variable where females, regardless of their learned-genetic beliefs, exhibited lower levels of superiority while males with genetic beliefs showed levels equal to the females' superiority and males with learned beliefs showed significantly higher levels of superiority.

Figure 4 shows the relationship between sex of subject, affect, and genetic-learned beliefs. In general, negative affect and learned beliefs subjects showed lower likelihood of having close friendships with any homosexual person. Affect had no effect with females who had genetic beliefs, while males with genetic beliefs showed statistically significant differences due to the affect factor.

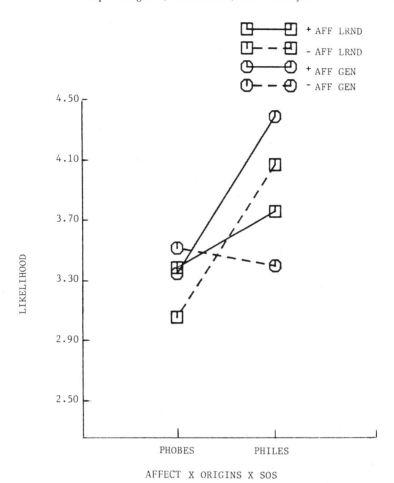

AFFECT X ORIGINS X SOS

FIGURE 3. The relationship of Affect, genetic-learned beliefs and SOS in responses to the question "have you ever been present in a social situation where homosexuals have been present?"

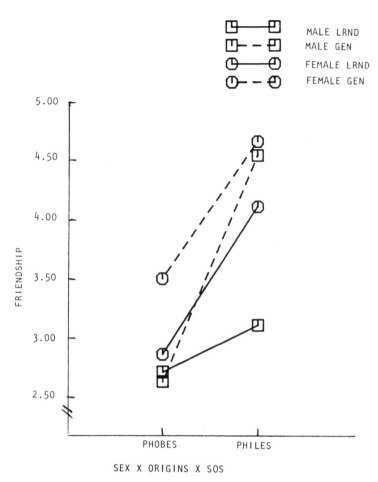

FIGURE 4. Sex differences within the genetic-learned factor in responses to the question "could you have a close friendship with a known homosexual?"

REFERENCES

Byrne, D. (1977). Social psychology and the study of sexual behavior. *Personality and Social Psychology Bulletin, 3,* 3–30.

Fisher, W. A., Byrne, D., & White, L. A. (1983). Emotional barriers to contraception. In D. Byrne and W. A. Fisher (Eds.), *Adolescents, sex, and contraception.* Hillsdale, NJ: Erlbaum.

Freund, K., Langevin, R., Gibiri, S., & Zajac, Y. (1973). Heterosexual aversion in homosexual males. *British Journal of Psychiatry, 122,* 163–169.

Kinsey, A. C., Pomeroy, W. B., & Martin, C. E. (1948). *Sexual behaviors in the human male.* Philadelphia: W.B. Saunders.

Langevin, R., Stanford, A., & Block, R. (1975). The effects of relaxation instructions on erotic arousal in homosexual and heterosexual males. *Behavior Therapy, 6,* 453–458.

Levitt, E., & Klassen, A. (1974). Public attitudes toward homosexuality: Part of 1970 national survey by the Institute for Sex Research. *Journal of Homosexuality, 1*(1), 29–43.

Morin, S. F., & Garfinkle, E. M. (1978). Male homophobia. *Journal of Social Issues, 34,* 29–47.

Wilson, S., Strong, B., Clarke, L., & Johns, T. (1977). *Human sexuality: A text with readings.* New York: West Publishing.

Changing Homophobic Attitudes Through College Sexuality Education

William J. Serdahely, PhD
Georgia J. Ziemba, MS
Montana State University

ABSTRACT. It was hypothesized that a unit on homosexuality (which emphasized role playing and the debunking of myths) in an undergraduate college sexuality course would alter students' homophobic attitudes. A modified version of the Hudson/Ricketts Index of Homophobia was used to measure homophobia. At the completion of the course, for those students in the treatment group with pretest scores above the median, the homophobic scores decreased significantly when compared to the scores of control counterparts. The results of this study also showed that there was no significant difference in homophobia scores at the end of the course for those students in the treatment group with pretest scores below the median when compared to the appropriate controls.

DEFINITION OF HOMOPHOBIA

George Weinberg (1972) receives credit for coining the term *homophobia,* by which he meant the fear felt by heterosexuals when in near proximity to homosexuals *and* the self-hatred experienced by gays because of their homosexuality. Rosan (1978) notes that "homophobia" is actually an abbreviated form of "homophilephobia," which literally means the fear of persons of one's own sex, clearly not the connotation given to these terms in common parlance nor in professional literature. Rosan points out that what is really meant by the terms *homophobia* (literally, the fear of that which is similar) and *homophilephobia* is an irrational dislike for those who are sexually attracted to persons of their own sex. It is because of the imprecision of the words, *homophobia* and *homophilephobia,* that Boswell (1980) suggests the substitute term *homosexophobia,* which literally means the fear of homosexuality.

Hudson and Ricketts (1980) differentiate between the terms *homonega-*

William J. Serdahely is Associate Professor of Health Education at Montana State University, Bozeman, Montana 59717. Georgia J. Ziemba is a statistician with the computing services at Montana State University.

109

tivity and *homophobia.* Homonegativity, for these authors, is a multidimensional set of responses involving *both* cognitive and affective reactions to homosexuality issues at the societal, legal, moral, and/or personal levels. Homophobia is more specific, representing the affective or emotional feelings of anxiety, disgust, aversion, anger, discomfort, and fear that heterosexuals may experience in dealing with homosexual persons. Hudson and Ricketts further expand Weinberg's definition of *homophobia* to include not only close or proximal contact with gays, but distal contact as well. It is the Hudson/Ricketts' definition of *homophobia* that is used throughout the remainder of this paper.

INTRODUCTION

Freedman (1978) points out that homosexuality, in and of itself, is not a sickness, but that homophobia is a "severe disturbance," damaging both homosexuals *and* heterosexuals (p. 320). Voeller (1980) characterizes homophobia as a human rights issue, noting that the methods of oppression and persecution of gays are identical to those used on other minority groups, such as Jews, blacks, and Native Americans. According to Marmor (1980a), homophobia "is a mental health issue of the first magnitude" (p. 21).

Due to the pervasive and invidious nature of homophobia, gays may be discriminated against in the areas of jobs, military service, housing, licensing and public accommodations. Gays may experience rejection from homophobic friends and relatives, most notably parents (Warren, 1980; Crooks and Baur, 1980). The hostility, contempt and disparagement (all components of the homophobic climate) endured by gays may lead to impaired self-concepts, with the concomitants of unhappiness, guilt, self-hatred, and thinking of oneself as being "evil" or "perverted" (Marmor, 1980a; Warren, 1980).

Both Warren and Marmor believe homophobia to be a fear that is deeply ingrained and commonly felt by heterosexuals in this society (Warren, 1980; Marmor, 1980b), a fear, according to Voeller, taught explicitly and implicitly through a variety of sources, including parents, friends, churches, and even the medical establishment. And, yet, in the opinion of Marmor, most gay men and lesbians "ask only to be accepted as human beings and allowed to live their lives free of persecution or discrimination" (p. 20).

Freedman (1978) states that little has been done to change the homophobic attitudes found in this country, much more clearly needing to be accomplished to ameliorate the current and widespread antigay biases. It was with Freedman's comments in mind that the present study was undertaken.

A UNIT ON HOMOSEXUALITY

For more than eight years, one of the authors has taught a lower division, undergraduate human sexuality course which always includes a unit on homosexuality. Over the course of these years, he has made several observations with respect to his students and their study of homosexuality:

1. many heterosexual, undergraduate students seem to be misinformed, intolerant, and prejudiced about homosexuality and homosexuals;
2. in general, male students seem to be more homophobic than female students; and
3. having gay speakers (provided by the local campus gay organization) talk to the class and answer questions seems to *increase,* rather than decrease, the homophobia of the class, an observation corroborated by Warren (1980, p. 137).

The present course of study of homosexuality in the undergraduate human sexuality course entails reading a chapter on homosexuality (Masters, Johnson, & Kolodny, 1982); doing two, dyadic role-playing situations in class; and discussing, in small groups, common myths about homosexuality. The technique of role playing is used here because of its purported advantage of assisting the development of empathy in the learner (Bruess & Greenberg, 1981). The group is divided into twosomes, and the two role-playing situations require *each* learner to play the role of a gay person, in one case wanting to tell one's parent about one's homosexuality, and in the other, "coming out of the closet" to one's best friend of the same sex who is heterosexual.

Based on one of the author's observations and discussions with his students, his *impression* is that these activities increase tolerance for gays and reduce homophobia. To determine the validity of this impression, he decided to measure his students' homophobia through the use of a questionnaire.

A HOMOPHOBIA QUESTIONNAIRE (IHP-M)

Smith appears to have been the first researcher to develop a homophobic scale (Smith, 1971; Weinberg, 1972). In 1976, Lumby used a modified version of Smith's questionnaire. But, neither Smith nor Lumby reported on the validity and reliability of their instruments.

Hudson and Ricketts (1980) developed an instrument which they called the "Index of Homophobia" (IHP). According to these researchers, IHP measures only homophobia, one of the several dimensions comprising the larger syndrome of homonegativity (as discussed previously).

Hudson and Ricketts report their IHP has a reliability of .901 and good factorial and content validity. However, of the 25 items included in the instrument, these authors say that five items fail to meet the criteria of their definition of homophobia. Five additional items are suggested as replacements, and Hudson and Ricketts report that Towne (1979) has shown these substitute items have excellent factorial validity (as well as better meeting the Hudson/Ricketts' homophobia definition).

The Hudson and Ricketts IHP was altered in this study to delete the five faulty items and to include the suggested replacements. The modified IHP (IHP-M) was given to a group of 34 persons, and the reliability of the IHP-M was calculated. (In their 1980 article, Hudson and Ricketts never reported calculating the reliability for a modified IHP which would include the five substitute items.)

Coefficient *alpha,* the same statistic Hudson and Ricketts used to calculate their IHP reliability, was found to be .950 for IHP-M, with a standard error of measurement (SEM) of 4.56. The original IHP was reported to have an SEM of 4.75. Because of the high reliability and good validity of the IHP-M questionnaire, this modified instrument was used in the present study.

METHODOLOGY

IHP-M was given at the beginning of Autumn Quarter, 1982, and again at the quarter's end, ten weeks later, to two groups of students. The treatment group was composed of 26 females and 15 males ($N = 41$) enrolled in a 200-level undergraduate sexuality course; the control group contained 29 females and 18 males ($N = 47$) taking a 200-level undergraduate drug education course. The mean age for the treatment group was 20.7 years, with an age range of 19 to 29; the mean age of the control group was 22 years, ranging in age from 18 to 47. Students in both groups came from a wide variety of academic majors, with no one curriculum predominating for either group. One of the authors of this paper was the instructor for both the sexuality and drug courses, with the treatment group receiving the homosexuality unit described above, and the control group receiving no instruction whatsoever on homosexuality. Homophobia scores were calculated by using the Hudson/Ricketts' formula, $S = \Sigma N - 25$ (Hudson and Ricketts, 1980). Using this formula means that the scores will fall within a range of points from zero to 100, as there are 25 items on the questionnaire, and the maximum score for any one item is 5 points.

Hudson and Ricketts (1980) divided the scores to their homophobia questionnaire into four categories. Scores in the 0 to 25 range were regarded as "high grade nonhomophobics," while the 25 to 50 point range represented the "low grade nonhomophobics." Persons receiving scores between 50 and 75 were said to be "low grade homophobics," with "high grade homophobics" scoring between 75 and 100 points (p. 360). These four categories were not used in the analysis of the data generated by IHP-M because the original questionnaire was never standardized. It was, therefore, felt that the cutoff points could not be considered valid.

Instead of the Hudson/Ricketts four categories, the pretest median for all respondents was used to divide the treatment and control students into two groups: those above, and those below, the median. Dividing the respondents according to the median was done for the following reason: If IHP-M is a measure of homophobia, and if the higher the IHP-M score means the greater the homophobia, and if the homosexuality unit is supposed to decrease homophobia, then it would be invalid to include all of the scores—those that are both high *and* low—in the analysis. It would be invalid because one would not expect the lower homophobia scores to change significantly. If the homosexuality unit is indeed accomplishing its objective of decreasing homophobia, then one would expect little or no change for those respondents with the lower homophobia scores, as these people, presumably, are relatively nonhomophobic. (Conversely, if the instructional unit increases homophobia, then the posttest scores for those treatment respondents below the median should increase.)

A Student's *t* test was used to determine whether or not statistically significant changes occurred between the treatment and control groups. First, the difference between each individual respondent's pretest and posttest score was calculated. Then, the average of the differences for the treatment group was determined, as well as the mean differences for the control group. Finally, a *t* test was used to compare the mean difference for the treatment group with that of the control group.

For the "above the median" category, the null hypothesis was that the treatment group's mean difference would be equal to or higher than that of the control group; the alternative hypothesis, that the treatment group's mean difference would be lower than that of the control group. Hence, a one-tailed test was used for the "above the median" comparison.

For the "below the median" category, the null hypothesis was that there would be no difference between the treatment group's mean and that of the controls; the alternative hypothesis, that there would be a difference between the two means. Hence, a two-tailed test was used for the "below the median" comparison.

RESULTS

The median was determined to be 73. Forty-three respondents had pretest scores above the median: 23 respondents from the treatment group, and 20 from the controls. Forty-five respondents comprised the "below the median" category: 18 respondents from the treatment group, and 27 from the controls.

For the "above the median" category, the mean difference in pre- and posttest scores was 0.6 for the control group, and -5.6 for the treatment group. For a separate variance estimate, a t value of 2.45 for 37.55 degrees of freedom was found, with a one-tailed probability of .01.

For the "below the median" category, the mean difference in pre- and posttest scores was -0.5 for the control group, and -0.3 for the treatment group. For a separate variance estimate, a t value of $-.06$ for 34.62 degrees of freedom was found, with a two-tailed probability of .950. When the variances of the two groups are significantly different, then the separate- not the pooled- variance estimate is suggested; hence, the fractional degrees of freedom. See Snedecor and Cochran, 1967, pp. 115–116.

The IHP-M mean pretest score for the control group ($N = 47$) was 69.40, with a standard deviation of 15.00. The IHP-M mean pretest score for the treatment group ($N = 41$) was 72.68, with a standard deviation of 12.27. A Student's t test was used to determine whether or not statistically significant differences existed between the control and treatment pretest scores. A t value of 1.11 (with 86 degrees of freedom and a significance of 0.2692) was determined, thereby showing no significant difference between the pretest scores for the control and treatment groups.

DISCUSSION

The "above the median" treatment group had an average decrease of 5.6 points, while the controls showed an average increase of 0.6 points. That is to say that not only did the treatment respondents' scores decrease after the treatment, but when compared to the controls, there was a statistically significant difference between the means ($p = .01$). Therefore, the null hypothesis that the treatment group's mean difference would be equal to or higher than that of the control group can be rejected in favor of the alternative hypothesis that the treatment group's mean difference is lower than that of the control group.

The "below the median" treatment group had an average decrease of only 0.3 points, with a 0.5 point decrease found for the controls. The difference between these two groups was not statistically significant. Therefore, the null hypothesis that there was no difference between the treatment group's mean and that of the controls cannot be rejected in favor of the alternative hypothesis.

The findings of this study suggest that the homophobic scores decrease for those students whose pretest scores are above the median and who are also exposed to the homosexuality unit. The findings also suggest that, for those students whose pretest scores are below the median, the unit does not increase their homophobic scores significantly, i.e., these respondents do not appear to become more homophobic after the treatment.[1]

NOTE

1. The classical regression approach to covariance analysis and interaction was also used to analyze the data, and the following model was proposed:

$$S_2 = a + b*S_1 + c*X_1 + d*X_1*S_1 + e,$$

where
S_2 = IHP-M posttest scores,
S_1 = IHP-M pretest scores, and
X_1 = 0 if in the control group, and
        1 if in the treatment group.

Whether considering the simplest first order model, S_2 versus S_1, or the full model written above, regression of the data through the origin improves the R-squared statistic (from a .63 to a .98 for the full model). The restricted model ("a" restricted to be zero) will be accepted since R-square, a measure of how well the model fits the data, is better.

Further analysis reveals that the interaction term, X_1*S_1, is statistically significant ($p = 0.045$). Hence,

$$S_2 = 0.997*S_1 + 15.047*X_1 - 0.249*X_1*S_1 + e$$

appears to fit the data best.

The fact that the coefficient of S_1 is essentially 1.00, and that the change in homophobia, $S_2 - S_1$, is of more importance than S_2 alone naturally induces the model:

$$S_2 - S_1 = c*X_1, + d*X_1*S_1 + e.$$

The results of the analysis on this model are:

$$S_2 - S_1 = 15.047*X_1 - 0.252*X_1*S_1 + e.$$

Again, the interaction term is statistically significant ($p = 0.039$) so the model should not be reduced. The difference model, $S_2 - S_1$, results in almost identical coefficients as the S_2 model and is consistent with the hypothesis of this study. Hence, the conclusions will be discussed in reference to the difference model:

1) If an individual was in the control group, then, on the average, one would expect $S_2 - S_1 = 0$; that is to say that one would expect no significant change in homophobic scores or attitudes.

2) If an individual was in the treatment group, then, on the average, $S_2 - S_1 = 15.047 - 0.252*S_1$. Hence, the more homophobic the individual is at the beginning of the sexuality course, the greater is the reduction in S_2 at the end of the course.

REFERENCES

Boswell, J. (1980). *Christianity, social tolerance, and homosexuality.* Chicago: University of Chicago Press.

Bruess, C. E., & Greenberg, J. S. (1981). *Sex education: Theory and practice.* Belmont, CA: Wadsworth.

Crooks, R., & Baur, K. (1980). *Our sexuality.* Menlo Park, CA: Benjamin Cummings.

Freedman, M. (1978). Towards a gay psychology. *The gay academic.* Palm Springs, CA: ETC Publications.

Hudson, W. W., & Ricketts, W. A. (1980). A strategy for the measurement of homophobia. *Journal of Homosexuality, 5*(4), 317–372.

Lumby, M. E. (1976). Homophobia: The quest for a valid scale. *Journal of Homosexuality, 2*(1), 39–47.

Marmor, J. (1980a). Epilogue: Homosexuality and the issue of mental illness. *Homosexual behavior.* New York: Basic Books.

Marmor, J. (1980b). Overview: The multiple roots of homosexual behavior. *Homosexual behavior.* New York: Basic Books.

Masters, W., Johnson, V., & Kolodny, R. (1982). *Human sexuality.* Boston: Little, Brown.

Rosan, L. J. (1978). Philosophies of homophobia and homophilia. *The gay academic.* Palm Springs, CA: ETC Publications.

Smith, K. T. (1971). Homophobia: A tentative personality profile. *Psychological Reports, 29,* 1091–1094.

Snedecor, G. W. & Cochran, W. G. (1967). *Statistical methods* (6th ed.). Ames, IA: Iowa State University Press.

Towne, S. (1979). *An analysis of relationships between beliefs, attitudes, intentions, and behavior with respect to homosexuals.* Unpublished doctoral dissertation, University of Hawaii at Manoa.

Voeller, B. (1980). Society and the gay movement. *Homosexual behavior.* New York: Basic Books.

Warren, C. (1980). Homosexuality and stigma. *Homosexual behavior.* New York: Basic Books.

Weinberg, G. (1972). *Society and the healthy homosexual.* New York: St. Martin's Press.

Homosexual Men and Women Who Served Their Country

Joseph Harry, PhD
Northern Illinois University

ABSTRACT. The present work examines the effectiveness of United States military policies in excluding homosexual men and women from the armed forces by comparing percentages of homosexuals who have served in the armed forces with matched samples of heterosexuals. Interview data on 1,456 respondents from 1969 and 1970 are reported. The data show that homosexual and heterosexual men seem equally likely to have served in the military, while lesbians were more likely than heterosexual women to have served. The data also indicate that the policies of excluding homosexuals from the services are ineffective. The explanation for this may be that many homosexuals may not be aware of their homosexuality at time of entry into the service, and, hence, cannot readily be identified either by themselves or others. It is also suggested that certain draft criteria have in fact increased the percentages of homosexuals serving in the military.

The present work aims to evaluate the effectiveness of United States military policies in excluding homosexual men and women from the armed forces. This is done through exploring two questions: (1) Are there differences in the percentages of homosexuals and heterosexuals who have served in the military when examined separately by sex? and (2) Among those homosexuals who have served, what percentages were subsequently separated from the service due to their homosexuality? Interpretations are then offered explaining the associations and percentages revealed in the data analysis.

All branches of the United States armed forces have by policy excluded homosexuals from military service. If their homosexuality is discovered at the time of induction, these persons are rejected; if it becomes evident later, they are then separated. While there was liberalization of these policies during the 1970s and early 1980s, it related to the type of

Joseph Harry is an Associate Professor in the Sociology Department of Northern Illinois University, DeKalb, IL 60115. Acknowledgment is extended to the Kinsey Institute for the Study of Sex, Gender and Reproduction for the data here employed and for partial support of the present work. Reprint requests may be sent to the author at the above address.

discharge given at time of separation, rather than to the question of separation itself (Snyder & Nyberg, 1980).

Data are minimal on the numbers of heterosexuals and homosexuals who have served in the military. Williams and Weinberg (1971) reported that 47% of a sample of 458 homosexual men had served in the military. However, there was no control group of comparable heterosexual males, and their sample was a quite young one, which effectively excluded many who would have served in the Korean conflict and World War II (Bell & Weinberg, 1978). Saghir and Robins (1973) found that 60% of a sample of 89 young homosexual men had served in the armed forces. However, comparisons with a comparable heterosexual control group were not possible due to wide age differences between their homosexual and heterosexual samples. It should be noted that, when comparing groups on the percentages who have served in the military, a control for age is mandatory since, after sex, age is the best predictor of military service.

Concerning the question of being discharged from the service, both Williams and Weinberg (1971) and Saghir and Robins (1973) reported that approximately three-fourths of the homosexual men in their sample who had served in the armed forces received honorable discharges and suffered no difficulties in the service due to their homosexuality. While these data suggest that there may be many homosexuals in the military who, by so serving, show that the exclusionary policy is ineffective, they do not speak to the question of rejection at time of induction versus later exclusion.

RESEARCH METHODS

The data to be presented are based on 2–5 hour interviews with 686 homosexual males, 337 heterosexual males, 293 lesbians, and 140 heterosexual women. These data were made available by the Kinsey Institute for the Study of Sex, Gender, and Reproduction at Indiana University. A detailed description of the sampling methods has been reported elsewhere (Bell & Weinberg, 1978). Interviews with the homosexuals were conducted in the fall of 1969, while interviews with the heterosexuals were conducted during the fall of 1969 and the spring of 1970. The males were probably draftees and the females volunteers.

The sampling of homosexuals first involved collection of a list of several thousand self-identified homosexuals living in the San Francisco Bay area who volunteered to be interviewed. These volunteers were obtained through a wide variety of sources. Respondents were stratified by age, sex, race, and education. Sampling for interviews was then done within these strata so as to achieve substantial heterogeneity on these demographic variables. The heterosexual samples were then selected so that their distributions would demographically match those of the homo-sexuals. In contrast to the homosexuals, the heterosexuals were obtained for study through a sampling of census tracts and blocks with quota sampling at the block level.

A homosexual orientation was operationalized in the following manner. Respondents were asked to rate themselves on two Kinsey hetero-sexual-homosexual rating scales for both sexual feelings and behavior. Those persons who obtained a combined score of four or greater were defined as homosexual; others were labeled heterosexual (Bell & Weinberg, 1978). As a result of this procedure the category "homosexual" includes some individuals who might be called bisexual. However, 91% of the homosexual males and 85% of the homosexual females rated themselves as Kinsey 5s or 6s for behavior ("exclusively homosexual" or "predominately homosexual, only incidentally heterosexual"). The corresponding figures for ratings of feelings were 84% and 77%.

RESULTS

Chi-square analyses are employed in the following analyses because of the several nominal variables. Table 1 presents responses to the question, "Have you even been in military service—including reserve and national guard membership?"[1] Data are shown for each sexual orientation for each sex. The lesbians appear significantly more likely to have served than heterosexual women. The probable reasons for this are varied. Lesbians may be freer than heterosexual women to enter military service because they are not oriented toward futures in marriage. Our operative assumption here is that it is the lack of anticipation of future marriage, not simply the present status of being single, which may free women to enter the military. Thirty-eight percent of the lesbians and 72% of the heterosexual females in the sample had been married, thus supporting the assumption that the lesser frequency of marital obligations of lesbians may permit them to enter military service more easily.

Turning to the males, Table 1 shows that homosexual and heterosexual men are equally likely to have served. The percentage of homosexual males who reported they had been in military service is somewhat higher than the 47% found by Williams and Weinberg (1971). However, in the Williams and Weinberg data, 8% of their male homosexual respondents were over 45 years of age, compared to 21% of the present sample. In the present data, age is curvilinearly related to having served for both homosexual and heterosexual males (see Table 2). The percentage who served peaks among the 45 to 54 year olds and then drops. That age group would most likely have served during World War II and was substantially excluded from the Williams and Weinberg data. Hence, the age dif-

Table 1

Ever in Military, Reason not Served, Type of Discharge, and
and Ever Sex on Active Duty by Sexual Orientation
for Males and Females (Percent)

| | Males | | Females | |
| | Sexual Orientation | | Sexual Orientation | |
	Gay	Non-Gay	Lesbian	Non-Lesbian
Ever in Military	57%	60%	15%	1%
n (100%)	686	337	293	140
	$x^2(1,\underline{1023})=0.58,p=ns$		$x^2(1,\underline{433})=17.86,p<.001$	
Reason Not Served Not Called, Exempt				
Deferred	35%	76%	X	X
Homosexuality Declared, Discovered	32%	0%	X	X
Other[a]	33%	24%	X	X
n (100%)	292	135	X	X
	$x^2(2,\underline{427})=76.09,p<.001$			
Percent Honorable Discharges	78%	94%	80%	X
n (100%)	388[b]	193[b]	41[b]	X
	$x^2(1,\underline{581})=23.96,\ p<.001$			
Ever Homosexual Sex on Active Duty	80%	7%	79%	X
n (100%)	377[c]	196[c]	43[c]	X
	$x^2(1,\underline{573})=276.79,p<.001$			

a. "Other" includes conscientious objectors, 1Ys, and non-homosexual 4Fs.

b. Two homosexual men, six heterosexual men, and two homosexual women
    were currently still in the service.

c. Fourteen homosexual men, five heterosexual men, and zero homosexual
    women had never spent a month on active duty while in the service.

ference between the present sample of homosexual males and those of
Williams and Weinberg may explain the difference in the percentages
who have served in the military. While Table 2 suggests an interaction effect, a log-linear test for interaction was run and no significant interaction
appeared.

The lack of difference between the percentages of homosexual and
heterosexual males who have served is somewhat puzzling since homosexuals might avoid military service by declaring their homosexuality. To
test the hypothesis that individuals may have declared themselves homo-

sexual in order to avoid military service, Table 1 presents sexual orientation as a possible reason for not serving, for those males who did not serve. One-third of the homosexuals (14% of all the homosexuals) declared themselves to be homosexual, or were discovered. (Of the 92 homosexuals in this category only seven had had their homosexuality discovered.) Since 14% of all the homosexual males avoided military service by declaring their homosexuality, we are left with the question of why the percentages of homosexual and heterosexual males who served are approximately equal. There also remains the question of why most homosexuals did not declare their homosexuality or bisexuality.

One hypothesis explaining why many homosexuals did not declare themselves is that, at the time they were called or volunteered, they did not know they were homosexual. The median age of "coming out" or fully realizing one's homosexuality and becoming socially and sexually active is approximately 19 or 20 (Dank, 1971; Harry & DeVall, 1978). This age coincides with the age when men have traditionally entered the service (Canby, 1972). Those who come to a realization of their homosexuality later presumably cannot declare it upon entering military service.

To examine this hypothesis, Table 3 analyzes data on "ever served" and "reason not served" by "age of self-definition as homosexual" and

Table 2

Ever in Military by Age for Gay and Non-Gay Males (Percent)

	Gays				
	Age				
	-24	25-45	35-44	45-54	55+
Ever in Military	19%	54%	78%	87%	53%
n (100%)	148	218	157	112	51
		$x^2(4,\underline{686})=156.29,\underline{p}<.001$			

	Non-Gays				
	Age				
	-24	25-45	35-44	45-54	55+
Ever in Military	30%	61%	73%	85%	65%
n (100%)	78	112	67	46	34
		$x^2(4,\underline{337})=47.03,\underline{p}<.001$			

Table 3

Ever in Military, Reason not Served, and Ever Homosexual Sex on
Active Duty by Age of Self-Definition as Homosexual and Age of Coming Out
(Gay Males Only)

	Age of Self-Definition			Age of Coming Out			
	-17	18-22	23+	Never	-17	18-22	23+
Ever in Military	49%	62%	71%	48%	42%	54%	70%
n (100%)	325	255	99	90	95	266	234
	$x^2(2,\underline{679})=19.45,\underline{p}<.001$			$x^2(3,\underline{685})=27.70,\underline{p}<.001$			
Reason Not Served							
Not Called, Exempt Deferred	35%	31%	52%	51%	34%	27%	39%
Homosexuality Declared, Discovered	38%	27%	10%	15%	47%	39%	18%
Other	27%	42%	38%	34%	18%	34%	42%
n (100%)	165	97	29	47	55	119	71
	$x^2(4,\underline{291})=14.59,\underline{p}<.01$			$x^2(6,\underline{292})=25.91,\underline{p}<.001$			
Ever Homosexual Sex On Active Duty	88%	79%	63%	67%	90%	89%	72%
n (100%)	148	155	68	39	39	141	157
	$x^2(2,\underline{371})=17.49,\underline{p}<.001$			$x^2(3,\underline{376})=19.16,\underline{p}<.001$			

"age of coming out." The question for age of coming out was: "At what age would you say you became part of a homosexual clique or crowd?" The self-definition measure involved two questions: (1) "How old were you when you first began to think of yourself as being sexually different?" and (2) "How old were you when you labeled the difference you felt 'homosexual'?" The second of these questions provides the measure of self-definition. (Seven men who said they never felt "sexually different" have been excluded.) Those who defined themselves as homosexual at later ages were more likely to have had military service. Similarly, those who became socially active homosexuals after the age of 22 were a good deal more likely to have served in the military.

The reasons that age of self-definition as homosexual and age of coming out are related to having had military service are explained in Table 3 by the associations of the former two measures with the stated reasons for not serving. Those who came to an early realization of their homosexuality, and those who came out earlier, are more likely to have declared their homosexuality to the military. The associations of age of self-definition and age of coming out with having had military service and with reasons for not serving probably understate the actual occurrences. If it were possible in the present data to relate the ages of self-definition and of coming out to the age at which the respondent first entered the service, these associations would probably be stronger.

The data therefore indicate that the military policy of excluding homosexual persons at time of entry was ineffective for both men and women. Only homosexuals are capable of excluding themselves. If they are not yet aware of their homosexuality, they are incapable of self-exclusion.

However, the services also attempt to separate homosexual individuals from service after entry. The data of Table 1 indicate that the services seem slightly more effective in separating homosexuals after entry, rather than excluding them before entry. The homosexual men were significantly more likely to have received other than honorable discharges. Nearly all of these discharges were due to their homosexuality. Still, the large majority of homosexual men receive honorable discharges, as shown in Table 1, and these data are in close agreement with the 76% receiving honorable discharges as reported by Williams and Weinberg (1971) and the 75% found by Saghir and Robins (1973).

The military discharges persons known to have engaged in homosexual activity while in the service. Homosexual activity was the usual basis for the other than honorable discharges given to homosexual men (Williams & Weinberg, 1971). Are these policies, however, effective? Of those homosexual males who did engage in homosexual activity in the service, 24% ($N[100\%] = 298$) received other than honorable discharges compared to 12% ($N[100\%] = 76$) of those who had not been sexually active during their time in the service ($X^2 = 5.14, df = 1, p < .03$). These data indicate a measure of effectiveness of the policy of separating homosexual persons known to have engaged in homosexual activity, but a lack of military effectiveness in the detection of that sexual activity. However, comparable data are not meaningful for the lesbians because of the small percentage who had been in the service and had not engaged in homosexual activity.

Whether or not homosexuals engage in sex with partners of the same sex while in the service may depend on how far along they are in the coming out process. To test this hypothesis, Table 3 shows that those who defined themselves as homosexual at later ages and those who came out later were somewhat less likely to have engaged in homosexual activities while in the service. Still, sizable majorities of all the groups shown had engaged in homosexual activity. Such activity in the service was also found to be an extension of homosexual activities prior to entering the service. Among the homosexual men who had engaged in homosexual activity six times or less during high school, 68% ($N[100\%] = 162$) continued while in the service, compared to 88% ($N[100\%] = 215$) of those who were more active during high school ($X^2 = 23.81, df = 1, p < .001$). It thus seems that homosexual behavior in the service is an extension of pre-service behavior. While the military attempts to reject persons who have engaged in homosexual behavior prior to induction, it has been shown that this effort is ineffective.

DISCUSSION

This study suggests that the military policies dealing with homosexuality are ineffective in keeping homosexuals out of the services. Homosexual men serve in the military in the same proportions as heterosexual men, while lesbians serve in greater proportions than heterosexual women. The large majority of both homosexual men and women receive honorable discharges while at the same time continue to engage in homosexual behaviors. Given the ineffectiveness of military policies excluding homosexuals, one must consider that, as Snyder and Nyberg (1980) suggest, these policies may serve other purposes. They may serve to reaffirm values of masculinity and heterosexuality.

It seems that military policies may actually increase the number of homosexual persons in the services. If lesbians disproportionately volunteer for military service, the policy of not drafting women may increase the percentage of lesbians in the service. The policy of exempting married men or men with dependents may also increase the number of homosexual men. Such exemptions have been intermittently allowed when the need for manpower was less than the available supply of single men, as occurred during the period 1963 to 1965 (Davis & Dolbeare, 1968). However, since homosexual men are far less likely than heterosexual men to have married (19% vs. 71% in the present data), the exemption of married men can only increase the percentage of homosexual men in the service. Exempting married men may account for the equal extent to which homosexual and heterosexual men have served. Since the data do not include information on the age at which respondents first entered the service, it is not possible to take into account age of entering the service relative to age of marriage. However, the "advantage" which homosexuals possess of being exempt from military service may offset the occasional "advantage" of exemptions for married men. These two factors therefore may cancel each other out. Explicit testing of this hypothesis must be left for future research.

The age at which men are drafted may also affect the numbers of homosexual men in the service. The data imply that if older men (in their mid-twenties) are drafted, the numbers of homosexuals will be reduced because most homosexual men come to a realization of their homosexuality by their mid-twenties and would be more likely to declare their homosexuality at time of classification or induction. However, the data also suggest that if older homosexuals were drafted they would be more sexually active than if they had been drafted at younger ages. Hence, if younger persons are drafted one obtains more homosexuals who are less sexually active; if older persons are drafted, one obtains fewer homosexuals, but those who are more sexually active.

CONCLUSIONS

This data analysis indicates that the policies for keeping homosexuals out of the military services are ineffective. Given that ineffectiveness, one may question whether these policies are justified. If these policies are to be continued, as is likely, it may be more realistic to recognize their political and symbolic functions rather than their stated purposes. It should also be recognized that other policies of the services, such as excluding women from the draft, exempting married men, and drafting at early ages, may increase the number of homosexual persons in the services.

NOTE

1. While the form of the question on having served in the military includes those who did not serve on active duty, in fact 96% of the gay men, 98% of the nongay men, and all of the lesbian women served on active duty.

REFERENCES

Bell, A., & Weinberg, M. (1978). *Homosexualities.* New York: Simon & Schuster.
Canby, S. (1972). *Military manpower procurement.* Lexington, MA: Lexington Books.
Dank, B. (1971). Coming out in the gay world. *Psychiatry, 34,* 180–197.
Davis, J., & Dolbeare, K. (1968). *Little groups of neighbors: The selective service system.* Chicago: Markham.
Harry, J., & DeVall, W. (1978). *The social organization of gay males.* New York: Praeger.
Saghir, M., & Robins, E. (1973). *Male and female homosexuality.* Baltimore: Williams & Wilkins.
Snyder, W., & Nyberg, K. (1980). Gays and the military: An emerging policy issue. *Journal of Political and Military Sociology, 8,* 71–84.
Williams, C., & Weinberg, M. (1971). *Homosexuals and the military.* New York: Harper & Row.

A Movement of Inverts:
An Early Plan for
a Homosexual Organization
in the United States

Erwin J. Haeberle, PhD, EdD
The Institute for Advanced Study of Human Sexuality

ABSTRACT. This is a translation of three letters, written in German in 1930, by Ernest F. Elmhurst, Magnus Hirschfeld, and Harry Benjamin. The letters deal with a hitherto unknown and apparently soon-abandoned plan to found an American homosexual organization.

The following correspondence from the files of Dr. Harry Benjamin, New York, reveals an early plan to found an American homosexual organization. The author of this plan was a German homosexual, Ernst Klopfleisch, who had immigrated to the United States in 1923 and adopted the new name Ernest F. Elmhurst. Apart from the single letter quoted below, nothing more is known at this time about Elmhurst or the further fate of his plan. It is obvious, however, that none of the correspondents knew anything about Henry Gerber (another German immigrant) and his Society for Human Rights, an earlier homosexual organization that had briefly flourished in Chicago (1924). While Elmhurst's plan was apparently soon abandoned, it is nevertheless of some historical significance, since it provides a second, and in this case a direct, link to the original German homosexual emancipation movement, in particular to Hirschfeld's Scientific-Humanitarian Committee.

The author wishes to express his sincere gratitude to Dr. Benjamin for permission to translate and publish the correspondence in this journal.

Erwin J. Haeberle is Director of Historical Research at the Institute for Advanced Study of Human Sexuality in San Francisco, Adjunct Professor at San Francisco State University and a research associate at the Kinsey Institute for Research in Sex, Gender and Reproduction. During the winter of 1983–1984 he was a visiting professor at the University of Kiel Medical School in Kiel, Germany. Reprint requests should be addressed to the author at the Institute for Advanced Study of Human Sexuality, 1523 Franklin Street, San Francisco, CA 94109.

127

THE LETTERS

The correspondence consists of three typewritten letters in German. The first of these, from Ernest F. Elmhurst, asks Magnus Hirschfeld for advice and help in founding an American homosexual organization. The scrambled and incomplete address reveals that Elmhurst knew of Hirschfeld's Scientific-Humanitarian Committee (the world's first homosexual rights organization), but somehow confounded it with Hirschfeld's Institute for Sexology. However, since both the Committee and the Institute (and indeed the headquarters of the World League for Sexual Reform) were housed in the same building, the letter had no difficulty reaching Hirschfeld.

Elmhurst had apparently been privately active in Germany developing a "gay resort" in the Harz Mountains (a popular resort area), but had been forced by local authorities to abandon this project. Indeed, it is possible that this episode was the reason for his leaving Germany and coming the United States.

Judging from the style of his letter, Elmhurst was not an intellectual, but a practice-oriented, rather unsophisticated enthusiast. The letter is written in stilted, convoluted language, and is occasionally ungrammatical and obscure. The translation has tried to be as faithful as possible to the original; only in a few instances has the sentence structure been simplified.

343 East 16th Street
New York, New York

January 22, 1930

Sanitätsrat Dr. M. Hirschfeld
Scientific-Hum. Institute
In den Zelten
Berlin, N.W.

Dear Sir:

After a lengthy weighing of the pros and cons, I have now decided anyway to turn to you with a letter which might mark the beginning of a "movement" or an organization of part of the inverts in the United States. During my seven years' stay, I have studied the psychology of the Americans sufficiently, recognized their strengths and weaknesses, learned to appreciate and respect their ideals—to the extent that they have any besides making money—and have finally arrived at the position that, where the base majority of the population shows, well into old age, marked symptoms of psychic bisexuality, the understanding of psychic bisexuality (and therefore also of homosexuality) is also much greater and more general than in any part of Western Europe. Not that the just mentioned majority shows an understanding of something which is not given to everybody at birth, and not because certain authorities have scientifically determined that man is principally a bisexual being; no, but simply because people here experience a freer education and development, which allows both bisexual symptoms existing in the depth of the human essence more or less to develop together. Thus, one also finds at least a toleration of the extreme inverted phenomena and much less of a pronounced hateful, hostile attitude toward inverts than I had observed in Germany.

As things stand here, the invert who is not altogether blind has a greater opportunity here than perhaps anywhere in the world to satisfy the feelings rooted in him. The great majority of bisexuals knows this in the reverse. Indeed, one could say that the invert runs a greater risk of ruining himself from over-association here, rather than from withering away for lack of empathy in a hostile environment. In smaller towns the situation is, without question, not quite as ideal as, for example, in New York, Philadelphia, Boston, Chicago, etc.

I have maintained that the number of admitted bisexuals—contrary to your survey of 1900—is definitely ten times greater than you tried to establish through your inquiries in Amsterdam and Berlin at the time. It is no exaggeration to say that 60 percent of the men would legitimize themselves as bisexual, if one tried to achieve such a result here. In view of the fact that the divorce rate is growing (in Kansas already 51 percent as of 1925), there is indirect proof that many unrecognized bisexuals in the general populace do not feel a strong basic attraction to the opposite sex, or else there would be attempts to resolve amicably the marriage-destroying contentions, most of which are economic in nature. On the other hand, since X and Y can exchange the same, or at least similar, feelings of love with a friend without enslaving obligations, why take the more expensive route, when the simpler alternative is so near and easy to obtain?

In 1926, I asked a sergeant of a regiment stationed near New York to find out quietly and objectively—taking all the time he needed—how many men in his company engaged in sexual intimacies with other men (by other men I mean mainly civilians). After three and a half months he told me what he found, emphasizing that he had examined each and every one thoroughly. He found that the whole company, except for four men, had been, or still were, intimate with other men. In 1929, I put the same question to an intimate friend of mine in military service, and he informed me that everyone in his company, except for one single man, maintained such intimacies. Should one therefore not contemplate the situation more seriously and ask: Where the general populace displays such a pronounced bisexual character, should one not found an organization or a club in which ideals like sports, intellectual competition, art, music, etc. could be cultivated? Since the specific invert possesses such a socially binding talent, could not only other homosexuals, but also—and this is more essential—a great number of bisexuals find and keep social connections, individuals who can never hope to find with a woman what their thirst for freedom requires. And among these very types the invert could find the permanent friend whom he had always wanted. On the other hand, giving the invert an opportunity to measure his abilities freely against those of the specific bisexual, might prove to be the most ideal way of emancipating the former by letting his ideals closely compete with those of bisexuals.

It would lead me too far afield to describe to you the innumerable possibilities for the activation of the invert. However, I consider it an easily accomplished beginning to own, even in the New World, some central place in the form of a large club building (similar to the YMCA or the YMHA here), with possibly an athletic club close to the large cities near the water or in the mountains. This could serve to give the invert that place in the world which he, with more or less justification, deserves according to his virtue.

The only opportunity to reach the inverts here, at the present time, is at the so-called costume balls, which are enormously successful, and are almost exclusively an enterprise of typical inverts and their supporters. This would be where to take the first step by distributing cards, which could be placed on the tables, announcing the idea of an organization. Thus, from among the guests of a dance, an organization could be formed that could be mentioned in the same breath along with all other venerable clubs and associations.

While it is true that, at first, such an organization would be a thorn in the side of certain government agencies which have become accustomed to regarding the inverts only as scum from the gutter, it requires no gift of prophecy to predict that certain authorities simply will have to change their positions on inverts and bisexuals a little. I do not doubt the success of such an organization, if it is undertaken from a central location like New York, for example. By renting a number of rooms in private clubs, some initial members could be attracted who would finance the initial organizational costs through membership fees. By arranging dances, like those at the Rockland Palace, for example, one could expect an enormous profit, which, in turn, could be the foundation for the next step forward. The collected addresses of those who are known as inverted or bisexual to our members could be the basis for a further expansion of the enterprise.

The possibility of forming a great international association or organization will under no circumstances materialize without the help of the United States. Therefore, for the time being, it is necessary to collect the now existing seizure [sic] points of our circle and to concentrate them on the new goal—namely, to connect the inverts of the New World with a central point in New York or Chicago. And the interested, pronounced bisexuals will respond to us here in this country in a more lively fashion than we ever dared to dream, and thus the hostile tendency of specifically heterosexual circles will not have to be feared all that much. With the slogan "Mind your own business," he will go where he belongs.

Now, Mr. Hirschfeld, it will be in your interest as well as mine to give me the address(es) of influential Americans you know, if possible, in scientific (and if not also financial) circles, where one could make a start with the project I have just tried to sketch for you. As you may remember, I (as Ernst Klopfleisch before my Americanization) tried to turn the *Kurhotel* in Altenau in the Harz Mountains into a summer gathering place for inverts in Germany, but the authorities in Clausthal lodged a protest and asked the main proprietor of the hotel to fire me immediately as the director, or else the hotel would be closed by the communal authorities. This proves that a similar project has been occupying my mind for years. Undoubtedly, I have learned from this experience, and would now begin a similar attempt with a little more finesse, and without giving serious cause for offense—which, by the way, I did not give then, either.

I would be happy to hear from you in this matter. Also, I would be very grateful if you would find the time to explain the idea introduced here to someone in New York. Also, if you have any further suggestions with regard to personalities who might sympathize with my idea, I hope you will inform me. The question revolved only around a single point: If the inverts with their ideals are an ethical group, they will be successful and prevail. If they are not an ethical group, they will not survive the hostilities and do not deserve to exist as an organization. But, should not whatever developed in Germany—if only with difficulty—also become possible in the U.S.A.? Indeed, I believe that one will encounter far fewer difficulties here than in the Old World. The only question is whether one turns one's passion into a virtue or a vice.

Looking forward to an extensive reply about this, I remain with best regards

> Yours sincerely,
> Ernest F. Elmhurst

Second is Hirschfeld's letter to Harry Benjamin, written on the rather elaborate letterhead of the World League for Sexual Reform, listing the three presidents of the League, August Forel, Havelock Ellis, and Magnus Hirschfeld as well as forty members of its international committee. The North American committee members listed are Harry Benjamin, William Robinson, and Margaret Sanger.

Berlin, Germany
March 1, 1930

Dear Colleague Dr. Benjamin:

Enclosed I am sending you, for your reaction, a letter we have received. I have told Elmhurst that the association of inverts which he desires is probably best and most easily organized within the framework of the World League for Sexual Reform. I have asked him to get in touch with you for an oral discussion of the matter.

With best regards,
Yours sincerely,
Dr. Magnus Hirschfeld

And third is the response, written by Harry Benjamin to Hirschfeld, which deals not only with Elmhurst's plan, but also with various other issues of mutual interest. The heterosexual Benjamin, who had no personal stake in the plan, but who, as one of the American pioneers of sexology, fully supported the reform goals of his European colleagues, clearly tried to oblige both Elmhurst and Hirschfeld. His negative evaluation must therefore be considered realistic. William J. Fielding, to whom Benjamin referred Elmhurst for further discussions, was a heterosexual writer of popular science books. A few months later, in the fall of 1930, Hirschfeld came to New York on Benjamin's invitation. It is not known whether there were any personal meetings with Elmhurst. In any case, Hirschfeld soon travelled on to Chicago and San Francisco, from where he embarked on his trip around the world via Japan, China, India, Egypt, and Palestine. He never returned to Germany.

New York City
June 10, 1930

Sanitätsrat Dr. Hirschfeld
c/o Institute for Sexology
Berlin N.W.
In den Zelten 10

Dear Esteemed Sanitätsrat:

Above all, I hope your stay in Switzerland has improved your health, and I hope to see you again in September, either in Berlin or Vienna.
I have been very sorry that you did not talk personally to my friend, the

well-known New York publisher Horace Liveright. Perhaps you have received the letter he brought you. I had urgently recommended to him the publication of your *Geschlechtskunde,* and he wanted to talk to you personally about it.

I have just written a few lines to Dr. Kauffmann in regard to the League; I hope he will convey the contents of my letter to you. Ernst *[sic]* Elmhurst, whose letter you sent me a few months ago, has visited with me a few times and explained his plans in great detail. However, I believe them to be practically unrealizable in New York. I have referred him to my friend William J. Fielding, since Elmhurst wanted to meet him. In my opinion, an honest and open association of inverts is impossible in America, whether within the framework of the World League or outside of it. I have advised Elmhurst to try starting very small, with a modest group of likeminded people. However, I am of the opinion that his slightly ambitious program cannot be realized in a way that even approximates his intentions. I hope to talk to you in detail about this and other matters in the fall.

The enclosed articles, which have just appeared, should certainly interest you. Laqueur and Dodds in London have already published confirmation of Funk's experiments.[1] I hope to speak briefly about the subject of ''Male Sexual Hormone'' at the Vienna Congress, and I won't need more than half an hour.[2]

With my best regards I remain

Your faithfully devoted,
Dr. Harry Benjamin

NOTES

1. Kasimir Funk, better known for his vitamin research, had, for the first time, produced ''androsterone,'' a male sex hormone extracted from male urine.

2. The congress mentioned here was the 1930 Congress of the World League for Sexual Reform.

A Bibliographic Guide to Government Hearings and Reports, Legislative Action, and Speeches Made in the House and Senate of the United States Congress on the Subject of Homosexuality

Gerard Sullivan, PhD (cand.)
University of Hawaii at Manoa

ABSTRACT. A thorough search was made of United States Federal Government publications in an effort to uncover government interest and action on homosexuality in the United States. No references were found prior to 1920 to government publications that refer to homosexuality. Since that time there has been sporadic interest in the subject, and from 1975 onwards it has been raised in Congress every year. There have been many hearings and reports that deal with the subject both directly and indirectly. Besides the bibliographic entries that follow, sources of information are listed and some annotation and discussion of the documents are included.

This bibliography is a research aid for those interested in studying the relationship between the U.S. Federal Government and civil rights for gay people. References to homosexuality in government publications have not been previously collected and published for use in this form. The bibliography is part of a larger study that examines government campaigns and social movements against gay people in the United States. As part of that work, an attempt was made to locate all federal government publications dealing with the subject of homosexuality. Government publications that deal with homosexuality include reports and monographs commissioned by government agencies, regulations and policies,

Mr. Sullivan is with the Sociology Department. Requests for reprints should be addressed to him at Porteus Hall 247, University of Hawaii at Manoa, Honolulu, HI 96822. Thanks are due to the reference librarians, especially Ms. Frances Jackson, of the Government Documents section of Hamilton Library, University of Hawaii for their patience and assistance. Recognition also goes to Peter Nelligan, Laureen Asato and Emma Porio for their help in preparing the manuscript.

and transcripts from Congressional Committee Hearings. This bibliography does not include military regulations, policies, reports or dispositions relating to homosexuality; court cases and decisions; or legislative interest and action on homosexuality at the state or county levels.

Legislation regulating sexual conduct usually comes under the purview of state legislatures in the United States. Nevertheless, over the years, the subject of homosexuality has received considerable attention from federal lawmakers, and more recently, government agencies. A substantial part of this attention has been by congressional committees and subcommittees dealing with appropriations and the criminal code for the District of Columbia. In other parts of the country, state governments would normally deal with these matters. In addition to this, however, the subject has been at issue in areas more usually considered the domain of Congress. These areas include civil rights legislation in recent years, and concern over security in the State and Defense Departments in the 1950s. This latter interest is fairly well known, and homosexuality was linked with communism in the eyes of some congressmen, senators and a sector of the public during the Cold War as a result of these investigations.

Most of the documents predating 1970 do not even recognize the existence of lesbians. It appears as if homosexuality was assumed to be a phenomenon which involved men only. Some of the more recent documents, however, refer to both lesbians and gay men.

Other trends are also noticeable in the references that follow. Before the 1970s, homosexuality was considered a perversion in most of the documents, and openly referred to as such. Congressmen did not appear to feel any hesitancy in expressing moral indignation at the idea of homosexuality, much less its practice. In several cases it was unreasonably linked with communism, and often with pornography, obscenity and blackmail. On a number of occasions congressmen openly and actively discriminated against homosexuals. Examples of this include attempts to purge the government of homosexual employees, the exclusion of "sexual deviates" from entry to the United States, and the attempt to revoke the charitable solicitations license of the Mattachine Society of the District of Columbia.

Since 1975, there has been considerable congressional treatment of the subject that has been positive and supportive. Though so far unsuccessful, attempts to have affectional and sexual preference included in the antidiscrimination legislation of the Civil Rights Act of 1964 have been made several times.

Major events that affect gay people have been referred to in the *Congressional Record,* including local government ordinances banning discrimination against gay people, recognition of the Metropolitan Community Church, and the American Psychiatric Association's decision to drop homosexuality per se from its diagnostic manual and to support antidiscrimination legislation. There is a clear correlation between the rise of the Gay Rights Movement and this change in the nature of congressional action. The influence of the "Christian New Right" has also been manifested since 1977 or so, and several negative comments have been recorded on the floor of the House and Senate and reported in the *Congressional Record.* There have also been successful attempts to deny certain federally funded government services such as legal advice and housing subsidies to gay clients.

The influence of the gay rights movement is also apparent in as much as leaders of the movement have testified at a number of hearings on legislation that has a potential effect on gay people. The assertion of gay people's rights in matters such as the television portrayal of homosexuals, and the right to be recognized as a "class" and included in the national census, is a recent phenomenon, but it may have an important effect on government policy.

MAJOR SOURCES OF REFERENCES

Below are listed indexes and other sources that were referred to in an effort to locate relevant documents.

—*Congressional Information Service Congressional Committee Hearings Index* (1959–1969)
—*Congressional Information Service Cumulative Service Index To Publications of the U.S. Congress* (1970–May, 1983)
—*Congressional Information Service U.S. Congressional Committee Prints Index until 1969* (1789?–1969)
—*Congressional Information Service U.S. Serial Set Index* (1789–1969)
—Congressional Quarterly's *Guide to Congress,* 3rd Ed. (1789–1982)
—*Congressional Record* (1918–23 June, 1983)
—*Cumulative Index of Congressional Committee Hearings 1935–1958*
—*Cumulative Subject Index to the Monthly Catalog of U.S. Government Publications 1900–1971*
—*Cumulative Title Index to U.S. Public Documents 1789–1976*
—*Government Reports Annual Index* (1965–18 Feb, 1983)
—*Index of Congressional Committee Hearings until 1935* (1789?–1935)
—*Monthly Catalog of U.S. Government Publications* (1976–June, 1983)

The *Congressional Record* includes bills and resolutions, remarks in the House and Senate, petitions and statements, as well as the text of articles and editorials, letters, studies, testimony, memoranda, addresses and ordinances referred to by members of Congress.

Especially prior to 1965 there was sometimes a hesitancy to use the word "homosexuality" and so a number of other alternative terms (invert, sex, pervert, immoral, sodomy, sexual deviate) were used in the search for documents in addition to "homosexuality." Some of these key words were more commonly used when referring to homosexuality.

The bound volumes of the *Congressional Record* complete with an annual index are not available for the most recent sessions of Congress. However, in their place, a daily paper copy does appear. Although the text of the two editions is the same, page references differ. In this guide, *Congressional Record* page references up until 31 December 1979 refer to the bound volumes. From 1 January 1980 onwards, references are to the daily edition page numbers.

CHRONOLOGICAL BIBLIOGRAPHY

In cases where the information is available, entries include the year of the item, the source, and the reference for location of the full document. Reports, hearings and monographs are referred to using the U.S. government documents Superintendent of Documents classification scheme which is commonly used by Government Documents Depository Libraries throughout the United States.

1921, Sixty-seventh Congress, First Session

Report
of the
Committee on Naval Affairs
of the
United States Senate
relative to
Alleged Immoral Conditions and Practices at the Naval
Training Station, Newport, Rhode Island

printed by the Government Printing Office, Washington D.C., for use by the committee, 1921

As Secretary of the Navy, Franklin D. Roosevelt authorized an investigation into homosexuality at the base. The inquiry involved entrapment and other questionable investigation techniques. Eighteen men were arrested. Some of them were held for long periods without charges being filed. The investigation was discredited after an Episcopal minister was arrested and his bishop and the local media came to his defense. They were very critical of the investigation and its methods.

1948, Eightieth Congress, Second Session

Congressional Record	*Congressional Record* page reference Volume *94*

Bills and Resolutions

House Bill HR 5809
A bill to provide for the treatment of sexual psychopaths
in the District of Columbia, and for other purposes
Referred to the Committee on the District of Columbia
Sponsored by Mr. Miller (R—Nebraska) 11 March 1948   2512

House Bill HR 6071
A bill to provide for the treatment of sexual psychopaths
in the District of Columbia, and for other purposes
Referred to the Committee on the District of Columbia
Sponsored by Mr. Miller (R—Nebraska) 31 March 1948   3884

Reported with amendments	4802
Amended and passed the House	4885
Referred to Senate Committee on the District of Columbia	4927
Reported with amendments	6267
Amended and passed the Senate	6310
House concurred in Senate amendment	6593
Examined and Signed	6747
	6851
Presented to the President	7114
Approved to become Public Law #615	7981

Report	U.S. Serial Set
made by	Superintendent
Mr. Miller (R—Nebraska)	of Documents
of the	Volume number
Committee on the District of Columbia	11211
of the	
House of Representatives	House Report
to accompany House Bill HR 6071	80-1787
regarding	
Treatment of Sexual Psychopaths in the	
District of Columbia	

22 April 1948, 11 pages

Miller's report advocates in part, increasing the penalties
for sodomy in the District of Columbia and providing a
more exact definition of the crime.

Report	U.S. Serial Set
made by	Superintendent
Mr. Kem (R—Missouri)	of Documents
of the	Volume number
Committee on the District of Columbia	11207
of the	
United States Senate	
to accompany House Bill HR 6071	Senate Report
regarding	80-1377
Treatment of Sexual Psychopaths in the	
District of Columbia	

21 May 1948, 12 pages

This report approves of Miller's suggestions to increase
sodomy penalties.

1950, Eighty-first Congress, Second Session

Congressional Record	*Congressional*
	Record
	page reference
	Volume *96*

Bills and Resolutions
    Senate Resolution 280
    to authorize an investigation of laws and procedures with
    respect to investigation and punishment of sexual
    perversion practices in the District of Columbia
    Submitted by Mr. Hill (D—Alabama)
    on behalf of a subcommittee of the District of Columbia
    Appropriations Committee
    19 May 1950   7329

    Passage of the resolution   7376
    Initiation of the investigation   7728
                                                            8208

Remarks in the Senate
    Mr. Brewster (R—Maine) and Mr. Tydings (D—Maryland)
    critical of the employment of homosexuals in the government.
    Remarks made in the context of a discussion on communism
    and national security 24 April 1950.   5575

    Mr. Hoey (D—North Carolina)
    Subcommittee on Investigations regarding the submission
    of Senate Document 241
    relative to
    Employment of Homosexuals and Other Sex Perverts
    in the Government
    15 December 1950   16587

Remarks in the House
    Mr. Miller (R—Nebraska)
    critical of employment of homosexuals in the government.
    Remarks made in the context of discussion on communism
    and nationalism
    31 March 1950   4527

    Mr. Hoffman (R—Michigan)
    critical of the employment of homosexuals in the government
    4 April 1950   4670

    Mr. Clevenger (R—Ohio)
    regarding the employment of homosexuals in the
    government   5401
    and in connection with communism and national
    security   5402
    19 April 1950   5403

Mr. Rich (R—Pennsylvania)
critical of the employment of sexual perverts in the
government
18 December 1950   16715

Extension of Remarks in the House
Mr. Miller (R—Nebraska)
critical of the employment of homosexuals in the
government. Remarks in connection with security risks.
Miller, a surgeon, had astonishingly ignorant and bigoted
attitudes about homosexuality
15 May, 1950   A3661

Mr. Hays (D—Ohio)
reporting Mr. Eric Sevareid's balanced discussion of the
investigation into the employment of homosexuals in the
government, broadcast over the CBS network
7 July 1950   A4960

Mr. Miller (R—Nebraska)
critical of the employment of homosexuals in the government
21 September 1950   A6775

Mr. Rich (R—Pennsylvania)
who submitted an article from the *Washington Times Herald*
on 16 December 1950 by Bert Wissman "Perverts in Federal
Agencies Called Peril to United States Security." Includes
a table of the departmental breakdown of alleged homosexual
employees
18 December 1950   A7755

Report	U.S. Serial Set
made by	Superintendent
Mr. McClellan (D—Arkansas)	of Documents
of the	Volume number
Committee on Expenditures in Executive Departments	11369
of the	
United States Senate	Senate Report
to accompany Senate Resolution 280	81-1746
regarding	
Employment of Moral Perverts by Government Agencies	

26 May 1950, 1 page

Report   Congressional
made by   Information
the Chairperson, Mr. Hill (D—Alabama)   Service
of the subcommittee of the   Micro-fiche #
Subcommittee on Appropriations for the District of Columbia   S4178
of the
United States Senate
regarding
Testimony on Subversive Activity and Homosexuals in
Government Service

May 1950, 7 pages

Hill's report investigates the incidence of homosexual
government employees and recommends that they
be dismissed.

Report   Congressional
made by   Information
Mr. Wherry (R—Nebraska)   Service
of the subcommittee of the   Micro-fiche #
Subcommittee on Appropriations for the District of Columbia   S4179
of the
United States Senate
regarding
Infiltration of Subversives and Moral Perverts into the
Executive Branch of the U.S. Government

17 May 1950, 16 pages

Wherry gives a full account of his investigations and is
enthusiastic about dismissing homosexual employees and
prosecuting for the crime.

Interim Report   U.S. Serial Set
made by   Superintendent
Mr. Hoey (D—North Carolina)   of Documents
of the   Volume number
Subcommittee on Investigations   11401
of the
Committee on Expenditures in Executive Departments
of the   Senate Document
United States Senate   241
pursuant to Senate Resolution 280
regarding
Employment of Homosexuals and Other Sex
Perverts in Government

15 December 1950, 26 pages

A detailed investigation of the employment of homosexuals
by the government. Contains some classic statements of prejudice
and ignorance. Presents statistics showing the number of
homosexuals separated in each government department and in the
military between 1947 and 1950. Makes recommendations
for future policy and procedures of dismissal.

Hearing (transcript)   Senate Committee
before a subcommittee of the   Hearings
Committee on Appropriations
of the   81st Congress
United States Senate
making appropriations for the Departments of State,   Senate Library
Justice, Commerce and the Judiciary for Fiscal Year   Volume number
ending 30 June 1951   943

Mr. Carran (D—Nevada), chairperson of the subcommittee   1950

See testimony given on 28 February 1950 by
Mr. John Peurifoy, Deputy Undersecretary of State, regarding
dismissal of homosexuals. Especially pages 597-8, 603-4.

1951, Eighty-second Congress, First Session

Hearing (transcript)	House Committee
before the	Hearings
Subcommittee on the Department of State	
of the	82nd Congress
Committee on Appropriations	
of the	Senate Library
House of Representatives	Volume number
regarding	1320
Department of State Appropriations for 1952	

Mr. Rooney (D—New York), chairperson of
the subcommittee　　　　　　　　　　　　　　　　　1951

See testimony on 2 March 1951 by Mr. Carlisle
Humelsine, Deputy Undersecretary for Administration,
Department of State, in which he states that 54 alleged
homosexuals were separated from the State Department
in 1950.
Especially pages 390–2.

1952, Eighty-second Congress, Second Session

Congressional Record	*Congressional*
	Record
	page reference
	Volume *98*

Extension of Remarks in the House
　Ms. Saint-George (R—New York)
　quoting an article from *Human Events* by Countess
　Waldeck, "Homosexuals International"
　Homosexuals are presented as sinful and linked with
　communism
　1 May 1952　　　　　　　　　　　　　　　　　　A2652

1953 (Presidential) *Executive Order 10450*	*Code of Federal*
	Regulations
"Security Requirements for Government Employment"	*Title 3*
Dwight D. Eisenhower	*The President*
27 April 1953	1949–1953
	Compilation

Hearing (transcript)	*Executive*
before the	*Sessions of the*
Executive Sessions of the Foreign Relations	*Senate Foreign*
Committee	*Relations*
of the	*Committee 1953*
United States Senate	*(Historical*
relative to	*Series)*
Loyalty-Security Problems of the Department	Volume 5
of State	

Mr. Wiley (R—Wisconsin), chairperson of	
the Committee	Government
First printed for use by the Senate Foreign Relations	Documents
Committee in 1953	Depository
	Libraries
Made public and published by the Government	Superintendent
Printing Office, Washington D.C. in February,	of Documents
1977	Call Number
Relevant testimony given on 5 February 1953	Y4.f76/2
See pages 67–108	Ex3/2/v5

1963, Eighty-eighth Congress, First Session

Congressional Record	*Congressional*
	Record
	page reference
	Volume *109*

Bills and Resolutions
    House Bill HR 5990
    A bill to amend the Charitable Solicitations Act
    to require certain findings before the issuance of a solicitation
    permit thereunder, and for other purposes
    Referred to the Committee on the District of Columbia
    Sponsored by Mr. Dowdy (D—Texas)
    1 May 1963   7511

Remarks in the House
    Mr. Waggonner (D—Louisiana)
    in which he refers to the *Washington Post* as a
    "radical left newspaper" because of an editorial
    opposing the revocation of the charitable solicitations
    permit of the Mattachine Society of
    Washington D.C.
    8 August 1963   14617

Extension of Remarks in the House
    Mr. Dowdy (D—Texas)
    providing further information about the Mattachine
    Society of Washington D.C.   A4211
    5 July, 1963   A4212

1964, Eighty-eighth Congress, Second Session

Congressional Record	*Congressional Record* page reference Volume *110*

Bills and Resolutions
    House Bill HR 5990
    A bill to amend the Charitable Solicitations Act
    of the District of Columbia to require certain
    findings before the issuance of a solicitations
    permit thereunder, and for other purposes
    Referred to the Committee on the District of Columbia
    Sponsored by Mr. McMillan (D—South Carolina)

Reported with amendment on 9 March 1964	4740
Objected to	16972
Amended and passed the House	18943
Referred Senate Committee on the District of Columbia	19112

Report	U.S. Serial Set
made by	Superintendent
Mr. McMillan (D—South Carolina)	of Documents
of the	Volume number
Committee on the District of Columbia	12619-1
of the	
House of Representatives	House Report
to accompany House Bill HR 5990	88-1222-1
regarding	
Amendments to the District of Columbia	
Charitable Solicitations Act	

6 March 1964, 8 pages

McMillan's report supports passage of the bill.

Report	U.S. Serial Set
made by	Superintendent
Mr. Multer (D—New York)	of Documents
and co-sponsored by 8 of the 24 members	Volume number
of the	12619-1
Committee on the District of Columbia	
of the	House Report
House of Representatives	88-1222-2
Report to accompany House Bill HR 5990	
outlining the views of a minority	
of the committee regarding	
Amendments to the District of Columbia Charitable	
Solicitations Act	

19 March 1964, 6 pages

Multer's report argues against passage of the bill.

Hearing (transcript)	House Committee
before	Hearings
Subcommittee Number 4	
of the	88th Congress
Committee on the District of Columbia	1st & 2nd Sessions
of the	
House of Representatives	Senate Library
relative to	Volume number
House Bill HR 5990	2073
A bill to amend the Charitable Solicitation Act	
of the District of Columbia	1963

Mr. Dowdy (D—Texas) chairperson of the
subcommittee

8, 9 August 1963 and 10 January 1964, 147 pages

The primary issue at the hearing was whether or not to
introduce legislation to revoke the charitable solicitations
permit granted to the Mattachine Society of Washington D.C.
Lengthy testimony was given by Franklin Kameny, then
president of the Mattachine Society of Washington D.C.

1965, Eighty-ninth Congress, First Session

Congressional Record

Congressional Record
page reference
Volume *111*

Bills and Resolutions
House Bill HR 2580
A bill to amend the Immigration and Nationality Act,
and for other purposes
Referred to the Committee on the Judiciary
Sponsored by Mr. Celler (D—New York)

The bill was amended in the House and then in
the Senate. Section 15(b) of the Senate amendments
would alter section 212(a)(4) of the Immigration and Nationality
Act (66 Stat 182; 8 USC 1182(a) (1)) to exclude sexual
deviates from entry to the United States. The House
agreed to the Senate amendments and the bill
was re-introduced.   25654

The bill passed both houses and was signed into law
to become public law 89-236 on 3 October 1965.   25925

Report	U.S. Serial Set
made by	Superintendent
Mr. E. Kennedy (D—Massachusetts)	of Documents
of the	Volume number
Committee on the Judiciary	12662-5
of the	
United States Senate	Senate Report
to accompany House Bill HR 2580,	89-748
A bill to amend the Immigration and Nationality Act	

15 September 1965, 59 pages

The Senate amended HR 2580 to alter section
212(a)(4) of the Immigration and Nationality Act to
exclude sexual deviates.

Report	U.S. Serial Set
made by	Superintendent
Mr. Celler (D—New York)	of Documents
of the	Volume number
Committee of Conference	12665-7
of the	
House of Representatives	House Report
to accompany HR 2580, the Immigration	
and Nationality Act	89-1101

29 September 1965, 15 pages

The House agreed to Senate amendments.

1967, Ninetieth Congress, First Session

Congressional Record	*Congressional Record* page reference Volume *113*

Extension of Remarks in the House Mr. Ashbrook (R—Ohio) comments on an article by Edward Fiske in the *New York Times* ''Episcopal Clergymen Here Call Homosexuality Morally Neutral'' 30 November 1967	34421

Ashbrook is disturbed by the declining influence of religion in establishing moral standards.

1970, Ninety-first Congress, Second Session

Congressional Record	*Congressional Record* page reference Volume *116*

Extension of Remarks in the House
   Mr. Rarick (D—Louisiana)
   on the Black Panther convention in Washington D.C.
   in which he quoes an article from the *Sunday Star*
   29 November 1970 "Twelve From Gay Lib Front
   Released After Brawl"
   30 November 1970   39213

1971, Ninety-second Congress, First Session

Congressional Record   *Congressional*
                                   Record
                            page reference
                              Volume *117*

Extension of Remarks in the House
   Mr. Rarick (D—Louisiana)
   Rarick cites an editorial "Fairness for Homosexuals"
   in the 2 February 1971 *Washington Post* and contrasts
   it with biblical passages condemning homosexuals.
   He also refers to newspaper articles that report that
   Franklin Kameny would run as an independent
   candidate for the District of Columbia delegate election,
   and that the Maryland legislature is considering a bill legalizing
   sexual acts between consenting adults.
   Rarick disapproves of both.   1831
   4 February 1971   1832

1972, Ninety-second Congress, Second Session

Congressional Record   *Congressional*
                                     Record
                            page reference
                              Volume *118*

Remarks in the House
   Mr. Koch (D—New York)
   deploring a vigilante attack on the Gay Activists'
   Alliance in New York City
   24 April 1972   14020

Monograph
"Homosexuality in Prisons" (with bibliography)
by Peter C. Buffum

Government
Documents
Depository
Libraries

sponsored by Law Enforcement Assistance
Administration, National Institute of Law
Enforcement and Criminal Justice,
U.S. Department of Justice

Superintendent
of Documents
Call Number

J1.36:73-3

February 1972, 48 pages

Report
of the
National Institute of Mental Health Task Force on
Homosexuality

Government
Documents
Depository
Libraries

"Final Report and Background Paper"

edited by John M. Livingood

Superintendent
of Documents
Call Number

sponsored by Office of Program Planning and
Evaluation, National Institute of Mental Health
A Department of Health, Education and Welfare
publication

HE 20.2402:H75/2

1972, 79 pages

1973, *Monograph*
"Not the Law's Business: An Examination of
Homosexuality, Abortion, Prostitution, Narcotics
and Gambling in the U.S."

Government
Documents
Depository
Libraries

by Gilbert Geis

Superintendent
of Documents
Call Number

sponsored by Center for Studies of Crime and
Delinquency, National Institute of Mental Health

HE 20.2420/2:
L44

1973, 262 pages

1974, Ninety-third Congress, Second Session

Congressional Record	*Congressional Record* page reference Volume *120*

Extension of Remarks in the House
Mr. Fraser (D—Minnesota)
in support of the Minneapolis City Council civil rights
ordinance prohibiting discrimination against homosexuals
which became law in April 1974. The ordinance is
reported in full.
2 May 1974   13057

Mr. Fraser (D—Minnesota)
in support of an amendment to the St. Paul City Council
civil rights ordinance prohibiting discrimination against
homosexuals
6 August 1974   27067

1975, Ninety-fourth Congress, First Session

Congressional Record	*Congressional Record* page reference Volume *121*

Bills and Resolutions
House Bill HR 166
A bill to prohibit discrimination on the basis of
affectional or sexual preference, and for other
purposes
Referred to the Committee on the Judiciary
Sponsored by Ms. Abzug (D—New York) and
Mr. J. Burton (D—California), Mr. Koch (D/L—New York),
Mr. McCloskey (R—California) and
Mr. Nix (D—Pennsylvania)
15 January 1975   188

1976, Ninety-fourth Congress, Second Session

Congressional Record	*Congressional Record* page reference Volume *122*

Bills and Resolutions
House Bill HR 13019
A bill to prohibit discrimination and for other purposes
Referred to the Committee on the Judiciary
Sponsored by Mr. P. Burton (D—California)
5 April 1976   9480

House Bill HR 13928
A bill to prohibit discrimination on the basis of affectional
or sexual preference, and for other purposes
Referred to the Committee on the Judiciary
Sponsored by Ms. Abzug (D—New York) and
Mr. AuCoin (D—Oregon), Ms. Burke (D—California),
Mr. Hawkins (D—California) and Mr. Miller
(D—California)
20 May 1976   14956

Remarks in the House
Mr. Koch (D/L—New York)
critical of the Supreme Court ruling on 29 March that
states may prosecute consenting adults for participating
in homosexual acts, and recommending passage
of HR 166
30 March 1976   8587

Extension of Remarks in the House
Mr. Koch (D/L—New York)
regarding the revision of the Job Corps health program
manual on sexual deviation   2673
5 February 1976   2674

Ms. Abzug (D—New York)
critical of the Supreme Court ruling on 29 March that
states may prosecute consenting adults for participation
in homosexual acts, and recommending passage
of HR 5452
31 March 1976   8925

Mr. Rangel (D—New York)
critical of the Supreme Court ruling on 29 March that
states may prosecute consenting adults for participating
in homosexual acts. Rangel emphasizes the implications
for citizens' rights to privacy. He refers to an editorial
in the *Washington Post* on 7 April 1976 that discusses
the issue.   9880
7 April 1976   9881

Mr. Koch (D/L—New York)
reporting on what U.S. cities are doing to end discrimination
based on affectional preferences. He refers to the
15 December 1973 American Psychiatric Association
resolution deploring discrimination against homosexuality,
and urges support of HR 166. Koch reports on current
city or county legislation in Detroit; Howard County,
Maryland; Austin, Texas; Portland, Oregon; Minneapolis;
San Jose; Alfred, New York; Cupertino, California; Mountain
View, California; St. Paul, Minnesota; Bloomington,
Indiana; District of Columbia; Santa Barbara,
California; Palo Alto, California; Madison, Wisconsin;
Seattle; Chapel Hill, North Carolina; Ann Arbor,
Michigan; Berkeley, California; and a detailed report
from the City of Detroit Human Rights Department   12037
on the subject.   to
30 April 1976   12044

Mr. Koch (D/L—New York)
again supporting HR 166 and reporting the results
of a recent poll conducted by the *New York Daily News*
showing that a majority of those interviewed disagreed
with the Supreme Court ruling that states may
prosecute consenting adults for participating in
homosexual acts.
17 May 1976   14085

Mr. Koch (D/L—New York)
recommending anti-discrimination legislation to
protect homosexuals and others, and reporting that
HR 166 was being considered by the Subcommittee
on Civil and Constitutional Rights chaired
by Mr. Don Edwards.
18 May 1976   14318

Ms. Abzug (D—New York)
recommending passage of HR 5452 and noting
distinguished organizations supportive of the bill.
Includes a statement by the New York City   23564
Association of the Bar supporting HR 5452.   23565
22 July 1976   23566

Hearing (transcript)   Government
before the   Documents
Subcommittee on District of Columbia Appropriations   Depository
of the   Libraries
Committee on Appropriations
of the   Superintendent
United States Senate   of Documents
relative to   Call Number
House Bill HR 13965
to amend the 1976 financial year and transition   Y4.Ap6/2
quarter budget requests for District of Columbia   D63/5
operating expenses   1976

Senator Chiles (D—Florida), chairperson   pages 128–147

Held on 24 May 1976 in Washington D.C.

Includes testimony by
Craig Howell, President, Gay Activists' Alliance
accompanied by Robert Hewes, Coordinator,
Gay Men's Venereal Disease Clinic

opposing D.C. budget cutbacks in VD programs for
homosexuals

Hearing (transcript)   Government
before the   Documents
Subcommittee on Communications   Depository
of the   Libraries
Committee on Interstate and Foreign Commerce
of the   Superintendent
House of Representatives   of Documents
relative to   Call Number
Consideration of federal and industry response
to public concern about the effects of televised   Y4.In8/4
violence and obscenity, and the reactions to network   94–140

implementation of the family viewing concept adopted
by the National Association of Broadcasters in 1975   see pages
                                                              248–257
Held in Denver and Los Angeles in July and August, 1976

Mr. Van Deerlin (D—California), chairperson   Committee
                                                              Serial

Includes statements by
Ginny Vida, Media Director, National Gay Task   94–140
Force; and   94th Congress
Newton E. Deiter, Gay Media Task Force

criticizing current programming and arguing for the
desirability of balanced television depiction of
homosexual lifestyles

Hearing (transcript)   Government
before the   Documents
Subcommittee on Alcoholism and Narcotics   Depository
of the   Libraries
Committee on Labor and Public Welfare
of the   Superintendent
United States Senate   of Documents
relative to   Call Number
Alcohol Abuse Among Women: Special Problems
and Unmet Needs

Held on 29 September 1976 in Washington D.C.   Y4.L11/2

Senator Hathaway (D—Maine), chairperson   AL1/12/1976

Includes a statement by Brenda Weathers, Director,
Alcoholism Center for Women Los Angeles,   see especially
California   pages 130–138

1977, Ninety-fifth Congress, First Session

Congressional Record

*Congressional
Record*
page reference
Volume *123*

Bills and Resolutions
House Bill HR 2998
A bill to prohibit discrimination on the basis of
affectional or sexual preference, and for other purposes
Referred to the Committee on the Judiciary
2 February 1977   3429
Referred to the Committee on Education and Labor
9 March 1977   6832
Sponsored by Mr. Koch (D/L—New York) and 24 House
members

House Bill HR 8268
A bill to prohibit discrimination on the basis of affectional
or sexual preference, and for other purposes
Referred jointly to the Committee on Education and Labor
and the Committee on the Judiciary
Sponsored by Mr. Koch (D/L—New York) and 14 House
members
13 July 1977   22734

House Bill HR 8269
A bill to prohibit discrimination on the basis of affectional
or sexual preference, and for other purposes
Referred jointly to the Committee on Education and Labor
and the Committee on the Judiciary
Sponsored by Mr. Koch (D/L—New York) and 18 House
members
13 July 1977   22734

Amendment to House Bill HR 7554
A bill making appropriations for the Department
of Housing and Urban Development and other agencies for the
fiscal year ending 30 September 1978, and for
other purposes
made by
Mr. Boland (D—Massachusetts)
of the
Committee on Appropriations

The "Stable Family Amendment" would prevent the
Department of HUD from providing services to
homosexual couples. Mr. Coughlin (Pennsylvania)
supported the amendment and quotes an article by
Judy Burke in the *Washington Post,*
"HUD to Allow Gays,   19076
Unmarried Couples."   19077

Bill with amendments passed in the House, 15 June 1977   19088
Reported with amendments in the Senate, 21 June 1977   20070

Amendment to House Bill HR 6666
A bill to amend the Legal Services Corporation Act
to provide authorization of appropriations for
additional fiscal years, and for other purposes.
made by
Mr. McDonald (D—Georgia)

The amendment would deny legal assistance with respect
to any proceeding or litigation arising out of disputes
or controversies on the issue of homosexuality
or so called gay rights.

Amendment passed in the House 27 June 1977   20919

(The bill was eventually defeated in committee.)

Remarks in the House
   Mr. Koch (D/L—New York)
   referring to the repeal of the Dade county ordinance
   protecting homosexuals from discrimination, and to
   lobbying efforts by people associated with the campaign to
   prevent the passage of HR 2998. Koch amended HR 2998
   to make it clear that it does not require affirmative action
   with respect to hiring of homosexuals.
   14 June 1977 ·   18855

Extension of Remarks in the House
   Mr. Waxman (D—California)
   paying tribute to the Reverend Troy Perry,
   founder of the Metropolitan Community Church
   9 June 1977   18358

Hearing (transcript)   Government
before the   Documents
Subcommittee of the Judiciary   Depository
of the   Libraries
Committee on the District of Columbia
of the   Superintendent
House of Representatives   of Documents
in conjunction with   Call Number
The District of Columbia City Council Judiciary Committee
and   Y4.D63/1
The District of Columbia Law Revision Committee (LRC)   95-1
relative to
District of Columbia Criminal Code Revisions   Committee
                                                   Serial
Held on 17 November 1977 in Washington D.C.   95-1

Includes statements by: 95th Congress
Mayo Lee, President, Gay Activists' Alliance;   see pages
Franklin E. Kameny; and   231-249
Willel W. Reitzer, of Universal Christian Publications

regarding LRC sexual offense recommendations relating
to homosexuality

1978, Ninety-fifth Congress, Second Session

Hearing (transcript)	Government
before the	Documents
Subcommittee on Domestic and International Scientific	Depository
Planning, Analysis and Cooperation	Libraries
of the	
Committee on Science and Technology	Superintendent
of the	of Documents
House of Representatives	Call Number
relative to	
Consideration of Research on Violent Behavior and	Y4.Sci2
Examination of Sexual Assault Prevention and Victim	95-64
and Offender Treatment Programs	
Held on 10, 11, and 12 January 1978 in New York City	Committee
	Serial
Mr. Scheuer (D—New York), chairperson	95-64

Includes statements by
David Rothenberg, Founder and Director, Fortune   95th Congress
Society; and Board Member, National Council on Crime   see pages
and Delinquency   464–488

recommending that homosexual assault in prison be
examined and the prison system re-evaluated

accompanied by Sergio Torres, former inmate,
giving a personal account of his prison experiences

Hearing (transcript)	Government
before the	Documents
Subcommittee on Communications	Depository
of the	Libraries
Committee on Interstate and Foreign Commerce	
of the	Superintendent
House of Representatives	of Documents
relative to	Call Number
Consideration of Recommendations Modifying House	
Bill HR 13015, the Communications Act of 1978,	
to Regulate Foreign and Interstate Telecommunications	Y4.In8/4
and Establish the Communications Regulatory	95-199
Commission to Replace the Federal Communications	
Commission.	

Mr. Van Deerlin (D—California), chairperson

Held in Boston, Chicago and Westwood, California in August 1978

Mr. Markey (D—Massachusetts), Mr. Russo (D—Illinois) and Mr. Waxman (D—California) presiding respectively

Includes a statement by David N. Drolet, Coordinator, Mass Caucus for Gay Legislation (Boston) on the potential impact of the bill on gay people, and opposed to the elimination of the public interest standard and de-regulation

Committee Serial 95-199

95th Congress

see pages 131–134

1979, Ninety-sixth Congress, First Session

Congressional Record

Congressional Record page reference Volume *125*

Bills and Resolutions
   Senate Bill S1808, The Family Protection Act
   A bill to strengthen the American Family and
   promote the virtues of family life through education,
   tax assistance and related measures
   Referred to the Committee on Finance.
   Sponsored by Mr. Laxalt (R—Nevada)
   24 September, 1979   25840

   2 additional sponsors announced Mr. Garn (R—Utah)
   and Mr. Cochran (R—Mississippi) 6 November 1979   31138
   1 additional sponsor announced Mr. Helms
   (R—North Carolina) 19 November 1979   33176
   1 additional sponsor announced Mr. Hatch (Utah)
   12 December 1979   35645

Senate Bill S 2081
A bill to prohibit employment discrimination on the basis
of sexual orientation
Referred to the Committee on Labor and Human Resources
Sponsored by Mr. Tsongas (D—Massachusetts), Mr.   34677
Weicker (R—Connecticut) and Mr. Moynihan
(D—New York)   34692

5 December 1979

House Bill HR 2074
A bill to prohibit discrimination on the basis of
affectional or sexual orientation, and for other
purposes
Referred jointly to the Committee on the Judiciary
and the Committee on Education and Labor
Sponsored by Mr. Weiss (D—New York)
8 February 1979   2301

40 additional sponsors announced 29 March 1979   6851
5 additional sponsors announced 24 May 1979   12626
5 additional sponsors announced 7 November 1979   31422
2 additional sponsors announced 19 December 1979   36991

House Concurrent Resolution 166
made by
Mr. McDonald (D—Georgia)
Expressing the sense of the congress that homosexual
acts and the class of individuals who advocate such
conduct shall never receive special consideration or a
protected status under the law
Referred to the Committee on the Judiciary
24 July 1979   20481

Remarks in the Senate
   Mr. Laxalt (R—Nevada)
   introducing the Family Protection Act (S 1808)
   Part of the act would restrict Legal Services Corporation
   from becoming involved in litigation for gay rights
   27 September 1979   26436

Mr. Tsongas (D—Massachusetts)
refers to the 1969 (1972?) National Institute of Mental
Health Task Force Report and the American Psychiatric
Association resolution which recommends homosexuals
not be discriminated against, and includes 14 letters from
prominent companies to the National Gay Task Force
regarding non-discrimination policies. He also discusses
court cases that have dealt with the rights of homosexuals   34693
to federal government employment.   to
5 December, 1979   34695

Mr. Moynihan (D—New York)
in support of S 2081
5 December 1979   34696

Mr. Weicker (R—Connecticut)
urging support of S 2081
5 December 1979   34708

Remarks in the House
　Mr. Weiss (D—New York)
　Critical of the FBI for discrimination against homosexuals
　in employment. He refers to the dismissal of John Calzada
　for alleged homosexuality, and asks support for HR 2074.
　22 May 1979   12060

Extension of Remarks in the House
　Mr. Ashbrook (R—Ohio)
　in support of the family as a basic social institution
　and against homosexuality, abortion and other so-called
　"threats" to the family
　16 November 1979   33022

Hearing (transcript) PART III	Government
before the	Documents
Subcommittee on Census and Population	Depository
of the	Libraries
Committee on the Post-Office and Civil Service	
of the	Superintendent
House of Representatives	of Documents
relative to	Call Number
Review of Bureau of Census Plans for Conducting	
the 1980 Census - Part III	Y4.P84/10
	96-14

Held in San Francisco, 17 April 1979

Mr. Garcia (D—New York), chairperson	Committee Serial 96-14
Includes statements by	
Kelly Harrington, Gay Class Advocate; and Futures Commodities Trading Specialist, U.S. Civil Service Office	96th Congress
arguing that gay people are a ''class'' and should be recognized by the Federal Government as such; and	see pages 79–82

Dan Basora, Human Relations Committee, Santa Clara County

Basora addresses the issue of sexual preference.

1980, Ninety-sixth Congress, Second Session

Congressional Record	*Congressional Record* page reference Volume *126*

N.B. From 1 January 1980 onwards, *Congressional Record* page references are to the daily edition and not to the bound edition as is the case up until 31 December 1979. Pagination of the daily and bound editions differ.

Bills and Resolutions
   Senate Bill S 1808
   A bill to strengthen the American family and promote
   the virtues of family life through education, tax
   assistance, and related measures.
   Referred to the Committee on Finance,
   Sponsored by Mr. Laxalt (R—Nevada)
   24 September 1979

   1 additional sponsor announced. Mr. Jepsen (R—Iowa)
   6 February 1980   S1135

Senate Bill S 2210
A bill to repeal section 212(a)(4) of the Immigration
and Nationality Act, as amended, and for other purposes
Referred to the Committee on the Judiciary
Sponsored by Mr. Cranston (California)
23 January 1980   S263

The intent of the bill was to reverse the current
exclusionary policy of the Immigration and Naturalization
Service toward lesbians and gay men on the basis that
such individuals suffer from a psychiatric disorder,
mental defect or disease. The policy is a result of Congressional
amendments to the Immigration and Nationality Act
in 1952 and 1965, designed to prohibit homosexuals
from entry to the United States.

House Bill HR 6303
A bill to repeal section 212(a)(4) of the Immigration
and Nationality Act, as amended, and for other purposes.
Referred to the Committee on the Judiciary
Sponsored by Mr. Beilenson (D—California) and Messrs.
Dixon (D—California) and Waxman (D—California)
28 January 1980   H294

8 additional sponsors announced 5 February 1980   H607
6 additional sponsors announced 5 March 1980   H1597
2 additional sponsors announced 12 March 1980   H1829
3 additional sponsors announced 28 March 1980   H2347
4 additional sponsors announced 17 April 1980   H2664
2 additional sponsors announced 29 April 1980   H3074
1 additional sponsor announced 20 May 1980   H3904

House Bill HR 7445, The Family Protection Act of 1980
A bill to strengthen the American Family and promote
the virtues of family life through education, tax assistance,
and related measures
Referred to the Committees on Education and Labor,
Ways and Means, the Judiciary, Agriculture, and
Armed Services
Sponsored by Mr. Symms (R—Idaho) and 9 House
members
22 May 1980   H4204

7 additional sponsors announced 2 July 1980   H6022
2 additional sponsors announced 24 September 1980   H9622

House Bill HR 7955
A bill to strengthen the American family and promote
the virtues of family life through education, tax
assistance, and related measures.
Referred to the Committees on Armed Services,
Education and Labor, Government Operations, the
Judiciary, and Ways and Means.
Sponsored by Mr. Paul (R—Texas)
19 August 1980   H7243

Public Law 96-536 of 16 December 1980 prohibits Legal
Services Corporation from using federal funds to provide
legal assistance for any litigation which seeks to adjudicate
the legality of homosexuality. House Bill HR 7584, an
appropriations bill providing funding for Legal Services
Corporation for fiscal year 1981, contains the restriction.
The bill was passed by the House and Senate and signed
into law.

Remarks in the Senate
Mr. Cranston (D—California)
in support of S 2210. Cranston gives a history of the policy
and its enforcement. He says the policy dates back to
amendments to the Immigration and Nationality Act made
in 1952 which were designed to exclude social psychopaths.
In 1965 the act was amended again to exclude sexual deviates.
Between 1971 and 1978, 31 people were denied entry to the
United States for reasons specified under Section 212(a)(4).
The text of the bill is given and he quotes from an article
in support of his position from the *Los Angeles Times*
on 31 December 1979, "A Matter For Congress' Attention."
23 January 1980   S268

Mr. Humphrey (R—New Hampshire)
in support of S 1808, the Family Protection Act. He quotes
from an article by Michael Novak from the Florida
Times-Union on 16 November 1979, "New Ideas Signal
a 'New Deal'"   S287
23 January 1980   S288

Mr. McClure (R—Idaho)
reports an article by Dr. Max Rafferty, "California
Educator Suffering Lightly in Sexual Escapade." Rafferty
tells of a teacher who was fired after it was found he was
having sexual relations with a 17-year-old male student.
However, his teaching license was not revoked and the
teacher is suing for re-instatement. Rafferty and McClure
agree that the teacher should have been fired.
28 February 1980   S1997

Mr. Humphrey (R—New Hampshire)
critical of the Carter administration's White House
Conference on Families. Humphrey gives a history and
interpretation of the conference. He is critical of the
inclusion of gay rights advocates and others, and quotes   S5009
13 letters and articles in support of his viewpoints.   to
Humphrey uses the issue in an attempt to discredit Carter.   S5036
9 May 1980
He includes an article by Susan Wells in the *Atlanta
Journal,* 12 March 1980, "State Conference Says
Homosexual Family Can Be Healthy Environment."   S5020
Humphrey also criticizes at length the 1977 National
Women's Conference. In particular he is upset because
he believes conservative women were not given fair
treatment and representation. He quotes 6 articles on the
subject. Humphrey also refers to an article by Jean
O'Leary and Ginny Vida, "Lesbians in the Schools."   S5032

Mr. Hollings (D—South Carolina)
opposing an amendment sponsored in the Senate
by Mr. Helms (R—North Carolina) to prohibit legal
representation by Legal Services Corporation in cases protecting,
defending or promoting homosexuality. The amendment
had been rejected earlier by the State and Justice
Department Committees and the full Appropriations
Committee
25 September 1980   S13389

Remarks in the House
Mr. McKay (D—Utah)
commenting that the family is the victim of "victimless
crimes" such as abortion and homosexuality
28 May 1980   H4251

Mr. Dannemeyer (R—California)
noting and commending the rejection of homosexuality
at Disneyland in California
16 September 1980   H8838

Extension of Remarks in the House
  Mr. Beilenson (D—California)
  in support of HR 6303. He cites articles from the
  Washington Post on 31 December 1979, "Medieval
  Barriers at the Border," and *Los Angeles Times* on
  31 December 1979, "A Matter For Congress' Attention"   E213
  29 January 1980   E214

  Mr. Waxman (D—California)
  in support of HR 6303 and announcing a petition signed
  by 133 of the 150 members of the Netherlands' Parliament
  urging the United States not to discriminate against
  foreign visitors on the basis of their sexual orientation
  11 February 1980   E505

  Mr. Symms (R—Idaho)
  in support of his amended version of the Family
  Protection Act
  22 May 1980   E2559

  Ms. Holt (R—Maryland)
  in support of HR 7445, the Family Protection Act of
  1980. Holt favors the act because it would provide
  tax breaks to families who support the elderly
  2 July 1980   E3408

  Mr. Weiss (D—New York)
  in opposition to the amendment sponsored by Mr.
  McDonald which would prohibit the Legal Services
  Corporation from providing legal representation in
  any case involving the rights of homosexuals
  28 July 1980   E3627

Mr. Murtha (D—Pennsylvania)
noting that the McDonald Legal Services Corporation
amendment had passed the House and comments that it
may be rejected by the Senate. Murtha quotes an article
by Joe Flower, "Gays in Business: The Prejudice and the
Power," which appeared in *San Francisco* magazine. He   E4635
wishes to recognize the achievements of gay people.   E4636
30 September 1980   E4637

Mr. J. Burton (D—California)
also submits Flower's article "Gays in Business: The
Prejudice and the Power," from *San Francisco* magazine.
Burton also wishes to recognize gay people and regrets
the passage of the McDonald Legal Services Corporation
amendment.
1 October 1980   E4697

Mr. Mitchell (D—Maryland)
critical of the Moral Majority and National Conservative
Political Action Committee. Mitchell cites two articles from
the Flint, Michigan *Journal,* "NCPAC Threat," and "Put
Those People in Their Place," which label these groups
as being on the "far right."
5 December 1980   E5311

Hearing (transcript)	Government
before the	Documents
Subcommittee on Employment Opportunities	Depository
of the	Libraries
Committee on Education and Labor	
of the	Superintendent
House of Representatives	of Documents
relative to	Call Number
consideration of House Bill HR 2074, prohibiting	
discrimination on the basis of sexual and affectional	Y4.Ed8/1
orientation	c49/3
HR 2074, The Civil Rights Amendment Act of 1979	

Held on 10 October 1980 in San Francisco

Mr. Hawkins (D—California), chairperson

"Homosexuality and the U.S. Military"
by Michael Thomas McIntyre, M.A. Thesis, Naval
Postgraduate School, Monterey, California

June 1980, 134 pages

1981, Ninety-seventh Congress, First Session

Congressional Record	*Congressional Record* page reference Volume *127*
Bills and Resolutions Senate Bill S 1708 A bill to prohibit discrimination on the basis of sexual orientation Referred to the Committee on Labor and Human Resources Sponsored by Mr. Tsongas (D—Massachusetts) and 6 Senators 6 October 1981	S11153
Senate Bill S 1378, The Family Protection Act A bill to strengthen the American Family and promote the virtues of family life through education, tax assistance, and related measures. Referred to the Committee on Finance Sponsored by Mr. Jepsen (R—Iowa) and Mr. Laxalt (R—Nevada) 17 June 1981	S6398
An additional sponsor announced (Mr. Garn, R—Utah) 16 July 1981	S7813
An additional sponsor announced (Mr. Hatch, R—Utah) 21 September 1981	S10198
An additional sponsor announced (Mr. Helms, R—N.C.) 15 October 1981	S11517

House Bill HR 311, the Family Protection Act
A bill to strengthen the American family and promote
the virtues of family life through education, tax
assistance, and related measures.
Referred jointly to the Committees on Agriculture,
Armed Services, Education and Labor, the Judiciary,
and Ways and Means
sponsored by Mr. Hansen (R—Idaho)
6 January 1981   H59

House Bill HR 1454
A bill to prohibit discrimination on the basis of affectional
or sexual orientation, and for other purposes
Referred to the Committee on the Judiciary and the
Committee on Education and Labor
Sponsored by Mr. Weiss (D—New York) and Mr.
Waxman (D—California) and 32 members of the House   H220
28 January 1981   H254

8 additional sponsors announced 10 March 1981   H 866
2 additional sponsors announced 18 March 1981   H1012
1 additional sponsor announced 8 April 1981   H1428
1 additional sponsor announced 12 May 1981   H2167
3 additional sponsors announced 16 July 1981   H4500

House Bill HR 3371
A bill to prohibit discrimination on the basis of
affectional or sexual orientation, and for other purposes.
Referred jointly to the Committee on the Judiciary
and the Committee on Education and Labor
Sponsored by Mr. Phillip Burton (D—California)
1 May 1981   H1724

House Bill HR 3524
A bill to repeal section 212(a)(4) of the Immigration
and Nationality Act, as amended, and for other purposes
Referred to the Committee on the Judiciary
Sponsored by Mr. Dixon (D—California) and 24 House
members
12 May 1981   H2166

2 additional sponsors announced 9 July 1981   H4198
2 additional sponsors announced 10 September 1981   H6143
1 additional sponsor announced 28 October 1981   H7879

House Bill HR 3955, the Family Protection Act
A bill to strengthen the American family and to promote
the virtues of family life through education, tax
assistance, and related measures
Referred to the Committees on Agriculture, Armed
Services, Education and Labor, the Judiciary, and
Ways and Means
Sponsored by Mr. Smith (R—Alabama)
17 June 1981   H3069

7 additional sponsors announced 9 July 1981   H4198
1 additional sponsor announced 21 October 1982   H7591

House Concurrent Resolution 29
Expressing the sense of Congress that homosexual acts
and the class of individuals who advocate such conduct
shall never receive special consideration or a protected
status under the law
Referred to the Committee on the Judiciary
Sponsored by Mr. McDonald (D—Georgia)
20 January 1981   H133

House Resolution 208
Disapproving the action of the District of Columbia City
Council in approving the District of Columbia Sexual
Assault Reform Act (D.C. Act 4-69) of 1981
Referred to the Committee on the District of Columbia
Sponsored by Mr. P. Crane (R—Illinois) and Mr. McDonald
(D—Georgia) and Mr. Marriott (R—Utah)
9 September 1981   H6072

Remarks in the Senate
Mr. East (R—North Carolina)
recognizing the Moral Majority as an important
contemporary force on American political and social process.
He quotes an article by Dr. James Thompson, "The Moral   S6408
Majority," printed in the *Rockford Papers,* May 1981.   to
17 June 1981   S6411

Mr. Jepsen (R—Iowa)
introducing the Family Protection Act (S 1378)
Senator Jepsen gives a detailed account of the provisions
of the bill. Section 108 of Title 1 would prohibit ''federal
funds from going to any public or private individual or
entity that presents that male or female homosexuality is   S6324
an acceptable lifestyle.'' Organizations promoting,   to
advocating or suggesting that homosexuality is a valid   S6344
lifestyle would be ineligible for federal government support. S6325
17 June 1981   S6338

Mr. Hatch (R—Utah)
in support of S1378, the Family Protection Act
21 September 1981   S10201

Mr. Tsongas (D—Massachusetts)
introducing S1708 and encouraging support for it. The
text of the bill is given and Tsongas lists major
corporations and municipalities that have policies against
discrimination on the basis of sexual orientation.
6 October 1981   S11154

Mr. Moynihan (D—New York)
in support of S 1708
6 October 1981   S11155

Mr. Garn (R—Utah)
in support of the Family Protection Act and recognizing
that it has been heavily criticized. He quotes an editorial
by Ian Binnie from the *Des Moines Register,* ''Kind
Words for the Family Protection Act'' which supports
the FPA.
21 October 1981   S11823

Remarks in the House
Mr. Weiss (D—New York)
seeking support for HR 1454
28 January 1981   H219

Mr. Smith (R—Alabama)
introducing the Family Protection Act of 1981 Title 1
of the act concerns "family preservation by restoring
parents' rights." Part of Title 1 restricts Legal Services
Corporation from becoming involved in litigation for
homosexual rights, abortion, divorce and busing. Title 3
would allow for parental approval of school text books
and involves other legislation dealing with sex education
and sex segregation in schools. Title 4 would allow for
voluntary prayer in schools. Title 5 would prevent federal
government regulation of religious institutions through
agencies such as the Internal Revenue Service. The act
would also provide tax breaks for families and seeks to
support families who assist elderly members or wish to
adopt children. Smith says the FPA is an effort to "turn   H3064
back to traditional American values."   H3065
17 June 1981   H3066

Mr. Siljander (R—Michigan), Mr. Dannemeyer
(R—California) and Mr. Lott (R—Mississippi)
in support of HR 311, the Family Protection Act   H3067
17 June 1981   H3068

Mr. Kastenmeier (D—Wisconsin)
noting that Public Law 96-536 states that Legal Services
Corporation (LSC) may not provide "legal assistance
for any litigation which seeks to adjudicate the legalization
of homosexuality." This amendment was passed by the
House and Senate in 1980 as part of an appropriations
bill. Mr. McDonald is now offering a further
amendment that LSC may not "provide legal assistance
to promote, defend or protect homosexuality."
Kastenmeier opposes the amendment.
18 June 1981   H3074

Mr. McDonald (D—Georgia)
in support of the proposed amendment   H3074
18 June 1981   H3076

Mr. Leach (R—Iowa), Mr. Railsback (R—Illinois),   H3075
Mr. John Burton (D—California), Mr. Studds   H3076
(D—Massachusetts), Mr. Frank (D—Massachusetts),   H3077
Mr. Pritchard (R—Washington), Mr. Waxman   H3078
(D—California) and Mr. Green (R—New York) are all
critical of the amendment.

Mr. Weiss (D—New York)
cites part of a letter from the Justice Department
to Senator Hollings (South Carolina) critical of
the amendment   H3077

A vote was taken and the McDonald amendment was
rejected 245 to 151   H3079

The debate continues for several more pages and   H3080
involves several other members. The original language   to
denying legal assistance for litigation seeking to   H3086
adjudicate the legalization of homosexuality
was retained.
18 June 1981   H3086

Mr. P. Crane (R—Illinois)
introducing House Resolution 208 which disapproves
the District of Columbia Sexual Reform Act. Crane
presents a petition signed by 10,000 D.C. residents
disapproving of the act which, among other things,
legalizes homosexual conduct.
1 October 1981   H6732

The debate on House Resolution 208 is a long one.
See pages H6731–H6762 and H6787. Much of the debate   H6731
centers around the right to self-determination by the   to
District of Columbia rather than on the content   H6762
of the Sexual Reform Act itself.
1 October 1981   H6787

Mr. P. Crane (R—Illinois)
presents a letter from Archbishop Hickey of the
District of Columbia disapproving of the Act
1 October 1981   H6746

Mr. McKinney (R—Connecticut)
against resolution 208. McKinney refers to an editorial
in the *Washington Post* which discusses Reverend Jerry
Falwell's opposition to the Sexual Assault Act which
Falwell says is "perverted." McKinney also gives an
outline of the Act and a listing of the organizations
which support it. The act decriminalizes homosexual acts
between consenting adults.
1 October 1981   H6752

A vote was taken and the resolution passed 281–119
1 October 1981   H6753

Extension of Remarks in the House
Mr. McDonald (D—Georgia)
citing the Moral Majority's response to criticisms
levelled against it by the American Civil Liberties
Union. McDonald is critical of the ACLU and quotes
from the 15 December 1980 issue of *The Moral
Majority Report* which says in part, "We favor
civil rights for homosexuals but oppose those who
choose to live a homosexual lifestyle from receiving
treatment as a minority group."   E615
23 February 1981   E616

Mr. McDonald (D—Georgia)
mourning the decline of moral values in America,
criticizing communism, and quoting from the January
1981 issue of the *Conservative Digest* by Dr. Jerry
Falwell, president of the Moral Majority. Falwell
includes some remarks on the Moral Majority's position
regarding homosexuality. (The Moral Majority was
founded in June 1979 by Falwell.)
25 February 1981   E704

Mr. Dixon (D—California)
in support of HR 3524   E2317
13 May 1981   E2318

Mr. Phillip Crane (R—Illinois)
in support of the Family Protection Act
22 June 1981   E3089

Mr. McDonald (D—Georgia)
quoting an article from the 21 September 1981 issue
of *Newsweek* by Jerry Falwell, "My Turn." Falwell
defends the Moral Majority and their right to express
their opinions, and outlines some of the positions
the Moral Majority takes on controversial issues. He also
comments on the appeal and membership of the Moral
Majority.
17 September 1981   E4308

Mr. Mazzoli (D—Kentucky)
in support of House Resolution 208 to disapprove
of the District of Columbia Sexual Assault Reform Act.
He reports that on 24 September 1981, the House
Committee on the District of Columbia voted 8–3
against House Resolution 208.
29 September 1981   E4476

Mr. Siljander (R—Michigan)
in opposition to the D.C. Sexual Assault Reform Act.
7 December 1981   E5615

Petitions
Petition POM-432 presented to the Senate
A petition from a citizen of Tacoma, Washington,
relating to the "Gay Bill of Rights"
Referred to the Committee on the Judiciary
24 September 1981   S10436

Petition POM-496 presented to the Senate
A petition from a citizen of San Antonio, Texas,
urging the Congress to veto the legislation of the
District of Columbia removing criminal penalties for
certain criminal acts (including sodomy).
Referred to the Committee on Governmental Affairs
16 October 1981   S11566

Petition POM-513 presented to the Senate
A petition from a citizen of San Antonio, Texas,
relating to House Bill 1454, the "Gay Bill of Rights"
Referred to the Committee on the Judiciary
19 October 1981   S11627

Petition POM-551 presented to the Senate
A petition from citizens of Cincinnati, Ohio,
relative to the "Gay Bill of Rights"
Referred to the Committee on the Judiciary
30 October 1981   S12661

Petition POM-628 presented to the Senate
A petition from a citizen of Arecibo, Puerto Rico,
urging rejection of "the Gay Bill of Rights"
Referred to the Committee on the Judiciary
2 December 1981   S14302

1982, Ninety-seventh Congress, Second Session

Congressional Record   *Congressional*
                                                         Record
                                                   page reference
                                                   Volume *128*

Bills and Resolutions
   House Bill HR 3524
   A bill to repeal section 212(a)(4) of the Immigration
   and Nationality Act, and for other purposes

   1 additional sponsor announced (Mr. Brodhead,
   D—Michigan)
   20 April 1982   H1503
   1 additional sponsor announced (Mr. Edgar,
   D—Pennsylvania)
   30 September 1981   H8131

   Amendment to House Bill HR 7205, (the Departments
   of Labor, Health and Human Services, and Education
   and Related Agencies Appropriations Act of 1983)
   that would appropriate an additional $2.6 million
   to the Center for Disease Control in 1983 for research
   on Acquired Immune Deficiency Syndrome (AIDS)
   by Mr. Roybal (D—California)
   1 December 1982   H8687

   The amendment passed the House on 1 December 1982   H8689

Remarks in the House
   Mr. Phillip Burton (D—California)
   against the exclusion of lesbians and gay foreign nationals
   by the Immigration and Naturalization Service. Burton
   quotes testimony by Mr. Greg Day, a gay activist, and
   Dr. David Kessler, a representative of the American
   Psychiatric Association. Both are critical of INS
   policy, which discriminates against gay people. The
   policy was first implemented after amendments to
   the Immigration and Nationality Act in 1965. Day's

testimony gives an outline of the enforcement and legal
challenges of the policy. Day and Kessler both
testified at a 14 July 1982 congressional briefing
on INS policy, held by Representative Dixon   H4530
(D—California), sponsor of HR 3524.   H4531
22 July 1982   H4532

Mr. Nachter (D—Kentucky),
Chairperson of the Appropriations Committee, in
support of the Roybal amendment to provide funds for
AIDS research
1 December 1982   H8688

Mr. Green (R—New York), Mr. Conte
(R—Massachusetts) and Mr. Weiss (D—New York) also
spoke in support of the Roybal amendment
1 December 1982   H8688

Extension of Remarks in the House
Mr. McDonald (D—Georgia)
critical of federal government grants to liberal
organizations. McDonald quotes an article from the
April 1982 issue of the *Conservative Digest,* "Leftist
Causes Your Money Supports." The article lists several
gay related organizations which accept federal funds,
including the Center for Homosexual Education,
Evaluation and Research in San Francisco.   E1721
22 April 1982   E1725

Mr. Fauntroy (D—District of Columbia)
in support of HR 3524. Fauntroy quotes the testimony
given by Professor Gordon at the 14 July congressional
briefing on INS policy. Gordon gives a brief history
of the INS exclusionary policy and legal challenges
to it, with special reference to homosexuality.   E3575
29 July 1982   E3576

Mr. Frank (D—Massachusetts)
in support of HR 3524. Frank quotes the testimony of
2 foreign visitors to the U.S., given at the 14 July
congressional briefing on INS policy. The testimony is
critical of INS exclusionary policies toward gay people.   E3704
5 August 1982   E3705

Mr. Weiss (D—New York)
in support of HR 3524. Weiss quotes the testimony of
2 foreign visitors to the U.S., given at the 14 July
congressional briefing on INS policy. The testimony is
critical of INS exclusionary policies toward gay people.   E4484
29 September 1982   E4485

Mr. Dornan (R—California)
on the virtue of morality and critical of the presence
of cocaine and homosexuality in the nation's capital
27 July 1982   E3512

Mr. Weiss (D—New York)
quoting an article by Ronald Gold in *Civil Liberties*
(November 1982) "Gay Rights is a First Amendment
Issue." Gold refers to the Family Protection Act and other
legislation at the federal, state and local levels. He argues
that gay people are being prevented from openly discussing
homosexuality.
7 December 1982   E4949

Petitions

Petition POM-676 presented to the Senate
A petition from a citizen of Cranford, New Jersey,
relative to the "Gay Bill of Rights"
Referred to the Committee on the Judiciary
28 January 1982   S92

Petition POM-970 presented to the Senate
A petition from a citizen of San Diego, California,
urging Congress to reject "the Gay Bill of Rights"
Referred to the Committee on the Judiciary
17 June 1982   S 7024

Petition POM-1195 presented to the Senate
A petition from a citizen of Kansas City, Missouri,
urging Congress to reject the "Gay Bill of Rights"
Referred to the Committee on the Judiciary
17 September 1982   S11718

Petition POM-1263 presented to the Senate
A petition from a citizen of Thousand Oaks, California,
urging Congress to reject "the Gay Bill of Rights" and
reaffirm traditional God-given morality.
Referred to the Committee on the Judiciary
1 December 1982   S13674

Petition POM-1278 presented to the Senate
A petition from a citizen of Columbus, Ohio,
ursing Congress to pass "the Gay Bill of Rights"
Referred to the Committee on the Judiciary
14 December 1982   S14731

Petition #593 in the House of Representatives
relative to HR 1454, gay rights
by Mr. Smith (Alabama) et al.
Referred to the Committee on the Judiciary
16 September 1982   H 7174

Hearing (transcript)   Government
before the   Documents
Subcommittee on Employment Opportunities   Depository
of the   Libraries
Committee on Education and Labor
of the   Superintendent
House of Representatives   of Documents
relative to   Call Number
Consideration of House Bill HR 1454, The
Civil Rights Amendment Act of 1981,   Y4.Ed8/1
prohibiting discrimination on the basis of sexual   C49/4
and affectional orientation

Mr. Hawkins (D—California), chairperson of the
subcommittee

Held on 27 January 1982 in Washington D.C.

Hearing (transcript)
before the
Subcommittee on Health and Environment
of the
Committee on Energy and Commerce
of the
House of Representatives
relative to
Kaposi's Sarcoma and Related Opportunistic Infections

Mr. Waxman (D—California) chairperson of the
subcommittee

Held on 13 April 1982 in Los Angeles

Government
Documents
Depository
Libraries

Superintendent
of Documents
Call Number

Y4.En2/3

97-125

Serial Number
97-125
97th Congress

Report
made by
Mr. Stokes (D—Ohio)
of the
Committee on Standards and Official Conduct
of the
House of Representatives
pursuant to House Resolution 518,
concerning alleged improper or illegal sexual
conduct . . . by members, officers, or employees
of the House
14 December 1982

House Report
97-965

97th Congress

1983, Ninety-eighth Congress, First Session (until 23 June 1983)

Congressional Record

Congressional
Record
page reference
Volume *129*

Bills and Resolutions
Senate Bill S 430
A bill to prohibit employment discrimination on the
basis of sexual orientation

Referred to the Committee on Labor and Human
Resources Sponsored by Mr. Tsongas (D—Massachusetts)
and Messrs. Cranston (D—California), Packwood
(R—Oregon), Moynihan (D—New York) and Kennedy
(D—Massachusetts)
3 February 1983   S972

1 additional sponsor announced (Mr. Inouye,
D—Hawaii)
24 February 1983   S1626

Senate Bill S1086
A bill to repeal section 212(a)(4) of the Immigration
and Nationality Act, as amended, and for other purposes
Referred to the Committee on the Judiciary
Sponsored by Mr. Cranston (D—California)
19 April 1983

The proposed legislation would prevent the Immigration   S4852
and Naturalization Service from discriminating   S4859
against homosexuals. The text of the bill is included.   S4860

House Bill HR 427
A bill to prohibit discrimination on the basis of
affectional or sexual orientation, and for other purposes
Referred jointly to the Committee on the Judiciary
and the Committee on Education and Labor
Sponsored by Mr. Weiss (D—New York) and Messrs.
Burton (D—California), Waxman (D—California) and
Lowry (D—Washington)
6 January 1983   H90

36 additional sponsors announced 8 March 1983   H940

House Bill HR 2624
A bill to prohibit discrimination on the basis of
affectional or sexual orientation, and for other purposes
Referred jointly to the Committee on the Judiciary
and the Committee on Education and Labor
Sponsored by Mr. Weiss (D—New York) and 58 House
members
19 April 1983   H2190

House Bill HR 2880
A bill to make individuals suffering from Acquired
Immune Deficiency Syndrome (AIDS) eligible for
coverage under the Medicare program
Referred jointly to the Committee on Ways and Means
and the Committee on Energy and Commerce
Sponsored by Mr. Weiss (D—New York) and Ms. Boxer
(D—California)
3 May 1983   H2600

Remarks in the Senate
Mr. Moynihan (D—New York)
in support of S 430. Moynihan comments that S 430
is identical to legislation introduced in the previous
two congresses
3 February 1983   S1007

Mr. Tsongas (D—Massachusetts)
listing several companies which have non-discrimination
policies toward gay people. The text of S430 is quoted.   S1006
3 February 1983   S1007

Remarks in the House
Mr. Weiss (D—New York)
relative to   H2585
Acquired Immune Deficiency Syndrome (AIDS)   to
3 May 1983   H2596

Weiss calls for financial support for research on AIDS.
He comments on bias and reluctance of government
agencies to provide support because many AIDS victims
are gay. He also refers to problems that AIDS victims
face. Weiss quotes the text of HR 2880.

Representatives speaking in support of Mr. Weiss:
Ms. Boxer (D—California)   H2586
Mr. Frank (D—Massachusetts)   H2586
Mr. Studds (D—Massachusetts)   H2587
Mr. Towns (D—New York)   H2592
Mr. Crockett (D—Michigan)   H2592
Mr. Waxman (D—California)   H2593
Mr. Roybal (D—California)   H2593
Mr. Edgar (D—Pennsylvania)   H2594
Mr. Addabbo (D—New York)   H2594

Mr. Edwards (D—California)	H2595
Mr. Lowry (D—Washington)	H2595
Ms. Schneider (R—Rhode Island)	H2595
Mr. Levine (D—California)	H2595
Mr. Rangel (D—New York)	H2596
Mr. Green (R—New York)	H2596
3 May 1983	

Articles Cited
Cahill, Kevin "Conquering AIDS" *New York Times*
22 April 1983   H2587

Nelson, Harry "Precursor to Fatal Illness Identified"
Los Angeles Times
21 April 1983   H2590

Colen, D.B. "A Small Casualty in AIDS War" *Newsday*
22 March 1983   H2591

Remarks in the House
Mr. Nachter (D—Kentucky)
of the
Subcommittee on Labor, Health and Human Services
in support of his amendment to a supplemental
appropriations bill which includes an additional
$12 million funding for AIDS research. Nachter
reports on government health agencies responses   H3336
to AIDS research.   to
25 May 1983   H3344

Representatives speaking in support of Mr. Nachter:	
Mr. Green (R—New York)	H3339
Mr. Miller (D—California)	H3340
Mr. Yates (D—Illinois)	H3340
Ms. Boxer (D—California)	H3340
Mr. Studds (D—Massachusetts)	H3340
Mr. Weiss (D—New York)	H3341
Mr. Lowry (D—Washington)	H3341
Mr. Conte (R—Massachusetts) Co-sponsor of the	H3341

amendment. Mr. Conte also reports on government
health agencies' responses to AIDS research.

Mr. AuCoin (D—Oregon)	H3343
Mr. Biaggi (D—New York)	H3344
Mr. Waxman (D—California)	H3344
25 May 1983	

The amendment passed in the House on 25 May 1983   H3362

Extension of Remarks in the House
Mr. Weiss (D—New York)
reintroducing legislation to prohibit discrimination
on the basis of sexual orientation in housing,
employment, education and public accommodations.
Weiss includes the text of the proposed legislation.
House Bill HR 427
3 January 1983   E17

Mr. Weiss (D—New York)
critical of exclusionary provisions in U.S. immigration
laws that deny entry to homosexuals. Weiss cites the
testimony of 2 foreign visitors to the U.S., given at
the 14 July 1982 congressional briefing on INS policy.
2 February 1983   E 268

Ms. Ferraro (D—New York)
critical of inadequate federal government funding
for AIDS research, and quoting the remarks of
Michael Callen, an AIDS victim, to the New York
congressional delegation.   E2403
19 May 1983   E2404

Ms. Schneider (R—Rhode Island)
in support of the supplemental appropriations bill
amendment that would provide increased funding for
AIDS research
26 May 1983   E2550

Petitions
Petition POM-154 presented to the Senate
A petition from a citizen of Los Angeles, California,
urging Congress to reject "the Gay Bill of Rights"
and reaffirm traditional God-given morality.
Referred to the Committee on Labor and Human Resources
10 May 1983   S6404

Petition POM-216 presented to the Senate
A petition from a citizen of Afton, Oklahoma,
urging Congress to reject "the Gay Bill of Rights"
and reaffirm traditional God-given morality.
Referred to the Committee on the Judiciary
9 June 1983   S8133

Report
made by
Mr. Dingell (D—Michigan)
of the
Committee on Energy and Commerce
of the
House of Representatives
to accompany House Bill HR 2350,
The Health Research Extension Act of 1983

House Report
98-191

98th Congress

16 May 1983

The incidence of AIDS is noted and there is a
recommendation for additional
research and funding.

See page 71

Report
made by
Mr. Dingell (D—Michigan)
of the
Committee on Energy and Congress
of the
House of Representatives
to accompany House Bill HR 2713,
relative to
Public Health Emergencies

House Report
98-143

98th Congress

16 May 1983

The bill and report is partly a response to the need for
additional funding for AIDS research.

Abstracts of Current Publications

Phillip Hecht, Abstracts Editor

The purpose of abstracts appearing in the *Journal* is to provide brief summaries of the most recent books and periodical literature on lesbianism, male homosexuality, gender identity, and alternative sexual lifestyles. The abstracts will include scholarly works in the following fields: the social and behavioral sciences, history, law, humanities, and psychology.

Chiswick, D. (1983). Sex crimes, *The British Journal of Psychiatry, 143,* 236–241.

"Crimes relating to sexual behavior account for only one percent of all indictable crimes." Using the Walmsey-White report (1979), Chiswick outlines the five major sex offense areas. Specific offenses such as rape, incest, buggery and sexual intercourse with a female under 13 years of age are defined and classified as serious sex offenses. Unlawful sexual intercourse with a female under 16 (but over 13) years old, indecent assault and indecency with children are classified as less serious sex offenses. The article characterizes these offenders and what roles psychiatry and the law can play in their treatment, particularly in preventing reconvictions.

Christie-Brown, J. R. W. (1983). Paraphilias: Sadomasochism, fetishism, transvestism, and transsexuality. *The British Journal of Psychiatry, 143,* 227-230.

This book discusses four paraphilias and their treatment using non-clinical population samplings. Sadomasochism, fetishism and transvestism are briefly defined with treatment varying from dynamic psychotherapy to behavior therapy. Transsexualism is more extensively covered due to "intense popular interest and publicity and the more vociferous demand of patients for medical treatment." Definitions of transsexualism center around the disturbance of gender development but often are complicated by other psychiatric disturbances within the same person. The program of treatment includes giving estrogens to males and testosterones to females prior to surgery.

191

Faderman, L. (1983). *Scotch Verdict.* New York: Morrow.

In 1811, there was an unusual lawsuit in Scotland. Jane Pirie and Marianne Woods, who ran a school in Edinburgh, were accused of lesbianism by one of their students, Jane Cumming. Lady Cumming Gorden, the student's grandmother, was primarily responsible for the withdrawal of all the students from the school. To restore their reputation and to seek recompense for the closing of their school, Woods and Pirie filed a lawsuit for libel against Lady Cumming Gorden.

Half of Faderman's book covers the reconstruction of the trial, including excerpts from testimonies and judges' opinions. Her goal is to find "whether they were really guilty of what they had been accused, what words were used to make such accusations in their day, how they defended themselves, how their judges responded, and what happened to women like them after such an experience in the early nineteenth century" (p. 18).

Several aspects of Scottish life in the early nineteenth century are analyzed: the role of women, especially the career opportunities available, the hearing, review, and appeal procedures, and attitudes toward sexuality.

Interspersed within the trial coverage are the viewpoints of Faderman and a friend, Ollie, as Faderman researches the trial. Events surrounding the lives of Jane Pirie and Marianne Woods are recreated from facts and speculation, and a case is built for the possibility that Jane Cumming lied when she told her grandmother of her teachers' affair. One major disagreement between Faderman and Ollie centers on whether the relationship between Pirie and Woods was sexual.

The sexual mores of nineteenth century Scotland are compared to twentieth century America. Much of the American viewpoint came from reactions to Lillian Hellman's play *The Children's Hour,* of the 1930s, and the movie adapted from it. Both were based on this case. The Scottish viewpoint, particularly on lesbianism, is exemplified by one judge's opinion: "The description of their behavior was so gross, bruttish, beastly and absurd that I could not give it the slightest credit. But still, I would be forced to believe it if well proved" (p. 233).

Golombok, S., Spencer, A., & Rutter, M. (1983). Children in lesbian and single-parent households: Psychosexual and psychiatric appraisal. *Journal of Child Psychology, 24,* 551–572.

Lesbian parenting has been viewed by some as a risk to child development because of the lack of same-sexed models, differential reinforcement of sex-typed behavior, and the omission of the Oedipal cycle. This empirical study deals with the psychosexual and psychiatric impact on children raised in a nontraditional family unit. Several lesbian households were compared to several single-parent households (heterosexual mothers without cohabitees). The sources for evaluation were mother and children interviews, and parent and teacher questionnaires.

The children's interviews emphasized gender identification and sex role behavior (also assessed on the interview with the mothers). The interviews and questionnaires involving the mothers supplied much of the information on the children's behavior, emotional state, and relationships. The instruments also included questions pertaining to background and personal feelings and attitudes about families. Separate interviews with the lesbian mothers assessed their sexual orientation and experiences and attitudes in bringing up children. Relationships between their partners who lived in the household and their children were also discussed.

The conclusions show that in comparing the lesbian and heterosexual households, there was little difference in the children's gender identity, sex-role behavior, sexual orientation, and emotional stability. There were more indications of psychological disorders in the heterosexual single-parent households. Some problems arose in the findings; for example, the questionnaires may not have been "sensitive" enough to spot disorders, sexual orientation findings were limited because many children were postpubertal, the subjects were not chosen at random, and the lesbian households all had experienced the presence of the fathers during some period.

Kaplan, H. S. (1983). *The evaluation of sexual disorders: Psychological and medical aspects.* New York: Brunner/Mazel.

This comprehensive work, analyzing various psychosexual dysfunctions, is divided into three major sections. The first section covers all of the psychological aspects of diagnosing sexual disorders. Several elements must be taken into consideration for every type of sexual dysfunction analyzed: the physiology, clinical features, and common organic and psychological causes. Major types of sexual dysfunctions, or disorders, include orgasmic phase, excitement phase, desire phase, functional dyspareunia, and phobic avoidance of sex. Differentiation between organic or psychogenic causes is essential in diagnosis. Case histories are included to show that symptoms may stem from underlying psychological causes. Other factors in evaluating sexual disorders include cultural impact, neuroses, sexual traumas, inadequate sexual techniques, couples with conflicting fantasies, power struggles, inadequate reciprocation, and incompatibility.

The method for the evaluation of sexual disorders includes seven steps: identifying the main problem and its history, analyzing the patient's current sexual behavior, conducting a complete medical examination, probing the patient's psychiatric nature, obtaining a psychosexual and family history, evaluating the relationship (because it may influence the patient's sexual dysfunction, and connecting all these methods together to decide what type of sex therapy is necessary.

Section Two analyzes the medical elements involved in sexual disorders. Females have specific diseases or use drugs that can impair orgasm and disturb the excitement phase. Males are also affected by drugs and diseases that contribute to ejaculatory disorders and impotence. Female dyspareunia involves pain on entry, in the midvaginal area, on deep thrusting, and during orgasm. Male dyspareunia includes pain on erection and intromission and during ejaculation. When sexual desire is affected, a complete physical examination, including laboratory tests, is necessary.

Section Three brings together psychological and medical factors involved in evaluating sexual disorders. Several syndromes are defined with corresponding medical and psychological treatment. In addition to the disorders mentioned above, she included paraphilias such as fetishism, transvestism, zoophilia, pedophilia, exhibitionism, voyeurism, sexual masochism, sexual sadism, atypical paraphilias, and ego dystonic homosexuality; sexual pain and disorders associated with genital muscle spasm including dyspareunia, uterine muscle cramps, vaginismus and ejaculatory pain; sexual phobias and unconsummated marriage.

Manos, N. (1983). Sexual life, problems, and attitudes of the prospective Greek physician. *Archives of Sexual Behavior, 12,* 435–443.

The results of a questionnaire on the sexual habits and attitudes of 82 male and 48 female Greek medical students included the following areas: (1) sexual experiences involving sexual intercourse, masturbation, oral sex, anal sex, and homosexual encounters; (2) sexual dysfunctions, including inhibited sexual excitement, premature ejaculation, inhibited female or male orgasm, and functional dyspareunia; (3) use of contraceptive measures, from withdrawal to abortion; and (4) attitudes of the medical students on oral sex, anal sex, abortion, and homosexuality. The respondents showed a liberal trend in their attitudes on sexuality, "to a similar degree or even higher level than ones reported for U.S. college and university students."

Peters, E. B. (1983). Freud's blind spot. *Christopher Street, 7*(5), 38–43.

This brief article charged that Freud's *Oedipus Complex* (based in part on Greek mythology) ignores the homosexuality of Laius, king of Thebes and father of Oedipus. Therefore, his hypothesis on infantile sexuality is inconclusive. The problem centers on the motive for the choice a child makes when he renunciates the love object relationship with the mother and establishes a new sexual identification with the father. Freud bases this choice on the fear of castration. Peters states that if Oedipus chose his father as a love object he would have been "induced" by Laius' homosexuality, not fear of castration. When Oedipus killed his father he thus committed the "supreme act of homophobia."

Roberto, L. G. (1983). Issues in diagnosis and treatment of transsexualism. *Archives of Sexual Behavior, 12,* 445–473.

The author suggests that we return to a very conservative use of sex reassignment surgery. She discusses the methods used in selection, diagnosis, and treatment involving transsexuals, recommending ways in which they could be improved.

Past survey methods reveal several problems, including a lack of variety of subject, insufficient numbers of questionnaires returned, unclear diagnostic criteria, and possible bias in unstructured psychiatric interviews where there is no "blind" interviewer. Various studies have attempted to create a separate classification system for transsexuals. One example is Meyer's (1974) listing of four common characteristics: inappropriateness or incapacity in the anatomically determined gender role, the belief that improvement will result from role reversal, choice of sexual partners of the same anatomic sex and inhibition of heterosexual interest, and desire for sex reassignment surgery.

Roberto believes a syndrome specifically for categorizing transsexuals should be formulated, but it must allow for diversity within that population. One idea is to group them on the basis of sexual behavior and partner choice. The two major transsexual classification systems are the DSM-III (American Psychiatric Association, 1978), and the Stanford University Gender Reorientation Program (Fisk, 1974). More unity is needed between these systems to make sure they are valid in diagnosing patients.

Transsexual diagnosis most often utilizes unstructured interviews where the patients explain the general aspects of their condition. The structured interview of Money and Primrose (1969) covering sexual history, psychosocial history, medical/development history, and fantasy/associational content would be "more thorough." Other criteria for better diagnosis includes the mental status examination, personality instruments, behavioral assessment, and the "real life test."

Types of treatment (described and critiqued) include intensive psychotherapy, supportive psychotherapy, group psychotherapy, behaviorally oriented psychotherapy, and gender reorientation with surgical sex reassignment. Although there has been a lack of controlled study on the effects of surgery, surgical and postoperative complications including psychological trauma have been reported.

The author's recommendations include early childhood interventions involving gender reorientation or modification of cross-gender identifications, more outcome and follow-up studies of the different types of treatment, longitudinal studies of gender-deviant children, strict rules for surgery to avoid the possibility of psychopathic deterioration, well defined follow-up programs for postoperative treatment, and accurate modes for measuring gender identity and gender role.

Senneker, P., & Hendrick, C. (1983). Androgyny and helping behavior. *Journal of Personal and Social Psychology, 45,* 916–925.

The results of a study where male and female subjects, classified as androgynous or sex-typed by the Bem Sex Role Inventory, were tested for reactions as bystanders to emergency situations. The goal was to test the validity of S.L. Bem's theory of androgyny and the accuracy of BSRI in measuring androgyny. The theory claims that there is a "greater behavioral flexibility to androgynous than to sex-typed individuals across a variety of situations."

The subjects were grouped with either four same-sexed or mixed-sexed partners or were entirely alone with a victim. The primary measurements were response time (speed of helping), and proportion of subjects helping. The following results were reported: a victim received more help from males than females; the larger the group the less help was given (diffusion of responsibility); and more help was received from androgynous than sex-typed subjects.

Stokes, K., Kilmann, P. R., & Wanlass, R. L. (1983). Sexual orientation and sex role conformity. *Archives of Sexual Behavior, 12,* 427–433.

The Bem Sex Role Inventory and Sexual Behavior Questionnaire were administered to a widely varied group of 186 male and female homosexuals, heterosexuals, and bisexuals. The purpose was to test the "validity of the stereotypical concept that homosexuals deviate from conventional sex-role standards in our society." Prior to this several studies were conducted using the following instruments: gender identity tests, the Bem Sex Role Inventory (BSRI), and Masculine-Feminine Scale of the Adjective Check List (Gough & Heilbrun, 1965). The results are contradictory and inconclusive, often showing only slight differences between homosexuals and heterosexuals.

The results of this survey show that the sex roles of homosexuals do not differ from heterosexuals and bisexuals. However, it does not prove that there cannot be a link between masculinity and female homosexuality or femininity and male homosexuality. Some problems involved with the findings include the small number of participants, the difficulty in finding bisexuals, and the possible imperfections of the BSRI in detecting feminine or masculine traits.

Weinberg, T., & Levi Kamel, G. W. (Eds.). (1983). *S and M: Studies in sadomasochism.* Buffalo, NY: Prometheus Books.

This is an anthology of several essays devoted to the study of sadomasochism as social behavior and subculture. In the past most studies were conducted on an individual basis using theoretical, psychological and moral viewpoints to construct causal explanations for sadomasochism as an illness. Sadomasochism is viewed as a subculture with its own "norms, values, language, justifications, publications and formally structured organizations" (p. 21). There is a unity in the relationship of the partners involved. Developing a sexology of sadomasochism along sociological lines can create a theory of S&M that will enable us better to understand related social phenomena.

The book is divided into four major areas: the first section, "Classical Perspectives on Sadomasochism" outlines the most important contributors to a theory of S&M. Krafft-Ebing, in his work *Psychopathia Sexualis,* describes sadism and masochism and recognizes the fantasy and nonphysical aspects of dominance and submission. Freud recognizes S&M as two parts of the same entity. Havelock Ellis refines the definitions of Freud and Krafft-Ebing by referring to pain as a sexual stimulant not involving cruelty. Paul Gebhard, a modern anthropologist, discusses the symbolic and complex nature of S&M as a "subcultural social behavior."

The second section deals with "S&M Identities." It focuses on the individual within the S&M scene. Lawrence Mass provides a convincing argument for the need to establish scientific research on S&M rather than relying on purely psychological interpretations. Andreas Spengler describes his empirical study of sadomasochists, emphasizing types of practices, the need for secrecy, partner seeking, and self-acceptance. G.W. Levi Kamel views the leather "career" as a series of six steps: disenchantment, depression, curiosity, attraction, drifting, and limiting. "Dialogue with a Dominatrix" by Howard Smith and Cathy Cox and "Autobiography of a Dominatrix" by Juliette are two essays that describe personal experiences of the individual within the S&M subculture.

"S&M Interactions," the third section, focuses primarily on the subcultural aspects of S&M. Thomas Weinberg's article analyzes the subcultural elements of the S&M world, especially the theatrics involved in "keyings" and setting the "frames." The diversity within the S&M subculture is illustrated by four S&M "careers" in an article by G.W. Levi Kamel and Thomas Weinberg. A very candid viewpoint of S&M is provided by Pat Califia. Gerhard Falk and Thomas Weinberg talk about the prevalence of sadomasochism in popular Western society as it appears in movies, literature, and music.

The last part is devoted to the "Social Organization of S&M." It shows how well established and organized the S&M subculture is. Weinberg and Falk address their essay to the topic of heterosexual S&M: its clubs, language, publications, and advertisements. G.W. Levi Kamel illustrates how highly organized gay S&M includes special patterns of restraint, humiliation, masculinity, along with mores for all phases of physical contact. In his essay on "sexual risk," John Alan Lee describes the network of protection factors which define the limits of behavior within the S&M encounters.

West, D. J. (1983). Homosexuality and lesbianism. *The British Journal of Psychiatry, 143,* 221–226.

Three major themes involving homosexuality are discussed: (1) homosexuality as compared to lesbianism, using in part the basic sociobiological differences between the sexes; (2) the origins of sexual orientation, involving several familiar theories including the establishment of gender identity, the relevancy of hormonal variations, cultural influences and the effects of parenting; and (3) problems faced by homosexuals stemming from general societal disapproval. These problems include particularly the clash between family and promiscuous lifestyles, as well as prostitution, sexually transmitted diseases, prison violence, and aging.